Corporate Crime, Law, and Social Control

Why do corporations obey the law? When companies violate the law, what kinds of interventions are most apt to correct their behavior and return them to compliant status? In this book Sally Simpson examines whether the shift toward the use of criminal law, with its emphasis on punishment and stigmatization, is an effective strategy for controlling illegal corporate behavior.

Simpson assesses the strengths and weaknesses of the criminalization of corporate misconduct and compares it with other approaches, such as civil and administrative legal interventions and cooperative crime control methods. She evaluates several theoretical assumptions about why criminalization should work and explains why it often does not. In reality, organizational actors pose challenges to deterrence; in light of the empirical record, the rational-actor assumptions underlying much crime control theory fall short of explaining illegal corporate behavior across the board.

Simpson concludes that strict criminalization models that rely on punishments will not yield sufficiently high levels of compliance. Empirical data suggest that in most cases cooperative models work best with most corporate offenders. Because some corporate managers, however, respond primarily to instrumental concerns, Simpson argues that compliance should also be buttressed by punitive strategies. Simpson's review and application of the relevant empirical literature on corporate crime and compliance, combined with her judicious examination of theory and approaches, make a valuable new contribution to the literature on white-collar crime and deterrence and criminal behavior more generally.

Sally S. Simpson is Associate Professor of Criminology and Criminal Justice at the University of Maryland.

Cambridge Studies in Criminology

Edited by

Alfred Blumstein, *H. John Heinz School of Public Policy and Management, Carnegie Mellon University*

David Farrington, *Institute of Criminology, University of Cambridge*

Other books in the series:

For Stas and Gabrys

Corporate Crime, Law, and Social Control

Sally S. Simpson

University of Maryland

CAMBRIDGE UNIVERSITY PRESS
Cambridge, New York, Melbourne, Madrid, Cape Town, Singapore,
São Paulo, Delhi, Dubai, Tokyo

Cambridge University Press
The Edinburgh Building, Cambridge CB2 8RU, UK

Published in the United States of America by Cambridge University Press, New York

www.cambridge.org
Information on this title: www.cambridge.org/9780521589338

First published 2002

A catalogue record for this publication is available from the British Library

Library of Congress Cataloguing in Publication data
Simpson, Sally S.
    Corporate crime, law, and social control / Sally S. Simpson.
       p.   cm. – (Cambridge studies in criminology)
    Includes bibliographical references and index.
    ISBN 0-521-58083-8 – ISBN 0-521-58933-9 (pb.)
    1. Corporations – Corrupt practices.   2. Commercial crimes.
    3. Commercial crimes – Prevention.   I. Title.   II. Cambridge studies in
    criminology (New York, N.Y.)
    HV6768.S56   2001
    364.16′8 – dc21   2001025804

ISBN 978-0-521-58083-0 Hardback
ISBN 978-0-521-58933-8 Paperback

Transferred to digital printing 2010

Contents

Preface

Corporate crime control is a deceptively complex topic. In spite of the many suggestions for how it might be accomplished (many of which are based on ideological preferences), few strategies have been explored empirically or systematically. This book began as a critical examination of the deterrence doctrine as it applied to corporations and their managers. Consistent with the "get tough on crime" philosophy of the 1970s and 1980s, many politicians, corporate crime scholars, and policy mavens determined that corporate violators would be (or at least should be) particularly susceptible to greater punishment threats – especially those found in criminal law. Given the rather unimpressive evidence regarding deterrence and traditional crime, I was curious as to whether the evidence was more convincing in the white-collar crime area. Further, I was attracted by the idea that corporations, as exceptionally powerful and often oblivious societal actors, require substantial curbs on that power for the common good. Criminal law seemed like a reasonable tool to achieve that rather modest goal. Lastly, as a student of corporate crime for fifteen years, it was comforting to know that my thoughts about corporate crime control were shared by many well-respected peers. The community of scholars who study in this area, at least those who are more critically oriented, are skeptical about the good intentions of corporate officers and challenge whether the companies they head are committed to socially responsible goals. While it was uncomfortable to jump on the punishment bandwagon, at least in this case, punitiveness made some sense.

I was thus surprised by the woeful lack of research on corporate deterrence, especially from a criminological perspective. Although the literature is replete with debates about "efficient" regulation, including econometric models of such, criminologists generally have had remarkably little to say about corporate deterrence. Even fewer have attempted to assess empirically the deterrence model as it applies to companies or corporate decision makers; of the few studies that do exist, evidence is far from unequivocal.

My purview of the relevant literature did, however, uncover the seminal work of Albert Reiss Jr. and John Braithwaite. Through their work came the idea of comparing and contrasting two models of corporate crime control – one based in deterrence and the other based in compliance. My thinking was also influenced by a question put to me by Amitai Etzioni, the noted George Washington University sociologist. He wondered why most studies of corporate offending focus primarily on deviant cases (often of a sensational nature) and not on law-abiding companies. He suggested that much could be learned about corporate crime by studying firms that obey the law.

Given the paucity of systematic research in this area, it was also important that my evaluations of these models be empirically grounded. Thus, in 1993 and 1998 I undertook two vignette studies that were administered to MBA and executive education students at four universities and a small group of managers at a Fortune 500 company. The results of these studies are used to assess the merits and deficiencies of both crime control strategies.

This work has taken almost a decade to come to fruition. Consequently, I am indebted to many who have helped the project along. Perhaps most important, I have had the benefit of extremely smart and resourceful research assistants and student collaborators. Lori Elis helped put together the vignettes (using a randomized design) and painstakingly made them legible in their questionnaire format. She also helped with some of the survey administration and preliminary data analysis for the first study. Her M.A. thesis was the first published work out of this data set. Nicole Leeper Piquero read over one of the first drafts of this book and made helpful comments. Laura Hickman, along with Nicky, learned random effects models and worked to translate the data from an SPSS format to LIMDEP and SAS. Most recently, Jennifer Castro reran all of the random-effects models, produced the tables for Chapter 7, and most of the appendices. She meticulously read the draft and prompted me to reconsider my conclusions. Finally, M. Lynn Exum worked closely with me to prepare and administer the second vignette survey. Although some of the items that he included in the survey did not perform as he would have liked, his commitment to the project never wavered. I thank all of these students (and former students) for their able assistance, good humor, and critical observations.

Numerous colleagues, at Maryland and other schools, contributed significantly to both my thinking about corporate crime control and the execution of the research. Many thanks to Craig Smith, Jeff Sonnenfeld, Diane Vaughan, Nikos Passas, David Weisburd, and Gil Geis for all their help in this endeavor. Also, I am grateful to Laureen Snider and Frank Pearce for providing challenging and provocative arguments that run counter to the conclusions I draw from these studies. Their research (and that of Diane Vaughan) has made me think much more carefully about the implications of my work.

I am indebted to Ray Paternoster for his statistical assistance and counsel, theoretical expertise, and wit. Lawrence W. Sherman, as chair of the Department of Criminology and Criminal Justice at Maryland, agreed to absorb the cost of the survey construction and administration. He even helped stuff envelopes one afternoon when the electrical power was out in the office. That, indeed, was assistance far beyond the call of duty.

Thanks go as well to David Farrington and Al Blumstein who, as editors of the Cambridge Studies in Criminology series, had helpful and encouraging comments on the first and second drafts of the original manuscript. Mary Child, the sociology editor at Cambridge, has guided the project with an accomplished hand and has been a source of calm when I was not.

Finally, my family has sacrificed and put up with me as I struggled to complete this project. Much love and sincere gratitude to Stas and Gabrys.

Criminalizing the Corporate Control Process

The modern tendency of the courts . . . has been widening the scope within which criminal proceedings can be brought against institutions which have become so prominent a feature of everyday affairs, and the point is being reached where what is called for is a comprehensive statement of principles formulated to meet the needs of modern life in granting the fullest possible protection of criminal law to persons exposed to the action of the many powerful associations which surround them.[1]

IMAGES of crime in the United States at the end of the twentieth century increasingly coupled the illegal practices of business executives with those of America's underclass. These mirror images of crime and criminals have had real consequences for how crime is understood and responded to in our society today. Crime in the suites and on the streets has been indelibly linked in the public mind. It has not always been so.

Neither street nor business crime is a new social problem. In fact, quite the opposite is true. Illicit drugs and the violence they spawn have concerned moral entrepreneurs and policy makers in this country for the better part of this century;[2] legislative attempts to curb the market powers of "robber baron" industrialists stimulated antitrust laws over a century ago.[3]

---

[1] *Russell on Crime*, 12th ed., ed. F. W. Cecil Turner, vol. 1 (London: Stevens Publishing, 1964), pp. 96–97.

[2] See, for instance, James Inciardi, *The War on Drugs: Heroin, Cocaine, Crime, and Public Policy* (Palo Alto, Calif.: Mayfield, 1986); Joseph Gusfield, *Symbolic Crusade* (Urbana: University of Illinois, 1963); Howard S. Becker, *Outsiders* (New York: Free Press, 1963); and Troy Duster, *The Legislation of Morality* (New York: Free Press, 1970).

[3] Corporations, until the early 1900s, were rarely subjected to criminal law. Strict liability was the preferred legal means to pursue acts of corporate malfeasance (William S. Laufer,

Historically, however, these populations of criminals were seen as distinct. For the most part, drug addiction (including alcohol) and violence were deemed problems for ethnics (Mexican, Chinese, Italian, Irish, and blacks) and immigrants (predominantly Catholic working class). The "real" crime problem was thought to rest with the constitutionally inferior and morally lax. Corporate criminals, on the other hand, were drawn from America's newly emerging capitalist Brahmins. Although perceived to be opportunistic and ruthless in their business practices, these entrepreneurs were part of the governing and newly emerging social elite. Consequently, popular definitions of and legal responses to crime and criminals were framed within divergent ideological and social-control orbits. Conventional crime was dealt with punitively, but corporate misbehavior was handled through administrative agencies or relatively lenient criminal statutes.[4]

Today, however, there is substantial overlap between conventional and white-collar crime control. Since the 1960s politicians and the general public have come to believe that the crime problem is pervasive and out of control. Citizens are bombarded with messages that create and reinforce this interpretation as media, politicians, and crime specialists document the illegal activities of business and street criminals. The crack-cocaine epidemic of the 1980s coupled with sensationalist reports of drug and school violence, rapes, robberies, and grisly serial murders comprises a large part of the cultural image of America's crime problem. But white-collar cases involving Michael Milken, Lincoln Savings and Loan, Archer Daniels Midland – even congressional leaders such as Dan Rostenkowski and former president Clinton – have contributed increasingly to this conception.

Public opinion polls show that over the past two decades white-collar crimes have attained greater significance in the mind of the populace. For instance, on a ranking scale where 1 is the most serious, the mean seriousness ranking of corporate and other white-collar offenses by the public was 91.75 in an 1972 study. This average shrunk to 79.71 in another survey

---

"Corporate Bodies and Guilty Minds," *Emory Law Journal* 43 [1994]: 647–730). The Sherman Act and Clayton Antitrust Act were passed into law in 1890 and 1914 respectively. There is some disagreement as to whether the legislation was truly populist or reflected the interests of the capitalist class; see Frank Pearce, *Crimes of the Powerful* (London: Pluto, 1976); and Gabriel Kolko, *The Triumph of Conservatism* (New York: Free Press, 1963).

[4] To be clear, corporate sanctions often include a criminal component. However, research demonstrates that civil and administrative remedies have been the preferred method of pursuing corporate violators. For instance, between 1890 and 1969, the ratio of civil to criminal cases brought by the Department of Justice in the antitrust area is 1.23:1 (Richard Posner, "A Statistical Study of Antitrust Enforcement," *Journal of Law and Economics* 13 [1970]: 385). See also Marshall B. Clinard and Peter C. Yeager, *Corporate Crime* (New York: Free Press, 1980).

conducted in 1979. Public ranking of the most serious corporate act, selling contaminated food that results in a death, decreased from a rank of twenty-sixth in 1972 to thirteenth in 1979.[5] A survey conducted in 1984 found that environmental crime was ranked seventh, "after murder, but ahead of heroin smuggling."[6] The perceived severity of environmental crimes by the general public has remained high in the 1990s, according to results from a survey commissioned by Arthur D. Little. When asked to evaluate how seriously authorities should respond to four types of corporate crime, 84 percent of respondents perceived environmental damage to be a serious crime, with three out of four believing that executive officers ought to be held personally accountable (liable) for such offenses.[7] In contrast, 74 percent of respondents ranked worker health and safety crimes to be serious, 60 percent felt that price fixing was a serious offense, and less than half (40 percent) held similar beliefs about insider trading.

Data from other Western nations also support the view that the general public is growing intolerant of certain types of white-collar crime. In Great Britain, for instance, respondents in a 1985 survey ranked murder with a weapon as the most serious offense but ranked fifth an example of mail-order fraud in which the offender set up a bogus mail-order company and fraudulently obtained £1,000 from private individuals.[8] Similarly, replication of the crime seriousness surveys in Brisbane, Australia, suggests that greater media attention for the past twenty years has produced respondents who view white-collar offenses to be more serious than their U.S. counterparts. The mean seriousness score for the Brisbane sample – again with 1 being the "most serious" ranking – was 74.23. This average is considerably lower than what the first U.S. survey found (91.75) and 5 points lower than the 1979 survey's average (79.71).[9]

Finally, the public may be more reactive toward corporate than non-corporate offenders. In their vignette survey, Miller, Rossi, and Simpson

[5] Peter H. Rossi, Emily Waite, Christina E. Bose, and Richard E. Berk, "The Seriousness of Crimes: Normative Structure and Individual Differences," *American Sociological Review* 39 (1974): 224–237; Francis T. Cullen, Bruce G. Link, and Craig W. Polznai, "The Seriousness of Crime Revisited," *Criminology* 20 (1982): 83–102.

[6] U.S. Department of Justice, *Bureau of Justice Statistics Bulletin*, January 1984, cited in Frederick W. Allison III and Elizabeth E. Mack, "Creating an Environmental Ethic in Corporate America: The Big Stick of Jail Time," *Southwestern Law Journal* 44 (1991): 1429.

[7] *The Corporate Board*, September–October 1991, 24–25.

[8] Michael Levi and S. Jones, "Public and Police Perceptions of Crime Seriousness in England and Wales," *British Journal of Criminology* 25 (1985): 234–250.

[9] Robert C. Holland, "Public Perceptions of White Collar Crime Seriousness: A Survey of an Australian Sample," *International Journal of Comparative and Applied Criminal Justice* 19 (1995): 91–105.

show that respondents prefer more severe sanctions "when either the crime victim, or the criminal offender is a corporation, and not an individual."[10] However, punitive attitudes vary by the degree of harm and the culpability of the act.[11] Surveys of business executives and criminal justice authorities also show similar variations in perceptions of white-collar crime seriousness and appropriate punishment.[12] Benson and Cullen, for instance, found that local prosecutors' perceptions of the corporate crime problem were a function of community characteristics. Local prosecutors in more populous jurisdictions, compared with those in suburban or rural areas, were more apt to regard corporate crime as a very or somewhat serious problem.[13] Although Benson and Cullen are unable to determine, based on their cross-sectional data, whether prosecutor's perceptions have changed over time, they cautiously interpret their data as suggestive that prosecutors become more concerned with corporate crime during their tenure in office. Specifically, prosecutors report that prosecutions have increased and that even more prosecutions are anticipated in the future.[14]

The criminal justice system is now playing a larger role in the war against corporate crime. Champions of this position claim that the criminal process offers a greater deterrent for corporations and managers than other control mechanisms.[15] But the shift of criminal justice to center stage raises important questions about the capacity of criminal law to prevent and control corporate illegality.

The goal of this book is to address, in detail, some of these concerns. A key premise of this investigation is that the criminal justice system will fail as a primary mechanism of corporate crime control, even though criminal law

---

[10] Joann L. Miller, Peter H. Rossi, and Jon E. Simpson, "Felony Punishments: A Factorial Survey of Perceived Justice in Criminal Sentencing," *Journal of Criminal Law and Criminology* 82 (1991): 396–415.

[11] Laura Schrager and James F. Short, "How Serious a Crime? Perceptions of Common and Organizational Crimes," in Gil Geis and Ezra Stotland (eds.), *White-Collar Crime: Theory and Research* (Beverly Hills, Calif.: Sage, 1980), pp. 14–31; James Frank, Francis T. Cullen, Lawrence F. Travis III, and John L. Borntrager, "Sanctioning Corporate Crime: How Do Business Executives and the Public Compare?" *American Journal of Criminal Justice* 13 (1989): 139–169.

[12] Studies are reported and summarized in Michael Levi, *Regulating Fraud* (New York: Tavistock, 1987), pp. 69–70 and 136–144.

[13] Michael L. Benson and Francis T. Cullen, *Combatting Corporate Crime: Local Prosecutors at Work* (Boston: Northeastern University Press, 1998), p. 51.

[14] Ibid.

[15] John Braithwaite, "The Limits of Economism in Controlling Harmful Corporate Conduct," *Law and Society Review* 16 (1981–1982): 481–504; John Braithwaite and Gilbert Geis, "On Theory and Action for Corporate Crime Control," *Crime and Delinquency* 28 (1982): 292–314; Francis T. Cullen and Paula J. Dubeck, "The Myth of Corporate Immunity to Deterrence," *Federal Probation* 49 (1985): 3–9.

offers the harshest formal sanction threat to corporate managers (and some claim the greatest deterrent) – namely, incarceration. The position against the use of criminal law to control corporate misconduct is, by no means, unique or unprecedented. In fact, more than two decades ago, Christopher Stone argued:

> Those who trust to the law to bind corporations have failed to take into account a whole host of reasons why the threat of legal sanction is apt to lack the desired effects when corporate behavior is its target – for example, limited liability, the lack of congruence between the incentives of top executives and the incentives of "the corporation," the organization's proclivity to buffer itself against external, especially legal threats, and so on.[16]

Stone asserts that the law will fail because it lacks the necessary flexibility to adjust to and permeate dynamic business organizations. While sympathetic to Stone's point, my view of criminal law is informed from a deterrence framework, a perspective that has been optimistically embraced by proponents of a punitive corporate control model but one that lacks supportive empirical evidence. To borrow a phrase from law professor John Coffee, "if such assertions could be cited as evidence, the case [for deterrence] ... would be strong indeed. In general, however, little is cited in support of this contention beyond anecdotal experiences and personal beliefs."[17]

Making a similar point, Charles Moore claims that the prospects for corporate deterrence are bleak because arguments in favor of corporate deterrence are founded on unrealistic views of the corporate actor and overly optimistic views of the legal system's capacity to control corporate behavior.[18] Moore's critique deals exclusively with the problems associated with deterring the corporate entity via criminal law (his position on deterrence is summarized in the third chapter of this book). The position I advance is that deterrence is unlikely for both the corporation *and* its officers

---

[16] Christopher D. Stone, *Where the Law Ends* (New York: Harper and Row, 1975), p. 93. See also John Braithwaite and Brent Fisse, "Self-Regulation and the Control of Corporate Crime" (pp. 194–220), and Michael Clarke, "Prosecutorial and Administrative Strategies to Control Business Crimes" (pp. 247–265), both in Clifford D. Shearing and Philip C. Stenning (eds.), *Private Policing* (Beverly Hills, Calif.: Sage, 1987).

[17] John Collins Coffee Jr. "Corporate Crime and Punishment: A Non-Chicago View of the Economics of Criminal Sanctions," *American Criminal Law Review* 17 (1980): 425. In making his point, Coffee was contrasting the deterrent value of fines with imprisonment and noting that commentators explicitly claim that only the latter can deter the businessman. Given the paucity of empirical evidence on the deterrent effects of any legal sanction brought against a firm or a manager, his words are equally apt here.

[18] Charles A. Moore, "Taming the Giant Corporation? Some Cautionary Remarks on the Deterrability of Corporate Crime," *Crime and Delinquency* 33 (1987): 379–402.

or managers. Punitiveness, as a strategy for corporate crime control, is not well grounded in the empirical literature and, in fact, is somewhat antithetical to the limited amount of research that has been conducted in this area. Research by Diane Vaughan, for instance, explicitly challenges the rational-choice foundation upon which corporate deterrence rests.[19]

For most corporate crime scholars, especially those of us who understand corporate crime as an abuse of power by capital,[20] an antideterrence position is an ironic one to assume[21] but one informed by both theory and scientific evidence. To lay the groundwork for the arguments and evidence against deterrence, we first need to identify the kinds of acts that corporations and their managers commit that are subject to criminal sanction and the characteristics that make these acts distinct from other kinds of crimes. Ironically, many of the uncommon features of corporate crime contribute to the belief that it is amenable to deterrence. Yet these same attributes suggest that corporate crime control will be more successfully achieved through processes other than the application of criminal sanctions to violators. Second, it makes little sense to argue that criminalization is a flawed policy unless it can be demonstrated that a trend toward criminalization actually is occurring. Thus, the latter part of this chapter is devoted to substantiating this position while attempting to explain why this change is happening now.

Definitions

What Is Corporate Crime?

Corporate crime is a type of white-collar crime. Edwin Sutherland introduced the latter concept to describe criminal activity by persons of high social status and respectability who use their occupational position as a means to violate the law.[22] As a subcategory of white-collar crime, corporate crime has been defined in many ways. Perhaps the simplest definition is that offered by Braithwaite: corporate crime is the "conduct of a corporation, or

---

[19] Diane Vaughan, *The Challenger Launch Decision: Risky Technology, Culture, and Deviance at NASA* (Chicago: University of Chicago Press, 1996); Diane Vaughan, "Rational Choice, Situated Action, and the Social Control of Organizations," *Law and Society Review* 32 (1998): 23–61.

[20] See, e.g., Frank Pearce and Laureen Snider, "Regulating Capitalism," in F. Pearce and L. Snider, *Corporate Crime: Contemporary Debates* (Toronto: University of Toronto Press, 1985), pp. 19–47.

[21] For a position counter to mine, see Laureen Snider, "The Corporate Counter-Revolution and the Disappearance of Corporate Crime" (paper presented at the annual meeting of the American Society of Criminology, Washington, D.C., 1998).

[22] Edwin Sutherland, *White-Collar Crime* (New York: Dryden Press, 1949).

of employees acting on behalf of a corporation, which is proscribed and punishable by law."[23]

Three key ideas are captured in this definition. First, by not speci- fying the kind of law that proscribes and punishes, Braithwaite accepts Sutherland's argument that illegality by corporations and their agents "differs from the criminal behavior of the lower socio-economic class prin- cipally in the administrative procedures which are used in dealing with the offenders."[24] Thus, corporate crime not only includes acts in viola- tion of criminal law, but civil and administrative violations as well. Second, both corporations (as "legal persons") and their representatives are rec- ognized as illegal actors. Which or whether each is selected as a sanc- tion target will depend on the kind of act committed, rules and quality of evidence, prosecutory preference, and offending history, among other factors.

Finally, Braithwaite's definition specifies the underlying motivation for corporate offending: on the whole, illegality is not pursued for individ- ual benefits but rather for *organizational* ends. Thus, in order to main- tain profits, manage an uncertain market, lower company costs, or put a rival out of business, corporations may pollute the environment, engage in financial frauds and manipulations, fix prices, create and maintain haz- ardous work conditions, knowingly produce unsafe products, and so forth. Managers' decisions to commit such acts (or to order or tacitly support oth- ers doing so) may be supported by operational norms and organizational subcultures.[25]

Perceptions of organizational needs have been empirically shown to in- fluence the corporate offending decision. Strains and pressures associated with decline *and* growth are linked to corporate illegality.[26] Interviews with middle and top managers at a steel manufacturing company conducted by this author, for instance, reveal how managers confront different realities under conditions of munificence and scarcity. In his description of how

---

[23] John Braithwaite, *Corporate Crime in the Pharmaceutical Industry* (London: Routledge and Kegan Paul, 1984), p. 6.

[24] Sutherland, *White-Collar Crime*, p. 9.

[25] James W. Coleman, *The Criminal Elite* (New York: St. Martin's Press, 1989).

[26] Marshall B. Clinard and Peter C. Yeager, *Corporate Crime* (New York: Free Press, 1980); Katherine M Jamieson, *The Organization of Corporate Crime* (Thousand Oaks, Calif.: Sage, 1994); Melissa S. Buucus and J. P. Near, "Can Illegal Corporate Behavior Be Predicted? An Event History Analysis," *Academy Management Journal* 34 (1991): 9–36; Sally S. Simpson, "The Decomposition of Antitrust," *American Sociological Review* 51 (1986): 859–879; Barry M. Staw and Eugene Swajkowski, "The Scarcity Munificence Component of Organizational En- vironments and the Commission of Illegal Acts," *Administrative Science Quarterly* 20 (1975): 345–354.

health and safety violations might occur, one manager said:

> There are no purists in a survival mode.... as soon as you're on the threshold [of economic constraints], then all of the shortcuts come out of the woodwork and we give them titles like "entrepreneur of risk," "risk analysis." We give them all kinds of fancy things to accommodate and legitimize the decision process.[27]

Such decisions have little to do with an individual employee's personal needs but a lot to do with organizational contingencies, priorities, and needs. In contrast, embezzlement – another type of white-collar crime – occurs when persons accept a position of trust within an organization but, by stealing from it, violate the financial trust placed in them.[28] Both this act and the conditions just described resulting in health and safety violations occur within a work setting. Each falls within the parameters of Sutherland's original definition. The difference between them lies in motivation and victim. Unlike corporate crime, embezzlement is motivated by an individual's needs (e.g., his or her debt, family considerations, perception of an unsharable problem, greed, revenge).[29] The primary victim of embezzlement is the firm itself.[30] Corporate crime, on the other hand, counts many victims, among them employees, other companies, the government, the environment, and consumers; however, because the act is undertaken in the pursuit of organizational goals, the company itself is not directly victimized.

Corporate offending occurs within an organizational context. This fact sets it apart from most other kinds of illegality. The organization comprises hierarchical, diverse, and often highly specialized positions. Work is autonomous, but it is also interactive and team-dependent. Organizations themselves are complex entities. Large corporations are divisible into subsidiaries; subunits such as sales and marketing, production, and finance; and smaller task groups. Like the organization as a whole, these units develop

---

[27] Sally S. Simpson, "Corporate Crime Deterrence and Corporate Control Policies: Views from the Inside," in Kip Schlegal and David Weisburd (eds.), *White-Collar Crime Reconsidered* (Boston: Northeastern University Press, 1992), pp. 296–297.

[28] Donald Cressey, *Other People's Money* (Glencoe, Ill.: Free Press, 1953), p. 12.

[29] Donald R. Cressey, *Other People's Money: A Study in the Social Psychology of Embezzlement* (1953; reprint, Montclair, N.J.: Patterson Smith, 1973); Dorothy Zeitz, *Women Who Embezzle or Defraud: A Study of Convicted Felons* (New York: Praeger, 1981); Kathleen Daly, "Gender and Varieties of White-Collar Crime," *Criminology* 27 (1989): 769–794.

[30] Certain types of white-collar crime, such as the recent savings-and-loan frauds, share elements of both embezzlement and corporate crime. Calvita and Pontell describe situations of "collective embezzlement" in which bank officers use institutional resources to enrich themselves at the expense of the bank, depositors, and the general public. See Kitty Calavita and Henry N. Pontell, "'Other People's Money' Revisited: Collective Embezzlement in the Savings and Loan and Insurance Industries," *Social Problems* 38 (1991): 94–112.

cultures and subcultures. It is here that most managers are socialized into organizational goals and subgoals. Here, too, employees learn the appropriate means and unique opportunities to achieve defined objectives and to respond to pressures – including criminal options. To understand corporate crime and to determine whether it is amenable to deterrence, one needs to examine how managers experience and express the moral imperatives of their work environment and how organizational needs are formulated and inculcated into managerial decisions.[31]

What Is Deterrence?

The idea of deterrence has its roots in utilitarian philosophy where individuals are seen as rational, pleasure-seeking, and self-interested. In accordance with hedonistic principles, individuals will maximize pleasurable experiences and avoid painful ones.[32] The traditional deterrence model assumes that fear of legal sanctions keeps persons law-abiding.[33] To the extent that formal punishment risk and consequence are assessed to be greater than the benefits of the criminal act, legality will prevail. The greater the certainty, severity, and celerity of punishment, the greater the putative deterrent effects for both offending individuals (specific deterrence) and the general public (general deterrence).

Deterrence theory emphasizes the formal legal system as the essential element in the crime inhibition process. Thus, fear of detection, arrest, and punishment resulting from conviction forms the core of a deterrence model.[34] For deterrence theorists, there is a straightforward answer to the question, Why do corporations obey the law? They do so because the threat of criminal sanctions is salient to the organization and its key managers. Yet managers and corporations may be inhibited from misconduct by other kinds of fears. For instance, threats to reputation, current or future employment, access to competitive resources (e.g., bids, contracts), friendship networks or associations, and family attachments can curb illegal conduct independent of legal sanctions. Managers and employees may not contemplate criminality because of moral habituation or a strong belief in the morality of the law. Traditional deterrence neglects these kinds of controls,

---

[31] Robert Jackall, *Moral Mazes: The World of Corporate Managers* (New York: Oxford University Press, 1988).

[32] Jeremy Bentham, *An Introduction to the Principles of Morals and Legislation*, ed. Laurence J. Lafleur (New York: Hafner, 1948).

[33] Jack Gibbs, *Crime, Punishment, and Deterrence* (New York: Elsevier, 1975).

[34] Johannes Andenaes, *Punishment and Deterrence* (Ann Arbor: University of Michigan Press, 1974).

which are arguably more important in corporate crime control (as they are in conventional crime control) for the majority of offenders. More than two centuries ago, Jeremy Bentham noted that punishment is unnecessary when other kinds of controls or interventions are successful.[35] Later in this work, I assert that greater enforcement effort should be centered on such informal controls and interventions.

Criminalization of Corporate Crime in the Post-Watergate Era

A "get tough on crime" rhetoric for criminals of all types is currently in vogue. On a practical level, this position has translated into mandatory and longer sentences for some kinds of offenders (e.g., drug offenders, recidivists, weapons offenses), a preference for prison time over less punitive alternatives, three-strikes legislation, and a return to the death penalty – with some advocates suggesting expansion of the circumstances under which a death sentence can be imposed (e.g., former president Bush's push to make drug trafficking a capital crime). For corporate offenders, it has meant more criminal instead of civil or regulatory cases brought against them; a push toward sentencing parity between white-collar and street criminals; and an increase in maximum penalty levels for a variety of organizational offenses (e.g., the Insider Trading and Securities Fraud Enforcement Act of 1988; Major Fraud Act of 1988; Money Laundering Control Act of 1986; Sherman Act).[36]

The punitive model of corporate crime control has support from both sides of the ideological spectrum. The reasoning behind this confluence, however, differs from side to side.[37] Several interpretations are offered to account for this punitive shift.

The Fairness Issue

The perceived inadequacies of the criminal justice process are at least partially responsible for both conservatives and radicals supporting a harsher

[35] Bentham, *Introduction.*

[36] Ilene H. Nagel and Winthrop M. Swenson, "The Federal Sentencing Guidelines for Corporations: Their Development, Theoretical Underpinnings, and Some Thoughts about Their Future," *Washington University Law Quarterly* 71 (1993): 224–225.

[37] Zimring and Hawkins have commented on how political ideology affects conservative and liberal images of crime causation. I extend their perspective to images of corporate crime control. Franklin E. Zimring and Gordon Hawkins, "Ideology and Euphoria in Crime Control," *University of Toledo Law Review* 10 (1979): 370–388. In a similar vein, the authors analyze the savings-and-loan crisis. See Franklin E. Zimring and Gordon Hawkins, "Crime, Justice, and the Savings and Loan Crisis," in Michael Tonry and Albert J. Reiss Jr. (eds.), *Beyond the Law: Crime in Complex Organizations* (Chicago: University of Chicago Press, 1993), pp. 247–292.

response to corporate crime. In direct contradiction to democratic principles, research indicates that justice has not been blind. Studies have found
that race, gender, and social class affect who will be charged, and how they
will be processed and punished.[38] For conservatives, illicit bias in the criminal justice process represents a potential threat to social order. It disputes
the ideology that all are equal before the law and that the state is neutral
in how the law is applied. "Disclosures of that bias undermined the law's
neutrality and thus challenged its legitimacy."[39]

A policy of punitiveness toward corporate offenders is supported by radicals as a means to curb corporate power and to achieve equity in criminal
justice sentencing. If poor minorities are going to be sent to prison, so too
should corporate offenders who are primarily white and middle or upper
class.[40] Corporate power and influence has, for too long, allowed violators
to manipulate the law, escape detection, negate harsh sentencing, or avoid
criminal processing. In his review of corporate criminalization, Sethi suggests that it is not coincidental that the trend toward harsher penalties for
corporate executives has occurred at a time "that business credibility in
the public eye is extraordinarily low" and political power elites have been
challenged by persons formerly disenfranchised.[41]

Paradoxically, the left has taken a criminalization position even though it
rejects punitiveness as an approach to conventional crime. In a recent book,
Michael Levi chastises advocates of more punitive responses to white-collar
criminals:

> One suspects that many white-collar crime writers who utilize seriousness
> survey findings to call for tougher policing and sentencing of white-collar
> "criminals" would be very much less happy to embrace public support for

---

[38] John Hagan, "Extra-Legal Attributes and Criminal Sentencing," *Law and Society Review* 8
(1974): 357–383; John Hagan, *Structural Criminology* (New Brunswick, N.J.: Rutgers University
Press, 1989); Kathleen Daly, *Gender, Crime, and Punishment* (New Haven: Yale University
Press, 1995); Michael Tonry, *Malign Neglect – Race, Crime, and Punishment in America* (New
York: Oxford University Press, 1995); Ilene Nagel, "The Legal/Extra-Legal Controversy,"
Law and Society Review 17 (1993): 481–515; Victoria L. Swigert and Ronald A. Farrell, Normal
Homicides and the Law," *American Sociological Review* 12 (1977): 96–102. See David Weisburd,
Stanton Wheeler, Elin Waring, and Nancy Bode, *Crimes of the Middle Classes* (New Haven: Yale
University Press, 1991), and Theodore Chiracos and Gordon Waldo, "Socioeconomic Status
and Criminal Sentencing," *American Sociological Review* 40 (1975): 753–772, for alternative
findings.
[39] Francis T. Cullen, William J. Maakestad, and Gray Cavender, *Corporate Crime under Attack: The
Ford Pinto Case and Beyond* (Cincinnati: Anderson, 1987), p. 13.
[40] Research by Kathleen Daly demonstrates that this generalized image of white-collar criminal
demographics appears to be more true for males than for female offenders. See Daly, "Gender
and Varieties of White-Collar Crime," *Criminology* 27 (1989): 769–793.
[41] S. Prakash Sethi, "Liability without Fault? The Corporate Executive as an Unwitting
Criminal," *Employee Relations Law Journal* 4 (1978): 208.

corporal or capital punishment for offenders coming from more deprived backgrounds. So the cry of *Vox Populi Supreme Lex* can turn out to be a hydra-headed monster, and those academics who are captivated by the notion that white-collar crime is high on the gravity list should beware of worshipping false and powerful gods.[42]

The proportionality and equity issues in the criminal justice response to white-collar or corporate versus conventional offenders have led to a push to eliminate or minimize disparities in the justice process.[43] As part of this effort, criminal laws have been rewritten or expanded so that white-collar offenses carry penalties similar to those of conventional crimes. For instance, former New York governor Cuomo pushed to redefine the seriousness of white-collar crime in New York State by contrasting the street thief ("a person who threatens violence to steal a wallet") with the one in the three-piece suit who defrauds millions by manipulating a ledger.[44]

Further, statutes originally intended to ease prosecution of organized crime are now used with some success against corporate criminals (e.g., the Racketeering Influenced and Corrupt Organizations Act). Perhaps the most famous use of RICO against a corporate offender was the pursuit and prosecution of Michael Milken, Wall Street's junk bond king, on securities fraud charges. On November 21, 1990, Milken was sentenced to ten years in prison for his participation in securities fraud, market manipulation, and tax fraud.[45] The threat of a RICO prosecution led Milken's employer, Drexel Burnham Lambert, to plead guilty to six felony counts of mail and wire fraud and securities fraud and to agree to major changes

---

[42] Levi, *Regulating Fraud*, pp. 74–75.

[43] Disparities clearly still exist. Tillman and Pontell's comparison of medicaid and grand theft cases in California shows greater leniency in the former – at least at early sentencing phases. In terms of time served, the white-collar offenders did not differ from their lower-class counterparts (Robert Tillman and Henry N. Pontell, "Is Justice 'Collar-Blind'?: Punishing Medicaid Provider Fraud," *Criminology* 30 [1992]: 547–574). Johnson also explores the question of whether adjudication and sentencing of white-collar and common offenders have become more "equitable" over a three-decade period. He compares aggregate sentencing data for corporate, white-collar, and common crime from the U.S. district courts, fiscal years 1964, 1974, and 1984 and discovers that although white-collar and corporate offenders are being brought to the courts more often and sentences appear to be harsher over time, offenders are still receiving more lenient sentences than common property offenders. Kirk A. Johnson, "Federal Court Processing of Corporate, White Collar, and Common Crime Economic Offenders over the Past Three Decades," *Mid-American Review of Sociology* 11 (1986): 25–44.

[44] Isabel Wilkerson, "Cuomo Asks New White-Collar Crime Terms," *New York Times*, February 2, 1986.

[45] Steve Coll and David A. Vise, "On the Trail of Ivan and Mike," *Washington Post Magazine*, September 29, 1991, p. 30.

in its organizational structure and oversight procedures.[46] Although there are movements to limit both the criminal and civil provisions of RICO, prosecutors have used the law successfully against a variety of white-collar or corporate offenses (especially in false advertising through mail or wire fraud and securities cases).[47]

In addition to these changes, the criminal justice system, at least at the federal level, is dramatically changing the process through which organizations are sanctioned for violations of criminal law. In 1991 Congress passed into law newly recommended guidelines for organizational sanctioning from the U.S. Sentencing Commission.[48] Responding to the belief that criminal organizations are sanctioned leniently and inconsistently, the commission recommended sentencing guidelines based, in part, on an optimal penalties approach. Optimal penalties specify that the sentencing process take into account the costs (or harm) associated with the illegal act *and* efforts to prevent, detect, and punish crime. This approach, at least theoretically, can impose extremely costly economic sanctions on the offending corporation. "There can be little doubt that the Organizational Guidelines taken as a whole greatly increase the potential sanctions for corporate misconduct including mandatory retribution, punitive fines capable of rising to hundreds of millions of dollars, and invasive probationary conditions."[49] These penalties are justified by the sentencing objectives of deterrence, proportionality, public protection, and restitution to victims.

The Relative Seriousness Issue

Proponents of more punitive approaches toward corporate offenders often argue that illegal acts by companies are more costly, both in terms of human lives and economically, than conventional crime.[50] Data drawn from

---

[46] Laurie P. Cohen, "Riding It Out: Fred Joseph Emerges Unscathed after Deal by Drexel and SEC," *Wall Street Journal,* April 17, 1989, p. A1; Mary Zey, "Reform of RICO: Legal versus Social Embeddedness Explanations" (unpublished manuscript, Department of Sociology, University of Wisconsin, Madison, 1991).

[47] Kay P. Kindred and Ronald R. Sims, "The Regulator's Perspective on Corporate Fraud," in Margaret P. Spence and Ronald R. Sims (eds.), *Corporate Misconduct* (Westport, Conn.: Quorum Books, 1995), p. 88.

[48] U.S. Sentencing Commission, *Guidelines Manual* (Washington, D.C.: U.S. Government Printing Office, 1991), chap. 8.

[49] Evelyn E. C. Queen, "Corporate Sentencing Guidelines," in Margaret P. Spencer and Ronald R. Sims (eds.), *Corporate Misconduct* (Westport, Conn.: Quorum Books, 1995), p. 58.

[50] For a critique of the left's embrace of white-collar crime and the tendency to ignore or simplify the crime issue, see Nicole Hahn Rafter, "Left Out by the Left: Crime and Crime Control," *Socialist Review* 16 (1986): 7–23.

178 corporate offenders in federal courts during the mid-1980s show that the average monetary harm per offense committed was $565,000.[51] In contrast, the average loss per burglary and per larceny during this time period was $1,000 and $400 respectively.[52] Moreover, a single decision to produce an unsafe product can maim or kill thousands of victims. Homicides in the United States hover around 22,000 persons per year, a number that is about one-fifth the number of persons who die on a yearly basis from diseases and injuries related to work.[53] When deaths and injuries due to unsafe products, environmental hazards, and other illegal corporate acts are added to the equation, corporate crime is perhaps the most dangerous and consequential kind of crime that occurs in our society.

The Economic Crisis Issue

Scapegoating also has played a role in the push for harsher criminal sanctions against both conventional and corporate offenders. Minorities (particularly African Americans) are blamed for the loss of working-class jobs and economic security (via "quota systems") for whites. At the same time, blacks are portrayed as our most dangerous criminals.[54] Corporate policies, such as debt financing and investment in junk bonds, have resulted in economic crises in some businesses and banking. Yet, despite bankruptcies and bailouts, CEOs and other top managers continue to earn multimillion dollar salaries and benefits or golden parachutes as their firms lose money, are taken over, or go bankrupt. At General Dynamics, for instance, while the work force was being cut by 18,000 in 1991, 23 top executives received $35 million in salary, bonuses, and stock options. This was three times the amount they had earned the prior year.[55] The savings-and-loan fiasco of the 1980s, in which thousands of victims and the general public directly or through bailouts lost billions of dollars due to unlawful risk taking and looting by bank executives, has contributed to the image of the profiteering

---

[51] Mark A. Cohen, "Corporate Crime and Punishment: A Study of Social Harm and Sentencing Practice in the Federal Courts, 1984–1987," *American Criminal Law Review* 26 (1989): 605–660.

[52] Federal Bureau of Investigation, *Uniform Crime Reports for the United States* (Washington, D.C.: U.S. Government Printing Office, 1988).

[53] Mark Green and John F. Berry, "White-Collar Crime Is Big Business," *Nation,* June 8, 1985, p. 707.

[54] Sentencing disparities between blacks and whites convicted of cocaine possession and trafficking illustrate the white majority concerns over dangerousness. See Michael Tonry, *Malign Neglect: Race, Crime, and Punishment in America* (Oxford: Oxford University Press, 1995).

[55] David A. Vise and Steve Coll, "The Two Faces of Greed," *Washington Post Magazine,* September 29, 1991, pp. 13–31; Elizabeth Holtzman, "When Management Falls Down on the Job," *Washington Post,* May 26, 1992, sec. A.

CEO and the powerless diffuse victim.[56] As reported in 1996, AT&T cut its work force by 40,000 at the same time that CEO Robert E. Allen received a pay package of $16 million. Richard Cohen observes, "The issue is not whether Allen deserved the package, but whether it was seemly for him to have taken it."[57]

Conservative politicians have recognized the power of race-based politics (Willie Horton was so effectively linked to Michael Dukakis that Republican pundits called him Dukakis's "running mate") and have exploited white working- and middle-class fear of blacks. The left manages the politics of class by building on working- and lower-class resentment of upper-class privilege.[58] Fear and resentment breed punitive responses toward members of those social groups held responsible for various societal ills. Sutherland was an early observer of this phenomenon:[59] "Fear and resentment develop... principally as the result of an accumulation of crimes, as depicted in crime rates or in general descriptions. Such resentment develops under those circumstances both as to white collar crimes and other crimes."

Governmental Mistrust Issue

Jack Katz has suggested that a social movement against white-collar crime emerged after the Watergate scandal at a time when the presidency lost "its considerable ability to protect lesser power centers from moral attack."[60] Consequently, those usually immune from scrutiny, such as government and business elites, found themselves illuminated by the public spotlight and under political and legal attack.[61] An essential part of this attack has

---

[56] For a discussion of the savings-and-loan cases, see Kitty Calavita and Henry N. Pontell, " 'Heads I Win, Tails You Lose': Deregulation, Crime and Crisis in the Savings and Loan Industry," *Crime and Delinquency* 36 (1990): 309–341; Calavita and Pontell, " 'Other People's Money' Revisited"; and Calavita and Pontell, "Thrift Fraud as Organized Crime," *Criminology* 31 (1993): 519–548.

[57] Richard Cohen, "Lifestyles of the Rich and Shameless," *Washington Post*, April 18, 1996, p. A25.

[58] See, for instance, Amitai Etzioni, "Going Soft on Corporate Crime," *Miami Herald*, April 15, 1990; Mark Muro, "What Punishment Fits a Corporate Crime?" *Boston Globe*, May 7, 1989; Philip Shenon, "The Case of the Criminal Corporation," *New York Times*, January 15, 1989.

[59] Sutherland, White-Collar Crime, p. 46.

[60] Jack Katz, "The Social Movement against White-Collar Crime," in Egon Bittner and Sheldon Messinger (eds.), *Criminology Review Yearbook*, vol. 2 (Beverly Hills, Calif.: Sage, 1980), p. 178.

[61] Ibid., pp. 166–171; Cullen et al., *Corporate Crime under Attack*. Academics are not immune to these forces. Vaughan (*The Challenger Launch Decision*), for instance, reflected on her initial inclination to define and comprehend the disastrous *Challenger* launch as an instance of intentional immoral wrongdoing. A careful consideration of the evidence, however, revealed a more complicated picture of how deviance came to be normalized in organizational policies and procedures – including safety regulations.

involved the use of criminal law (historically the social control tool of choice against the disenfranchised) against business and government criminals. Cases studies of the Ford Pinto criminal prosecution and the Imperial Food Products manslaughter convictions seem to suggest that local prosecutors are the "key actors in socially constructing corporate violence as lawlessness," setting precedents (legally and otherwise) for criminalization.[62]

This phenomenon was, by no means, restricted to the United States. In his review of the rise and fall of the fraud issue in the Netherlands, Brant ironically observes:

> Far from defining the black, the poor, the long-haired hippy, the working class, the lumpenprolitariate, the lunatic fringe or any other traditional and easily available scapegoat of capitalism as a threat to societal values, ... the fraud panic at its height was about the pillars of Dutch society.... the way of coping most frequently resorted to was criminal law.[63]

Whether the social movement against white-collar crime has had any long-term institutional effects is debatable. In the United States, Katz saw signs of its demise during the Carter administration.[64] In the Netherlands, after an expansion of criminal law into all areas of white-collar and corporate crime during the 1980s, Brant claims that the 1990s saw a reversal in the cycle.[65] Others claim that post-Watergate effects on the sentencing of white-collar offenders have been mixed. More white-collar criminals may have gone to prison, but for less time than comparable (and less educated) conventional offenders.[66] One fact, however, is indisputable. Criminal law is utilized in *corporate* crime cases more than ever before.

The Facts of Criminalization

Prior to 1982, the Environmental Protection Agency (EPA) relied primarily on civil penalties to discipline environmental law violators.[67] This fact is not surprising given that the agency did not have any criminal investigators on

---

[62] John P. Wright, Francis T. Cullen, and Michael B. Blankenship, "The Social Construction of Corporate Violence: Media Coverage of the Imperial Food Products Fire," *Crime and Delinquency* 41 (1995): 33; Cullen et al., *Corporate Crime under Attack*.

[63] C. Brant, "The System's Rigged – or Is It?" *Crime, Law and Social Change* 21 (1995): 105.

[64] Katz, "Social Movement," p. 178.

[65] Brant, "The System's Rigged."

[66] John Hagan and Alberto Palloni, "'Club Fed' and the Sentencing of White-Collar Offenders before and after Watergate," *Criminology* 24 (1986): 603–621; Johnson, "Federal Court Processing."

[67] Frederick W. Addison III and Elizabeth E. Mack, "Creating an Environmental Ethic in Corporate America: The Big Stick of Jail Time," *Southwestern Law Journal* 44 (1991): 1427–1448.

staff until December 1981.[68] Once on board, however, these investigators took advantage of the criminalization of a number of environmental statutes (including the Clean Water Act and the Comprehensive Environmental Response Compensation and Liability Act) to increase both the number of criminal cases pursued by the EPA and more punitive outcomes. Sentences have become harsher and penalties more severe. For some environmental crimes the likelihood of going to prison, even for first-time offenders, has increased dramatically.[69] In 1984 the *total* length of prison time imposed on all violators by federal courts was two years. By 1989 this number had risen to almost thirty-seven years. Fines rose during this period as well – from $198,000 in 1984 to $11.1 million five years later.[70]

Although some suggest that criminal law is used mostly for egregious environmental violations and that the upward trend in punishment is modest[71] or leveling off,[72] a deterrence rationale is often invoked to justify stricter criminal penalties.[73]

The EPA is not alone in this trend. During the 1990s, health care fraud was a top priority with the Department of Justice. In the five-year period between 1992 and 1997, criminal convictions increased threefold.[74] A review of official data by Salinger shows that criminal prosecutions of price-fixing cases, after leaping to a peak during World War II after fifty years of sporadic enforcement efforts, increased steadily in the decades following the war.[75] Gallo, Dau-Schmidt, Craycraft, and Parker tracked Department of Justice criminal antitrust cases from 1955 through 1993. They concluded that "each half-decade in the 1980s have at least twice the number of cases brought in any of the previous half-decades, with a peak number of 404 criminal cases brought in the 1980–84 period."[76]

[68] Robert W. Alder and Charles Lord, "Environmental Crimes: Raising the Stakes," *George Washington Law Review* 59 (1991): 792.

[69] Addison and Mack, "Creating an Environmental Ethic in Corporate America," pp. 1442–1443.

[70] Ibid., p. 1427.

[71] Adler and Lord, "Environmental Crimes," p. 781.

[72] Ibid., p. 794.

[73] Ibid., p. 790.

[74] Malcolm K. Sparrow, "Fraud Control in the Health Care Industry: Assessing the State of the Art," *National Institute of Justice Research in Brief* (Washington, D.C.: U.S. Department of Justice, December 1998).

[75] Lawrence M. Salinger, "Antitrust Enforcement: An Analysis of Ninety-Nine Years of Federal Criminal Price-Fixing Cases, 1990–1988" (Ph.D. dissertation, Washington State University, 1992).

[76] Joseph C. Gallo, Kenneth G. Dau-Schmidt, Joseph L. Craycraft, and Charles J. Parker, "Criminal Penalties under the Sherman Act: A Study of Law and Economics," in Richard O. Zerbe Jr. (ed.), *Research in Law and Economics*, vol. 16 (Greenwich, Conn.: JAI Press, 1994), p. 26.

This upward trend in antitrust criminal prosecutions has abated some-what in the 1990s. Geis and Salinger, for instance, show that antitrust crim-inal prosecutions have decreased substantially from peak periods in the 1980s.[77] This decline may reflect a deterrent effect associated with the "enforcement seige" of the 1980s or a declining number of contested merger cases following passage of the Hart-Scott-Rodino law in 1986.[78] It may also indicate that the Department of Justice has reached a saturation point, given case increases during the 1980s absent comparable increases in bud-get and resources. Yet, even with lower overall numbers, criminal antitrust cases constitute a larger percentage of total cases. Gallo and associates show that criminal antitrust enforcement during 1993 reached 90 percent of total Department of Justice cases.[79]

The shift toward criminal prosecutions has not escaped the attention of business, either. Noting that the number of white-collar crimes pursued by federal authorities between 1970 and 1984 "increased three-fold," corpo-rate attorneys William Knepper and Dan Bailey highlight the areas in which corporations and corporate officials are criminally liable.[80] They are quick to note that an important part of this trend is the prosecution of direc-tors and officers responsible for "the governance and management of their corporation."[81]

The emphasis on prosecuting individuals instead of firms is shown in Department of Justice antitrust cases as well as EPA cases.[82] Between 1955 and 1993, 47 percent of Department of Justice antitrust cases involved in-dividual criminal defendants (mostly executive officers).[83] In cases where a verdict was rendered, the Department of Justice could boast an 82 per-cent success rate for cases in which an individual was a defendant.[84] "Since 1970, the number and percentage of individuals imprisoned and the av-erage prison term per individual has been significantly greater than prior to 1970."[85] Of the sixty-seven defendants convicted of or pleading guilty

[77] Gilbert Geis and Lawrence S. Salinger, "Antitrust and Organizational Deviance," in Peter A. Bamberger and William J. Sonnenstuhl (eds.), *Research in the Sociology of Organizations: Deviance in and of Organizations*, vol. 15 (Stamford, Conn.: JAI Press, 1998), pp. 71–110.

[78] Ibid., pp. 92–93.

[79] Gallo et al., "Criminal Penalties," p. 27.

[80] William E. Knepper and Dan A. Bailey, *Liability of Corporate Officers and Directors*, 4th ed. (Charlottesville, Va.: Michie Company, 1988).

[81] Ibid., p. 232.

[82] Addison and Mack, "Creating an Environmental Ethic in Corporate America," p. 1427, n. 4.

[83] Gallo et al., "Criminal Penalties," p. 31.

[84] Ibid., p. 36.

[85] Ibid., pp. 47–48.

for environmental offenses in fiscal year 1986, only twenty-two (less than one-third) were corporations. In a large majority of cases (73–84 percent), corporate officers are charged when the corporation is charged.[86] And, like the shift toward criminal over civil or administrative adjudication of cases, going after managers and directors is justified by a deterrence argument.

> The Justice Department and EPA strongly believe that members of the reg-
> ulated community will be less likely to consider willful or calculated evasion
> of environmental standards when they know that discovery might lead to a
> prison term. It is no accident, therefore, that three times as many individuals
> have been prosecuted by the Environmental Crimes Section as corporate de-
> fendants.... It has been, and will continue to be, Justice Department policy
> to conduct environmental criminal investigations with an eye toward identi-
> fying, prosecuting and convicting the highest-ranking, truly responsible cor-
> porate officials.[87]

Sentencing standards changed for both individual and corporate environmental criminals in 1987 with the sentencing guidelines for individuals going into effect in November and the Criminal Fines Improvements Act differentiating individual from corporate fine levels. As a result of these changes, average fines and sentenced jail time for both corporate and individual EPA violators have increased.[88]

The spectacular levels of fraud uncovered in the savings-and-loan industry also had an impact on criminalization. Congress, in 1989, passed the Financial Institutions Reform, Recovery, and Enforcement Act. This act enhanced the prosecutorial budget of the Department of Justice by $225 million – granted exclusively to pursue financial fraudsters. According to Calavita and Pontell, the act was successful. "By 1992, over eight hundred S&L offenders had been convicted, with 77 percent receiving prison terms."[89]

The 1991 sentencing guidelines for organizations increased the fine amounts for corporations sentenced for other types of felonies and class A misdemeanors (excluding antitrust and most environmental offenses). Research conducted on request for the U.S. Sentencing Commission found that preguidelines fines were substantially less than the actual dollar cost of

---

[86] Adler and Lord, "Environmental Crimes," p. 845.
[87] Addison and Mack, "Creating an Environmental Ethic in Corporate America," p. 1440, n. 115.
[88] Adler and Lord, "Environmental Crimes," pp. 790–799.
[89] Kitty Calavita and Henry N. Pontell, "Saving the Savings and Loans? U.S. Government Response to Financial Crime," in Frank Pearce and Laureen Snider (eds.), *Corporate Crime: Contemporary Debates* (Toronto: University of Toronto Press, 1995), p. 199.

the original offense, and that there were substantial sentencing disparities in the system.[90] Postguidelines studies, using data from 1984–1996, found fines (criminal and total pecuniary) to be higher for the guidelines-constrained sentences than for other observed sentences. However, because all fines rose after 1991 (both those constrained and unconstrained by the guidelines), it is unclear whether the guidelines are directly responsible for sanction increases.[91]

Conclusions

The social control of corporate offending increasingly is utilizing a strategy of criminalization. But what are the perceived benefits of prosecuting a case criminally rather than administratively or civilly? Generally, the application of criminal sanctions is thought to be stigmatic – that is, offenders are shamed by a "criminal" label. Civil or regulatory interventions are generally nonstigmatic and conciliatory. Ostensibly, the shame associated with criminal processing imposes additional inhibitory effects beyond (or as a consequence of) those attached to official discovery and processing.[92] Equally important for deterrence adherents is that criminal convictions often carry harsher penalties than those available through other legal means, especially for individuals who are convicted and sentenced to jail or prison. Reasonably, it is thought that harsh sanctions are more powerful deterrents than punishments that are inconsequential.

The primary aim of this work is to review, evaluate, and consider the corporate crime deterrence model. In the next chapter, the deterrence doctrine is traced from the late eighteenth century to its most recent permutations. Unlike other justifications for punishment that are not amenable to empirical verification and remain philosophical, deterrence propositions are testable.[93] Therefore, in Chapter 2 studies of conventional and corporate offenders are evaluated as to whether results are generally supportive of the doctrine. Chapter 3 gives special attention to some of the

[90] Mark A. Cohen, Chih-Chin Ho, Edward D. Jones III, and Laura M. Schleich, "Report on the Sentencing of Organizations in the Federal Courts, 1984–1987," in U.S. Sentencing Commission, *Discussion Materials on Organizational Sanctions* (Washington, D.C., 1988). See also Nagel and Swenson, "The Federal Sentencing Guidelines for Corporations."
[91] Cindy R. Alexander, Jennifer Arlen, and Mark A. Cohen, "Regulating Corporate Criminal Sanctions: Evidence on the Effect of the U.S. Sentencing Guidelines" (unpublished Working Paper, 1997).
[92] Sutherland, *White-Collar Crime*, pp. 43–44; Marshall B. Clinard, *The Black Market* (New York: Holt, Rinehart, 1952), pp. 59–60, 243–245.
[93] William J. Chambliss, "Types of Deviance and the Effectiveness of Legal Sanctions," *Wisconsin Law Review* 25 (1967): 703–704.

problems associated with applying criminal law to corporations (as criminal actors) and to corporate managers, while civil (primarily tort) and regulatory law are examined as possible sources of deterrence in Chapters 4 and 5 respectively.

The discussion in Chapter 6 shifts away from the purely legal realm toward crime control alternatives, especially the role of informal sanction threats and enforced corporate self-regulation. Alternatives to formal legal sanctions are evaluated in the context of recent assertions that corporate crime regulation is a dialectical process – a process that acknowledges that state imposition of harsh punishment may, in fact, be counterproductive[94] and that deterrence and compliance are best understood as complementary crime control strategies.[95] Different arguments promoting and challenging the wisdom of self-regulation are reviewed, including the notion that organizational personnel are most aware of corporate crime when it occurs and therefore are the best people to pinpoint organizational vulnerabilities and identify culpable parties.[96] Additionally, we examine the deterrence argument in light of recent research that questions whether corporate deviance (and managerial decision making) is the product of cost-benefit calculations.

In Chapter 7, original research is used to evaluate deterrence and cooperative models of corporate crime control. Results support the inhibitory effect of individual shame, prosocial habituation, and informal sanctions on corporate offending for most, but not all, offenders. Criminal and other legal sanctions appear to play an important crime inhibition role among those who do not view corporate crime as morally abhorrent. Finally, Chapter 8 offers policy implications in light of survey results along with suggestions for new research directions.

---

[94] Toni Makkai and John Braithwaite, "The Dialectics of Corporate Deterrence," *Journal of Research in Crime and Delinquency* 31 (1994): 366.

[95] John Braithwaite, *To Punish or Persuade* (Albany, N.Y.: SUNY Press; 1985).

[96] See, e.g., ibid. and John Braithwaite, "Taking Corporate Responsibility Seriously: Corporate Compliance Systems," in Brent Fisse and Peter A. French (eds.), *Corrigible Corporations and Unruly Law* (San Antonio: Trinity University Press, 1985), pp. 39–61; and *Crime, Shame, and Reintegration* (Cambridge: Cambridge University Press, 1989), pp. 129–151.

CHAPTER TWO

Deterrence in Review

GIVEN THE importance of a deterrence framework perspective as a rationale for bringing more criminal law into the corporate crime control process, the philosophy of deterrence deserves a more systematic treatment. Accordingly, in this chapter, we focus exclusively on the deterrence doctrine. Specifically, I trace the philosophical development of deterrence from the simple views of rationality and hedonism put forth by eighteenth-century utilitarians to the various positions advocated today by social scientists; and then examine what studies tell us about the relationship between formal legal sanctions and control of conventional crime, and the deterrent effects of criminal justice processing for corporate offenders.

Rationality and Crime

The Classical School

The origins of deterrence lie in the so-called classical school of criminology. Cesare Bonnesana Marchese de Beccaria (1738–1794) and Jeremy Bentham (1748–1832), the two philosophers most strongly identified with this tradition, were influenced by Enlightenment ideas about human nature and the development of society. Beccaria argued that human beings, upon joining society, gave up certain individual freedoms in exchange for the protection and security that society offered. The social contract that was established from this exchange gave the state the authority to establish law and to punish violators.[1]

---

[1] Cesare Beccaria, *On Crimes and Punishments*, trans. Henry Paolucci (Indianapolis: Bobbs-Merrill, 1963).

Classical criminologists assumed that all persons were capable of criminality because of a "natural" human tendency to pursue pleasurable activities. This natural hedonism, however, was tempered by rationality. Individuals would weigh the benefits of crime against the consequences of punishment before a course of action was decided.[2] If the consequences of crime (i.e., punishment) outweighed its benefits (pleasurable anticipated outcomes), classicists surmised that illegal conduct would be inhibited. Conversely, if the threat of punishment was dwarfed by crime's pleasures, then criminality was undeterred.

Several factors were thought to influence the deterrent value of punishment. First, and most important, a more certain punishment offered a greater threat than one less certain. So too, when punishment was swiftly applied, the association between the criminal act and its costs would be more clearly associated in the minds of the deviants. A third element of the punishment triad, severity, was also identified as essential to deterrence. However, given that punishment at the time was excessively harsh (e.g., England had more than two hundred capital offenses, and death by execution occurred every six weeks in early eighteenth-century London), severity was thought to be more effective when it was proportional to the seriousness of the offense.[3] Bentham, for instance, felt that punishment should not produce more pain than was necessary to prevent crime. If excessively severe, the positive gains from the necessary evil of punishment would be defeated.[4] The utilitarians (as classical criminologists came to be called) wrought significant legal and constitutional changes across Europe, Great Britain, and the United States, but their ideas fell into disfavor. High crime rates and scientifically oriented research temporarily, at least, derailed armchair theorizing about hedonism, rationality, and the benefits of a reasoned system of punishment.

By the late nineteenth century, a new social-scientific criminology was emerging. "Positive" criminology sought to identify the biological, psychological, and sociological determinants of crime. It would be another seventy years before utilitarian ideas reemerged to gain a significant toehold in the study of crime.

The Neoclassical School

Modern deterrence theory is indebted to the classical school for many of its basic ideas about crime causation and the role of punishment in inhibiting

---

[2] Jeremy Bentham, *An Introduction to the Principles of Morals and Legislation*, ed. Laurence J. Lafler (New York: Haftner, 1948).

[3] Beccaria, *On Crimes and Punishment*.

[4] Bentham, *Introduction*.

illegal conduct. However, Andenaes suggests that early deterrence theory was primarily concerned with "mere deterrence" or the frightening effects of punishment, ignoring punishment's other preventative effects.[5] He argues that, in addition to deterrence, punishment has moralizing and habituation effects.[6] Thus, punishment or its threat can inhibit individuals from violating the law because: (1) they fear the consequences of punishment, (2) law and its application have an educative influence on citizens, and (3) a person's prosocial habits are reinforced. These outcomes can occur at the individual level (specific prevention) or at a broader societal level (general prevention).

Specific deterrence is concerned with how individuals respond to punishment. That is, do individuals subjected to sanctions adjust or modify their actions after punishment? General deterrence assumes that the application of sanctions to law violators will prevent others from engaging in similar offenses. Thus, when a criminal is put to death, not only will she or he not offend again (specific deterrence), but the actual execution will send a message to the rest of society that the death penalty is a cost to be considered when contemplating a capital offense. If this communication is received and crime inhibited, general deterrence has been achieved.[7]

Beccaria and Bentham's simple conception of rationality also has been elaborated by neoclassical theorists. Human rationality is characterized as partially determined and bounded (or limited).[8] Decision choices are limited by the amount, quality, and type of knowledge individuals process. Persons vary in their capacities to incorporate and evaluate material relevant to their decision choices. Importantly, the concept of bounded rationality suggests that decisions may not be "optimal" in the real world but structured by the information available to, as well as the capacities and experiences of, the decision maker.

Choices can be influenced by demographic, environmental, and situational experiences. Past experience with criminality and the criminal justice system, for instance, can modify a person's perceptions of sanction likelihood and cost.[9] Thus, experienced persons will be more realistic in their

---

[5] Johannes Andenaes, *Punishment and Deterrence* (Ann Arbor: University of Michigan Press, 1974).

[6] Ibid., p. 6.

[7] See Raymond Paternoster, *Capital Punishment in America* (New York: Lexington Books, 1991), for a recent review of these positions.

[8] Derek B. Cornish and Ronald V. Clarke (eds.), *The Reasoning Criminal: Rational Choice Perspectives on Offending* (New York: Springer-Verlag, 1986).

[9] Linda Saltzman, Raymond Paternoster, Gordon P. Waldo, and Theodore G. Chiricos, "Deterrent and Experimental Effects: The Problem of Causal Order in Perceptual Deterrence Research," *Journal of Research in Crime and Delinquency* 13 (1982): 172–189; Pamela Richards

assessments of sanctions than those with little crime or formal criminal justice experience.[10]

Deterrence theory has been influenced and expanded by economic arguments about decision choices. These influences are particularly salient in the corporate crime area. Such models assume that complex social phenomena such as feelings, moral values, taste, and convenience are reducible to quantifiable elements of cost and benefit. Economists working within this tradition argue that these preferences along with more traditional economic considerations influence individual choices. Gary Becker's economic model views crime and crime control in the following manner:

> The approach taken here follows the economists' usual analysis of choice and assumes that a person commits an offense if the expected utility to him exceeds the utility he could get by using his time and other resources at other activities. Some persons become "criminals," therefore, not because their basic motivation differs from that of other persons, but because their benefits and costs differ.[11]

The economic approach to deterrence (also known as the Chicago school perspective or utility models of crime and punishment) has had little influence on conventional criminal justice policy – in part because evidence supporting the model's assumptions is equivocal or policy recommendations are seen as premature.[12] However, economic utility models have been salient in the debate over sentencing guidelines for organizational offenders.[13] Preliminary drafts of the sentencing guidelines, based on an optimal penalties approach, determined punishments by multiplying the harm of the act by the probability of conviction. From this perspective, fines are viewed as the most appropriate punishment ("taxes") for corporate criminals as

and Charles Tittle, "Gender and Perceived Chances of Arrest," *Social Forces* 59 (1981): 1182–1199.

[10] The concept of bounded rationality is defined by Herbert A. Simon as a simplified model of an actor's real situation. "He behaves rationally with respect to this model, and such behavior is not even approximately optimal with respect to the real world." See his *Models of Man* (New York: Wiley, 1957), p. 199.

[11] Gary S. Becker, "Crime and Punishment: An Economic Approach," *Journal of Political Economy* 76 (1968): 176.

[12] Pamela Lattimore and Ann Witte, "Models of Decision Making under Uncertainty: The Criminal Choice," in Derek B. Cornish and Ronald V. Clarke (eds.), *The Reasoning Criminal: Rational Choice Perspectives on Offending* (New York: Springer-Verlag, 1986), pp. 129–155; Daniel Nagin, "Criminal Deterrence Research at the Outset of the Twenty-First Century," in Michael Tonry (ed.), *Crime and Justice: A Review of Research*, vol. 23 (Chicago: University of Chicago Press, 1998), pp. 1–42.

[13] For example, Mark A. Cohen, "Corporate Crime and Punishment: A Study of Social Harm and Sentencing Practice in the Federal Courts, 1984–1987," *American Criminal Law Review* 26 (1989): 605–660; Richard Posner, "Optimal Sentences for White-Collar Criminals," *American Criminal Law Review* 17 (1980): 409–418.

monetary costs can be calculated and incorporated into the firm or managerial decision choice. The final version of the guidelines, however, moved away from a strict optimal penalty approach, in large part because it was too difficult to estimate sanction probability for the myriad of offenses in which organizations engaged. "Estimates about the probability of detection based on non-random survey responses were judged to be too 'rough,' bordering on mere assumptions; empirical verification of these rough estimates was impossible."[14] It is important to recognize, as well, that corporate leaders and business advocates complained vociferously that the optimal penalty approach would produce excessively punitive fines (over deterrence).[15] A modified deterrence model was adopted by the commission instead in which the seriousness of the offense (calculated by illicit gains to the firm or economic losses) is used to make a base-fine calculation. The base fine is then increased or decreased (multiplied) by a culpability score, which is determined by the number of aggravating or mitigating factors (measures of a firm's "good citizenship").[16] "The culpability score is the means by which the fine provisions of the Guidelines implement the sentencing purposes of *just punishment and deterrence.*"[17]

A final modification of the classical deterrence perspective by modern theorists is the assumption that deterrence may vary by crime type. Some have suggested that the greatest deterrent impact should occur when criminal acts are instrumental and calculative in nature.[18] Theft, therefore, should be more amenable to deterrence than rape, drug trafficking more responsive than drug use, and most kinds of corporate crime more deterrable than most forms of violent crime.

Empirical Support for Deterrence

Conventional Crime

The reemergence of the deterrence doctrine in the late 1960s spawned extensive tests of deterrence hypotheses, especially those related to certainty

---

[14] Ilene H. Nagel and Winthrop M. Swenson, "The Federal Sentencing Guidelines for Corporation: Their Development, Theoretical Underpinnings, and Some Thought about Their Future," *Washington University Law Quarterly* 71 (1993): 219.

[15] Comments heard by this author at the February 14, 1990, public hearings dealing with organizational sanctions.

[16] Nagel and Swenson, "The Federal Sentencing Guidelines for Corporation," pp. 233–336.

[17] Ibid., p. 233 (emphasis added).

[18] Charles Tittle, "Crime Rates and Legal Sanctions," *Social Problems* 16 (1969): 409–423; Steven Burkett and David A. Ward, "A Note on Perceptual Deterrence, Religiously Based Moral Condemnation, and Social Control," *Criminology* 31 (1993): 119–134. For contrary empirical evidence, see Gary F. Jenson, Jack P. Gibbs, and Maynard Erickson, "Perceived Risk of Punishment and Self-Reported Delinquency," *Social Forces* 57 (1978): 57–78.

and severity of punishment, formal versus informal sanctions, and variation in deterrent effects across crime types. This research has taken two distinct paths: general deterrence studies that employ aggregate data to assess the relationship between actual punishments and levels of criminal activity (*objective* deterrence) versus investigations that assess how subjective judgments of punishment risk and consequence influence the criminality of individuals (*perceptual* deterrence). Objective and perceptual studies utilize distinct research strategies. According to the objective deterrence literature, this approach assumes that the actual threat of punishment certainty associated with committing a crime (usually measured as "the ratio of prison commitments or arrests to total crimes in an area under study")[19] and its degree of severity (measured as the aggregate length of a sentence served for the particular crime of interest)[20] will affect some objective measure of crime such as, say, the official homicide rate.

In general, objective deterrence research shows only mixed support for deterrence arguments. Early studies, typically unsophisticated methodologically,[21] were more apt to find inverse relationships between sanction certainty and severity (occasionally) and the incidence of crime. More recently, research designs that incorporate econometric estimation techniques and include relevant control variables have failed to replicate the deterrent effects found in initial studies, particularly those of sanction severity.[22] Daniel Nagin, in his review of this literature, cautioned against prematurely concluding that deterrence hypotheses are supported by the data. "Taken as a whole, the evidence might be judged as providing reasonably definitive support of the deterrence hypothesis. . . . However, the evidence is not as definitive as it might appear."[23] Others found the evidence more compelling. For instance, a mere two years after Nagin's influential assessment, Cook claimed that deterrence studies support the idea that punishment works for some crimes. The fact that crime rates increased substantially during naturally occurring events (e.g., police strikes) was also compelling evidence in favor of deterrence. Based on his review, Cook concluded, "the criminal justice system, ineffective though

---

[19] Franklin E. Zimring, "Policy Experiments in General Deterrence: 1970–1975," in Alfred Blumstein, Jacqueline Cohen, and David Nagin (eds.), *Deterrence and Incapacitation: Estimating the Effects of Criminal Sanctions on Crime Rates* (Washington, D.C.: National Academy of Sciences, 1978), p. 171.

[20] Raymond Paternoster, "The Deterrent Effect of the Perceived Certainty and Severity of Punishment: A Review of the Evidence and Issues," *Justice Quarterly* 4 (1987): 173.

[21] Early studies usually relied on cross-sectional data; bivariate correlations; few, if any, controls; and/or overlapping measures of the independent and dependent variables.

[22] Paternoster, "The Deterrent Effect."

[23] Daniel Nagin, "General Deterrence: A Review of the Literature," in Blumstein et al., *Deterrence and Incapacitation: Estimating the Effects of Criminal Sanctions on Crime Rates*, p. 111.

it may seem in many areas, has an overall crime deterrent effect of great magnitude."[24]

Yet, among most criminologists and sociologists, the theoretical and methodological problems associated with objective deterrence studies led most researchers to abandon objective deterrence in favor of perceptual deterrence. An obvious exception to this trend involves the death penalty scholars.[25]

The perceptual approach to deterrence questions whether, in fact, the objective application of sanctions influences behavior at all. Jack Gibbs argues that the objective likelihood of sanction is important only to the extent that a person's perceptions of his or her own punishment risks are affected by it.[26] This subjective deterrence position is neatly summarized by Raymond Paternoster: "deterrence was most likely to depend on what the certainty and severity of punishment were *thought* to be rather than on their objective or actual levels. When the deterrence doctrine was restated in this way, researchers began to examine it as a *perceptual process.*"[27]

Operationally, perceptual deterrence studies employ survey techniques in which respondents are asked to estimate their own punishment risks. For instance, subjects might be asked what they think the chances are that they will be arrested if they commit a particular criminal or deviant act; or, given X probability of being caught, would they commit a criminal or deviant act. Subjects might then be queried about how costly arrest would be for them. These estimates are then juxtaposed against self-reported criminal participation to see whether perceptions of punishment threat influence a person's behavior.

It is difficult to summarize findings from the perceptual deterrence literature because research designs, variables of interest, operationalization, and statistical methods vary greatly from study to study. Yet, after several decades of research in this area, some relatively consistent patterns have emerged.

Uncommitted. Among the criminally uncommitted, legal sanctions are of little consequence to decision processes. To use Cook's terminology, this group will find the profit or pain associated with criminal opportunities "highly

---

[24] Philip J. Cook, "Research in Criminal Deterrence: Laying the Groundwork for the Second Decade," in Norval Morris and Michael Tonry (eds.), *An Annual Review of Research*, vol. 2 (Chicago: University of Chicago Press, 1980), p. 213.

[25] See, e.g., Ruth D. Peterson and William C. Bailey, "Felony Murder and Capital Punishment: An Examination of the Deterrence Question," *Criminology* 29 (1991): 367–418.

[26] Jack Gibbs, *Crime, Punishment, and Deterrence* (New York: Elsevier, 1975), p. 115, n. 6.

[27] Paternoster, "The Deterrent Effect," p. 174 (emphasis in original).

unattractive."[28] In general, the law-abiding are relatively unaffected by variations in the threat of punishment because the idea to commit a criminal act simply never occurs to them. This tendency toward moral habituation, as Andenaes would call it, is demonstrated in Quint Thurman's study of tax evasion. Thurman found that among a randomly generated sample of respondents, almost three-fourths (more than 73 percent) were disinclined to cheat on their taxes *regardless* of any variation in punishment certainty or severity. Even under conditions of minimal sanction risk, his respondents overwhelmingly indicated that they would not falsify tax documents.[29] Similarly, in their factorial survey, Bachman, Paternoster, and Ward discovered that formal sanction threats mattered little to a group of male college students who considered sexual offending to be morally wrong. Conversely, among students who were not morally offended by rape scenarios, more instrumental concerns (including legal sanction risks) weighed more heavily in respondents' self-reported offending probabilities.[30]

Committed. Fear of formal legal sanctions does not significantly alter the behavior of persons firmly committed to a criminal life-style. In fact, among this group of offenders, criminal opportunities will be assessed as highly desirable and worthwhile.[31] Ironically, John Conklin notes that many criminals fail to take sanction threats into account *because to do so would reduce a criminal's confidence that the illegal act could be completed successfully.*[32] Under this condition, the choice to engage in crime appears to be "irrationally rational."

On the other hand, many career criminals assume that getting caught is just one of the many risks of their chosen profession. This does not mean that punishment inevitability renders them imprudent. Ethnographic accounts of professional thieves, for instance, show that much planning and thorough preparation goes into selecting a likely target, the appropriate time for the act, and the necessary tools to ensure a successful outcome.[33]

---

[28] Cook, "Research in Criminal Deterrence," p. 218.

[29] Quint Thurman, "General Prevention of Tax Evasion: A Factorial Survey Approach," *Journal of Quantitative Criminology* 5 (1989): 127–146.

[30] Ronet Bachman, Raymond Paternoster, and Sally Ward, "The Rationality of Sexual Offending: Testing a Deterrence/Rational Choice Conception of Sexual Assault," *Law and Society Review* 26 (1992): 343–372.

[31] Cook, "Research in Criminal Deterrence," p. 218.

[32] John E. Conklin, *Criminology* (New York: Macmillan, 1986), p. 386.

[33] Neal Shover, *Great Pretenders* (Chapel Hill: University of North Carolina Press, 1996), pp. 156–157; Harry King and William J. Chambliss, *Harry King: A Professional Thief's Journey* (New York: John Wiley & Sons, 1984); and Richard P. Rettig, Manual J. Torres, and Gerald R. Garrett, *Manny: A Criminal-Addict's Story* (Boston: Houghton Mifflin, 1977).

Safecrackers, for instance, take pains to avoid discovery and, depending on the level of risk, may adjust their criminal participation accordingly. It is unlikely, however, that professional thieves will cease criminal activities completely. Instead, some level of restricted deterrence (lessening the frequency of participation) or displaced deterrence (a shift of target, locale, or timing of the act) may be achieved by increasing the likelihood of discovery.

Deterring the criminally committed is a difficult task indeed. Part of the problem may lie with what Jack Katz calls "the seductions of crime." To the extent that sanction risk is a factor at all in the crime calculus, deterrence theorists might have it on the wrong side of the cost-benefit equation. Part of the attractiveness of crime might be that it is risky, thrilling, and seductive.[34]

Marginally Committed. Among persons marginally committed to criminal activity, shifts in punishment risk seem to affect behavior. For these "indifferent" individuals, even a small change in risk factors can affect behavior.[35] Tittle and Rowe have suggested that there is a tipping point in the deterrence process – a risk level that, once reached, renders the criminal act too costly to consider.[36] Klepper and Nagin find, for instance, that increasing sanction certainty from zero to a nonzero possibility acts as a powerful deterrent among persons who were inclined to cheat on their taxes.[37] The authors speculate that the characteristics of their sample (i.e., middle-class, mid-career master's students) may account for this dramatic result. For persons who have much to lose by discovery, merely increasing sanction likelihood above zero produces a risk they are unwilling to take.

It is important to distinguish, however, perceived losses stemming from criminal justice processing from other kinds of threats associated with offending. Among persons who might be motivated to commit crime under the right kinds of conditions (such as the respondents described earlier), extralegal (informal) costs associated with criminal behavior may be enough to constrain them from doing so. For instance, the perceived costs to reputation, self-esteem, salient personal attachments, and future opportunities

---

[34] See, e.g., John Hagan, *Structural Criminology* (New Brunswick, N.J.: Rutgers University Press, 1989), pp. 153–154. In his book *The Seductions of Crime* (New York: Basic Books, 1988), Jack Katz describes the "sneaky thrills" of shoplifting, vandalism, and joyriding but also the rational irrationality of robbery and murder.

[35] Cook, "Research in Criminal Deterrence," p. 218.

[36] The tipping point that they observe is an aggregate one; however, rational-choice theory would predict that individuals have tipping points as well (e.g., the point at which costs exceed benefits or vice versa). Charles R. Tittle and Alan R. Rowe, "Certainty of Arrest and Crime Rates: A Further Test of the Deterrence Hypothesis," *Social Forces* 52 (1974): 455–462.

[37] Steven Klepper and Daniel Nagin, "Tax Compliance and Perceptions of the Risk of Detection and Criminal Prosecution," *Law and Society Review* 23 (1989): 209–240.

are, in general, more threatening and inhibitive of misconduct than formal legal sanction certainty or severity.[38] Klepper and Nagin fail to control for these kinds of costs in their study. Thus, it is possible that their findings are spurious.[39]

Others, however, examine both kinds of costs. In their study of deterrence, Harold Grasmick and Donald Green examine the potential inhibitory effects of both formal and informal sanctions on past or estimated future participation in eight illegal activities. They find that formal legal sanctions, moral commitment to law-abiding behavior, and the threat of social disapproval from significant others inhibited "those people who, for whatever reason, are *ever-motivated* to commit illegal acts" (emphasis added). Like Thurman's study of tax cheats and Bachman and associates' respondents contemplating the possibility of sexual offending, Grasmick and Green conclude that among the noncriminally motivated population, inhibitory factors such as these "should be irrelevant in the production of conformity to legal norms."[40]

More recent studies – in the rational-choice tradition – also demonstrate that both formal sanction threats and self-imposed costs (such as feeling shame or guilt) discourage offending.[41] There is some disagreement as to whether informal costs inhibit crime independent of formal sanctions. Criminologists Kirk Williams and Richard Hawkins suggest that extralegal inhibitors are activated by the risk of formal legal processing. So, for instance, a person fears the loss of reputation as a direct consequence of

---

[38] Raymond Paternoster, "Decisions to Participate in and Desist from Four Types of Common Delinquency: Deterrence and the Rational Choice Perspective," *Law and Society Review* 23 (1989): 7–40; Harold G. Grasmick and Donald E. Green, "Legal Punishment, Social Disapproval and Internationalization as Inhibitors of Illegal Behavior," *Journal of Criminal Law and Criminology* 71 (1980): 325–335; Irving Piliavin, Rosemary Gartner, Craig Thornton, and Ross L. Matsueda, "Crime, Deterrence, and Rational Choice," *American Sociological Review* 51 (1986): 101–119.

[39] In an extension of their earlier work, Klepper and Nagin find that sanction severity (criminal prosecution given detection) also has a deterrent impact on tax cheaters. They suggest that this result (which is fairly anomalous in the perceptual deterrence literature) is due to the fact that their measure of severity fails to unpack legal from other attendant costs related to prosecution including stigmatic, attachment, and commitment costs. See Steven Klepper and Daniel Nagin, "The Deterrent Effect of Perceived Certainty and Severity of Punishment Revisited," *Criminology* 27 (1989): 721–746.

[40] Harold G. Grasmick and Donald E. Green, "Legal Punishment, Social Disapproval and Internationalization as Inhibitors of Illegal Behavior," *Journal of Criminal Law and Criminology* 71 (1980): 335.

[41] See, e.g., Harold G. Grasmick and Robert J. Bursik Jr., "Conscience, Significant Others, and Rational Choice: Extending the Deterrence Model," *Law and Society Review* 24 (1990): 837–861; Bachman et al., "The Rationality of Sexual Offending"; Daniel S. Nagin and Raymond Paternoster, "Enduring Individual Differences and Rational Choice Theories of Crime," *Law and Society Review* 27 (1993): 467–496.

arrest and prosecution.[42] Although research into this question is far from conclusive, preliminary tests conducted by authors other than Williams and Hawkins suggest that informal sanctions operate relatively independently of legal threats and are generally more powerful in their constraints.[43]

Crime Benefits. Deterrent effects will vary depending on the motivations and opportunities for criminal behavior (the benefits of crime) and other opportunity structures. As indispensable as the concept of benefit is for a deterrence framework (at least deterrence recast in rational-choice or economic utility terms), few studies of deterrence actually measure the potential gains of crime – and most of these employ objective deterrence research designs. These investigations suggest that both formal sanctions *and* economic opportunities (operationalized as income from legal activity, the legal wage rate, and employment chances) are inversely related to the incidence of crime.[44] Thus, crime decreases with both punishment certainty and severity (the fear factor) *and* with better opportunities for legitimate employment and income.

Perceptual studies are also beginning to explore the role of opportunity and benefit in assessing criminal possibilities. Klepper and Nagin, for instance, characterize their taxpayers as "gamblers" who consider the costs and benefits of false reporting carefully before taking a chance on noncompliance. "Like the findings of other studies on the 'rational' criminal, our results portray an image of an informed, rational taxpayer who structures his noncompliance gambles to keep the risks of detection and criminal prosecution down to acceptable levels."[45]

W. Kip Viscusi replicates the importance of benefit using a different segment of respondents. Among inner-city black youths, Viscusi shows that illegalities that are perceived to be extremely risky (i.e., likely to result in

---

[42] See Andenaes, *Punishment and Deterrence*, pp. 34–83, Kirk R. Williams and Richard Hawkins, "Perceptual Research on General Deterrence: A Critical Review," *Law and Society Review* 20 (1986): 545–572.

[43] Daniel S. Nagin and Raymond Paternoster, "On the Relationship of Past and Future Participation in Delinquency," *Criminology* 29 (1991): 163–189. Bachman et al., "The Rationality of Sexual Offending."

[44] A brief summary of this literature is provided by Steven Klepper and Daniel Nagin, "The Criminal Deterrence Literature: Implications for Research on Taxpayer Compliance," in Jeffrey A. Roth and John T. Scholz (eds.), *Taxpayer Compliance*, vol. 2 (Philadelphia: University of Pennsylvania Press, 1989), p. 135. See also W. Kip Viscusi, "Market Incentives for Criminal Behavior," in R. Freeman and H. Holzer, (eds.), *Inner-City Black Youth Unemployment* (Chicago: University of Chicago Press, 1986).

[45] Klepper and Nagin, "Tax Compliance," p. 238.

arrest, conviction, and prison) require compensatory benefits. One way to think about these "risk premiums" is in deterrence terms. Viscusi suggests:

> Legitimate and illegitimate activities both have upward-sloping income-risk profiles. The primary distinguishing characteristic of illegitimate activities is that the risk premiums have an additional policy implication in that they imply that enhanced criminal enforcement will raise the risks to crime, thus diminishing its attractiveness.[46]

Finally, Piliavin and his colleagues examine the hypothesis that persons will engage in crime if the expected utility of crime is greater than the expected utility of other alternatives, taking into account formal and informal sanction risk. They use three distinct groups of persons with severe unemployment problems: adult offenders with a history of incarceration; adults who are known drug users; and adolescent school dropouts age seventeen to twenty, one-half of whom have arrest records. The study finds perceptions of neither formal nor informal sanction threats influence the crime choice. Instead, the opportunities and benefits associated with the illegal act are more salient to the decision process.[47]

Type of Crime. Deterrent effects vary by crime type. Recall that it is assumed in the deterrence literature that some crimes are more readily deterrable than others. Tax noncompliance falls neatly into the rational and therefore more deterrable kind of crime category. Studies consistently support this portrait, with almost all concluding that fear of detection deters most tax cheating.[48]

Other crimes, however, do not fit as cleanly – theoretically or empirically – into these simplistically drawn categories of rationality. For instance, crimes of passion are thought to involve more emotion than calculus; addictive or compulsive acts, like shoplifting or illicit drug use, imply compulsion and randomness, not calculation. Yet, these illegal acts, though not apparently as rational as tax fraud, involve decision choices and thus may be subject to instrumental and moral considerations.[49] Ronald Clarke and Derek Cornish suggest that rationality and deterrence must be understood in broad terms.

> Even if the choices made or the decision processes themselves are not optimal ones, they may make sense to the offender and represent his best efforts at

---

[46] Viscusi, "Market Incentives for Criminal Behavior," p. 337.

[47] Piliavin et al., "Crime, Deterrence, and Rational Choice."

[48] See Roth and Scholz, *Taxpayer Compliance*; Klepper and Nagin, "Tax Compliance," p. 209.

[49] Andenaes, *Punishment and Deterrence*, p. 86; Bachman et al., "The Rationality of Sexual Offending"; Paternoster, "Decisions to Participate."

optimizing outcomes. Moreover, expressive as well as economic goals can, of course, be characterized as rational. And, lastly, even where the motivation appears to have a pathological component, many of the subsequent planning and decision-making activities (such as choice of victims or targets) may be rational.[50]

This approach assumes that all violating behavior involves some kind of informed choice, but that the factors that influence choices vary across crime type and across decision points (i.e., decisions to engage in crime, persist in crime, exit from crime). As Andeneas points out, "the question is not whether punishment has deterrent effects, but rather under what conditions and to what extent the deterrent purpose is effected."[51]

Some of these ideas are tested by Paternoster, who examines how factors thought to affect the crime choice vary across different decision points.[52] Using a sample of high school students, Paternoster assumes that decisions to engage or not in crime involve a dynamic, not static, process and that multiple decision points are involved. Therefore, he examines whether the decision to participate in crime (yes or no) at one point in time modifies the crime choice later. Other factors that might influence the crime choice at that particular moment – such as material conditions, ties of affection to significant others, formal sanction risks, demographic characteristics – are also inspected.

Four kinds of delinquent acts are considered, including marijuana use, drinking liquor, theft, and vandalism. Paternoster ascertains that the initial decision to offend (nonoffenders who become offenders between $time_1$ and $time_2$) is unrelated to adolescent perceptions of formal legal sanctions' certainty or severity regardless of crime type. Other factors, such as being female, holding strong moral beliefs, high levels of parental supervision, and a lack of participation in social activities, are more inhibitory of crime at this stage than fear of punishment. But even these influences vary in significance and magnitude across the crimes under study.

When he allows perceptions of risk to change over time, later stages of decision making show some deterrent effects for sanction certainty but not severity (i.e., decisions to initiate an offense given no prior delinquency and decisions to desist from crime). These risks, however, are offense-specific (marijuana use and vandalism when initiation decisions occur and alcohol use when desistance occurs) and relatively weak compared with other

---

[50] Clarke and Cornish, *The Reasoning Criminal*, pp. 163–164.
[51] Andenaes, *Punishment and Deterrence*, p. 84.
[52] Paternoster, "Decisions to Participate."

considerations "such as the level of participation of their peers and the degree of peer approval for such behavior."[53]

Nagin and Paternoster attempt to disentagle whether stable individual differences or the perceived costs and benefits of crime (including both legal and extralegal) affect decisions to engage in different types of crime – theft, drunk driving, or sexual assault. The study found that all three crime types were predicted by indicators of low self-control *and* the perceived costs and benefits of crime. Shame also significantly predicted involvement in theft and drunk driving, but was unrelated to sexual assault.[54]

In sum, the importance of formal legal sanctions for deterring criminal conduct appears to depend on one's commitment to criminal activities, the influence of other inhibitory mechanisms in one's life (e.g., informal sanctions, educative and habituative influences), the perceived benefits of illegal conduct relative to its costs, and alternative opportunity structures. Restraints over behavior (including formal sanction threats) differ across crime types and criminal decision points. When sanction threats are taken into account by potential offenders, certainty of punishment tends to matter more than sanction severity.

The body of evidence, then, tends to only weakly support a deterrence perspective.[55] It is important to note, however, that this review has been concerned primarily with the success of "mere" deterrence (as defined by Andeneas). The educative and morally habituative effects of formal legal sanctions – on both specific and general deterrence – are less amenable to empirical validation even though the greatest impact of formal legal sanctions may be in their symbolic representation of societal mores.

Corporate Crime

Unfortunately, few statistical studies explicitly test a deterrence model for corporate offending. Because of this fact, justifications for corporate crime deterrence are either based on assumptions about the white-collar offender or have been drawn from the conventional crime literature and extrapolated to the corporate setting.

---

[53] Ibid., p. 38.

[54] Nagin and Paternoster, "Enduring Individual Differences."

[55] Nagin's recent assessment of the deterrence literature is more positive. "I now concur with Cook's more emphatic conclusion that the collective actions of the criminal justice system exert a very substantial deterrent effect." Daniel S. Nagin, "Criminal Deterrence Research at the Outset of the Twenty-First Century," in Michael Tonry (ed.), *Crime and Justice: A Preview of Research*, vol. 23 (Chicago: University of Chicago Press, 1998), p. 3.

Drawing first on earlier work by Chambliss,[56] Cullen, Maakested, and Cavender suggest that corporations and their managers will be deterred from crime because corporate criminal acts are not crimes of passion but are deliberate acts that weigh potential costs against economic gains; because corporate crimes are situationally opportunistic; and because executives are not committed to a "life of crime." Thus, the crime act is no different than other business decisions where economic gains are considered against potential losses. It is likely to occur when the circumstances are perceived to be conducive. Based on these assumptions, Cullen et al. offer three reasons why criminal law should deter corporate offending.[57]

First, when criminal law is used against organizational entities, it forces firms to treat prosecution as an organizational contingency – something to be taken into account as a possible outcome if criminal options are considered in the decision process. Because criminal prosecution is more punitive and stigmatizing than other control mechanisms, the strategic contingency produced by this fact simply cannot be ignored by managers.

Second, corporate criminal prosecutions will demarcate the ethical and acceptable boundaries of corporate conduct. When criminal sanctions are brought against specific offenders, the punished will learn the boundaries of appropriate behavior and adjust future actions accordingly. Further, unsanctioned firms, by observing the punishment of others, are sensitized to the existing boundaries. Prosocial and habituative behavior will be reinforced among the law-abiding. Among the criminally active, law will bring educative and moralizing influences.

Third, the threat of criminal prosecutions will strengthen alternative systems of corporate crime control. To the extent that criminal prosecutions are more feared than other sanction sources, corporations will buttress their internal compliance systems and cooperate more with regulatory agencies to avoid criminal sanctions.

Sutherland noted years ago that managers are well integrated into their respective communities. Many have families. They attend church and PTA meetings and view themselves as respected and ethical community members.[58] Such good societal members have much to lose by engaging in crime. If criminal prosecution threatens these valued commitments,

---

[56] William J. Chambliss, "Types of Deviance and the Effectiveness of Legal Sanctions," *Wisconsin Law Review* 25 (1967): 712–717.

[57] Francis T. Cullen, William J. Maakestad, and Gray Cavender, *Corporate Crime under Attack* (Cincinnati: Anderson, 1987), pp. 342–353.

[58] Edwin Sutherland, *White-Collar Crime* (New York: Dryden Press, 1949).

achievements, and attachments, maximum deterrent effects should be realized.[59]

Objective Deterrence Studies. Most corporate crime deterrence studies fall within the "objective" research category. Of the five studies that will be reviewed here, two examine the deterrent impact of formal legal sanctions on antitrust offending,[60] one focuses on home repair fraud,[61] and another explores whether governmental regulation affects coal mine safety.[62] A final study assesses recidivism in a sample of white-collar offenders, some of whom are corporate criminals.[63] Clearly, given their diverse foci, variables of interest and time periods vary across analyses.

Beginning first with the antitrust studies, Michael Block, Frederick Nold, and Joseph Sidak examine whether horizontal minimum price-fixing is influenced by civil and criminal adjudication. Arguing that it is difficult to test a simple deterrence model because of industry diversity (of products, costs, and demand), they limit their study to the collusion-prone white pan bread industry. In their test, Block and his colleagues assume that price-fixers are risk-neutral – neither risk seekers nor risk-adverse. Additionally, they assume that information about prosecution is rationally incorporated into assessments of risk. "Colluders . . . estimate the probability that they will be apprehended in a particular period. In this formulation, whenever colluders are apprehended, colluders estimate of the probability of apprehension increases."[64]

After statistically adjusting for factors that can influence product price markups (such as energy and labor costs), the researchers discover that bakers are quite sensitive to fluctuations in sanction certainty (measured as

---

[59] Using interview data with imprisoned white-collar offenders, Benson and Cullen explore whether white-collar offenders are especially sensitive to prison (i.e., the experience is more painful for them than for other offenders). They discover that, for a variety of reasons, these high-status offenders appear to adjust better to prison than lower-class offenders. See Michael L. Benson and Francis T. Cullen, "The Special Sensitivity of White-Collar Offenders to Prison: A Critique and Research Agenda," *Journal of Criminal Justice* 16 (1988): 207–215.

[60] Michael Kent Block, Frederick Carl Nold, and Joseph Gregory Sidak, "The Deterrent Effects of Antitrust Enforcement," *Journal of Political Economy* 89 (1981): 429–445; Sally S. Simpson and Christopher S. Koper, "Deterring Corporate Crime," *Criminology* 30 (1992): 201–229.

[61] Ezra Stotland, Michael Brintnall, Andre L'Heureux, and Eva Ashmore, "Do Convictions Deter Home Repair Fraud?" in Gilbert Geis and Ezra Stotland (eds.), *White Collar Crime: Theory and Research* (Beverly Hills, Calif.: Sage, 1980), pp. 252–265.

[62] Michael S. Lewis-Beck and John R. Alford, "Can Government Regulate Safety? The Coal Mine Example," *American Political Science Review* 74 (1980): 745–756.

[63] David Weisburd, Elin Waring, and Ellen Cyat, "Specific Deterrence in a Sample of Offenders Convicted of White-Collar Crimes," *Criminology* 33 (1995): 587–607.

[64] Block et al., "The Deterrent Effects of Antitrust Enforcement," p. 137, f. 23.

the number of Department of Justice price-fixing prosecutions and changes in the department's enforcement capacity) and sanction severity – especially those posed by private class action suits that are seen as more costly to colluders than criminal prosecutions. These deterrent effects are both general and specific. Thus, when prosecutions increased, price markups in general decreased (general deterrence). So too, once prosecuted, colluders reduced price markups in the year following adjudication (specific deterrence).

The strong deterrent effects noted by Block and his colleagues are not reproduced in a study of antitrust offending by this author and Christopher Koper.[65] Following the antitrust offending of a group of companies after each had committed at least one serious anticompetitive act (primarily price-fixing, monopolization, and illegal corporate mergers and interlocks), we examine whether criminal, regulatory (Federal Trade Commission), and civil sanctions brought in the criterion case affect the likelihood that a company will reoffend.

Unlike Block, Nold, and Sidak, our design controlled for crime opportunities (e.g., company size) and a proxy measure of the economic benefits of antitrust offending (economic health of the firm, its primary industry, and the U.S. economy). In general, only modest support was found for a deterrence model. Specifically, past guilty verdicts and a change in antitrust penalties from misdemeanors to felonies inhibited recidivism, but other deterrence variables failed to affect corporate recidivism or had contradictory effects. Importantly, criminal sanctions relative to civil and regulatory interventions did not produce a deterrent effect. In fact, criminal sanctions *increased* reoffending likelihoods. Industry characteristics and economic conditions, on the other hand, were stronger by far in their effects on firm reoffending. These results lead us to conclude:

> There is evidence to suggest that among a group of prior offenders, formal sanction severity is a stronger inhibitor of reoffending than our measures of sanction certainty or celerity. And yet, among this select group, the motivations and opportunities for crime apparently outweigh the costs incurred by firms as a result of offending in the first place. It seems that a firm's cultural and economic climates exert a greater influence to reoffend than the legal environment exerts pressure not to.[66]

Whereas the antitrust studies show somewhat contradictory results in terms of the deterrent effect of formal legal sanctions, the other two objective deterrence studies are more consistent in their support of a deterrence

---

[65] Simpson and Koper, "Deterring Corporate Crime."
[66] Ibid., p. 220.

model. For instance, Stotland, Brintnall, L'Heureux, and Ashmore assess whether sanction certainty (the number of convictions) and severity (the number of jail sentences, fines, restitutions, and sentences actually served) affect the level of home repair frauds reported to the attorney general's office or the Department of Consumer Affairs in Seattle, Washington.

After statistically controlling for the number of homes in the area, changes in the amount of home repair work over the time period in question, the case load (excluding home repair fraud) of the two offices, press releases by the prosecutor warning the public about the frauds, and the possibility that complaints may rise immediately following a conviction, a deterrent effect was established. "A tendency toward an upward rise of home repair fraud was reduced by convictions."[67] In other words, the rate of increase in these cases over time was slowed by convictions, but not reversed.

Taking a different approach, but staying within the objective deterrence tradition, Michael Lewis-Beck and John Alford investigate whether government regulation of coal mine safety has reduced the rate of fatalities in this industry. They examine the consequence of three legislative acts: the first major piece of safety legislation, the Mine Inspection Act of 1941; the 1952 Federal Coal Mine Safety Act; and the Federal Coal Mine Safety Act of 1969. Using a statistical technique that allows them to examine the short- and long-term impact of each piece of legislation, the researchers claim that legislation does have a long-term deterrent effect on the number of fatalities per million man-hours worked per year. They qualify their results, however, noting that the 1952 act had no discernible impact on their dependent variable. This failure of deterrence is due, they argue, to the fact that the legislation was poorly conceived and enforced. Absent the support of the union, management, and the Bureau of Mines, the act was more of a symbolic response to public demands for government intervention (following a series of mine explosions in 1951) than it was a powerful tool to be used against mine owners who placed firm profits over worker safety.

Although Lewis-Beck and Alford do not directly test for the deterrent impact of sanction certainty and severity, several conclusions can be drawn from their more general study. First, legislation need not be severe in order to deter. The 1941 act, for instance, reduced fatalities not because it carried with it seriously consequential outcomes. In fact, just the opposite was true. Mine safety inspector recommendations were *not* mandatory. But, because the 1941 act was the first law giving federal mine inspectors the right to enter the mines, investigate accidents, and make safety recommendations,

[67] Stotland et al., "Do Convictions Deter Home Repair Fraud?" p. 262.

its impact was quite powerful. Most mine operators made at least minor improvements to look better to inspectors. Further, the law was educative. It identified an important area of concern and socialized owners "to the more public role of promoter and protector of safety."[68]

Their data also suggest, however, that harsher and more certain sanctions may be required to force long-term changes in the way business conducts its day-to-day working practices. The 1969 law, relative to the other two acts under study, expanded the powers of federal inspectors, standardized health and safety requirements for all mines, and is viewed as a tougher law overall.

The last study to be discussed uses a criminal career model to follow the post conviction offending of a group of white-collar offenders who had come before the federal courts in fiscal years 1976–1978.[69] Offenders were selected for study if they had committed one of eight categories of offenses: antitrust, securities fraud, mail and wire fraud, false claims and statements, credit and lending institution fraud, bank embezzlement, income tax fraud, and bribery. One of the aims of the researchers was to compare the failure likelihoods of offenders sentenced to prison with those who had other sentencing outcomes. (Information about length of sentence or time at risk was not available.) It was presumed that there would be greater specific deterrence for imprisoned white-collar offenders (given that this outcome is the most punitive of the sentencing options). Yet, the data showed no specific deterrent effect of prison on recidivism. In fact, recidivism was somewhat higher for white-collar offenders sentenced to prison compared with those who were not (though not significantly so). This fact is true regardless of whether comparisons were made among groups ranked low, moderate, or high in their mean probability of imprisonment.[70]

Perceptual Deterrence Studies. Much like the conventional crime literature, corporate crime studies that examine deterrence as a perceptual process are much less supportive of traditional deterrence arguments than are those taking an objective approach.[71] It is important to recognize, however, there are fewer perceptual studies from which to drawn conclusions.

---

[68] Lewis-Beck and Alford, "Can Government Regulate Safety?" p. 751.

[69] Weisburd et al., "Specific Deterrence."

[70] For an update of this study, see David Weisburd and Elin Waring (with Ellen F. Chayet), *White-Collar Crime and Criminal Careers* (Cambridge: Cambridge University Press, 2001).

[71] This statement is not true when other kinds of workplace crime are investigated. In their study of employee theft, Richard C. Hollinger and John P. Clark found that employees were deterred from theft when they perceived sanction certainty to be high (sanction source was not specified) and sanction severity to be costly (whether dealt with informally, within the organization, or by the police). These effects were greatest for older workers. See Hollinger and Clark, "Deterrence in the Workplace, Perceived Certainty, Perceived Severity, and Employee Theft," *Social Forces* 62 (1983): 398–418.

The most systematic and carefully drawn research was undertaken by Braithwaite and Makkai.[72] These Australian criminologists test a deterrence model of corporate compliance by examining perceptions of *organizational* sanction risk among 410 nursing home chief executive officers. They utilize a variety of statistical models and respondent subsamples (e.g., "rational" versus emotional respondents, those who believe regulations are legitimate versus those who do not) but ultimately conclude that sanction certainty and severity fail to produce significant deterrent effects.

In a recent update of their study (using panel data instead of the cross-sectional results discussed earlier), Makkai and Braithwaite find that informal sanctions – specifically, self-disapproval – affects future compliance levels. "Nursing homes run by managers who report at Time 1 that one should feel guilty about noncompliance have less noncompliance in their organization at Time 2."[73] Overall, however, the deterrence model fails to account for compliance among this group of respondents.

Similarly, experiments conducted by Jesilow and associates find little evidence that either formal or informal sanctions (publicity) influence the decision of auto repair shops to engage in fraud.[74] Contrasting "honest" and "dishonest" businesses, the researchers find a weak association between firm size and honesty (smaller businesses were more honest). They also uncover significant differences between businesses in their views of sanction severity that are contradictory of the deterrence hypothesis. For example, they found that *dishonest* concerns were more likely than honest repair shops to view the punishments meted out by the Bureau of Automotive Repair as severe – just the opposite from what a deterrence perspective would anticipate.

The perceptual deterrence literature would lead us to believe that most corporate decision makers, even though they share many characteristics thought to maximize deterrent effects, are unaffected by formal punishment risks and outcomes. Yet some caution is necessary before we conclude that deterrence fails miserably in the corporate crime area. Failure to uncover perceptual deterrence effects may be due in part to sample characteristics. For instance, respondents in the Braithwaite and Makkai and the Jesilow studies are drawn from the top levels of management. Interviews with managers have revealed that middle managers, who are subjected to

---

[72] John Braithwaite and Toni Makkai, "Testing an Expected Utility Model of Corporate Offending," *Law and Society Review* 25 (1991): 7–39.

[73] Toni Makkai and John Braithwaite, "The Dialectics of Corporate Deterrence," *Journal of Research in Crime and Delinquency* 31 (1994): 360–361.

[74] Paul Jesilow, Gilbert Geis, and Mary Jane O'Brien, "Experimental Evidence That Publicity Has No Effect in Suppressing Auto Repair Fraud," *Sociology and Social Research* 70 (1986): 222–223; Paul Jesilow, Gilbert Geis, and Mary Jane O'Brien, "'Is My Battery Any Good?' A Field Test of Fraud in the Auto Repair Business," *Crime and Justice* 8 (1985): 1–29.

greater pressures to offend, appear more cognizant of sanction threats than top executives.[75] But even here, threats to organizational reputation and managerial self-respect, job prospects, and significant relationships inhibit misconduct more than the possibility of criminal sanctions. And, unlike the typical depiction of business people in the corporate crime literature as "profit-seeking sociopaths,"[76] managers – regardless of level – do express concerns about the ethical implications and consequences of their day-to-day business decisions. These sentiments are captured poignantly by the comments of a mining supervisor whose decisions literally can mean the difference between life and death for his employees.

> If there were a disaster or one of the men got hurt, you know, morally you think about it. . . . My father had two people work for him that were killed and I saw how it affected him. It took him years to get over it. I've had two of my employees killed and I keep thinking back, "What could I have done differently?"[77]

These data suggest that debates about why corporations obey the law should be sensitive to a variety of decision costs and rewards, not just managers' fears of formal sanction threats (i.e., "mere" deterrence).

Conclusions

Our review of the conventional and corporate crime deterrence literature suggests that after much study and investigation, the evidence in favor of deterrence still is equivocal. The strongest support comes from perhaps the weakest of research designs – those that employ cross-sectional "objective" measures of sanction risk and consequence. As perceptual critics note, deterrence is likely to depend on what punishment risks and outcomes are *thought* to be, not what they actually are.[78] Such studies find little evidence that criminal behavior is restrained by the threat of formal sanctions among populations who are committed to a criminal life-style or morally habituated.

[75] Sally S. Simpson, "Corporate-Crime Deterrence and Corporate-Control Policies: Views from the Inside," in Kip Schlegel and David Weisburd (eds.), *White-Collar Crime Reconsidered* (Boston: Northeastern University Press, 1992), pp. 287–306.
[76] Cullen, et al., *Corporate Crime under Attack*, p. 350.
[77] Sally Simpson, unpublished research, Department of Criminology and Criminal Justice, University of Maryland, College Park, MD 29742.
[78] Gordon P. Waldo and Theodore G. Chiricos, "Perceived Penal Sanction and Self-Reported Criminality: A Neglected Approach to Deterrence Research," *Social Problems* 19 (1972): 522–540.

In the case of corporations, the contradictory findings between the objective and perceptual deterrence findings raise intriguing questions. If individual managers are unaffected by the threat of formal sanctions (as the perceptual deterrence literature indicates), what do the prodeterrence patterns in the aggregate studies really mean? It may be that the relationships between crime and punishment certainty and severity observed in the objective data would disappear if other factors were included in the statistical analyses. But let us assume for a moment that both sets of findings are accurate. Is it possible for corporations to respond to sanction threats absent perceptual deterrence on the part of managers? These seemingly incongruent findings make sense if one closely inspects how criminal sanction risks are communicated within a company. First, it is possible that a majority of managers do not contemplate crime and therefore are not sensitive to sanction threats. Like Thurman's sample of respondents who refuse to cheat on their taxes under any circumstances, many corporate managers may never consider the crime option. It is further likely that most managers do not believe that they *personally* are at risk for *corporate* crime prosecution. Thus, they do not fear or adjust their behaviors based on the possibility that the company may be penalized (like Braithwaite and Makkai's nursing home executives). The organizational entity, on the other hand, is more often the target of criminal cases. When a firm is perceived by management to be at risk for prosecution, directives will be issued and corrective action taken.[79] However, managerial control units are themselves selectively comprised. Only some managers – those who are responsible for controlling adherence to standards – will be sensitive to *corporate* prosecution risks.

Another possible interpretation for the contradictory objective and perceptual deterrence findings is that the relationships between sanction threats and criminality have been misspecified. Few studies of corporate crime deterrence include variables that tap the potential rewards of crime relative to its costs. Further, measures of informal sanctions (whether independent or interactive with formal sanction threats) are too rarely scrutinized for their inhibitory effects on managers. Finally, because both the firm and individuals may be affected by informal threats, each should be considered as a potent source of crime control.

Deterrence studies of corporate crime need to take all of these factors into account before firm conclusions can be drawn about the applicability

---

[79] Robert N. Anthony, *The Management Control Function* (Boston: Harvard Business School Press, 1988).

of a deterrence model to corporate offending. However, the questions raised by our review of the deterrence literature suggest that punitive policy recommendations based in a deterrence framework also are premature. In the next chapter we consider some other reasons why criminal law may not be the best mechanism for preventing and controlling corporate illegality.

CHAPTER THREE

Assessing the Failure of Corporate Deterrence and Criminal Justice

FINDINGS from the empirical literature imply that the traditional deterrence model is severely challenged. In this chapter I offer explanations for why criminal sanction threats fail to deter corporations and their managers from violating the law. These interpretations range from suggestions that the problem does not rest with the deterrence model per se but rather with how the criminal justice system responds to the corporate offender, to arguments that theoretical deterrence and its rational-choice assumptions are fundamentally flawed.

Two levels of analysis are relevant for our discussion. We first review why criminal law fails to deter the corporate entity and then shift to a discussion of deterrence and the corporate manager.

Criminal Law and the Corporation

A common explanation for the failure of corporate deterrence is that criminal penalties are not imposed often or severely enough to insure compliance. If, the argument goes, criminal sanctions were threatening enough that firms and their representatives were forced to take notice of them, deterrence would work.[1] This reasoning deserves greater examination.

---

[1] Explanations vary as to why criminal sanctions are rarely imposed and, if levied, render relatively paltry punishment. Some implicate the dominance of capitalist interests in a bourgeois state, assuming instrumental or structural perspectives. See, e.g., Harold C. Barnett, *Toxic Debts and the Superfund Dilemma* (Chapel Hill: University of North Carolina Press, 1994); Laureen Snider, "The Rise and Fall of the Canadian Regulatory State" (paper presented to the annual meetings of the American Society of Criminology, Chicago, 1996; Frank Pearce and

Legal System Problems

Implementation Failure. This position, rather than dismissing the deterrence doctrine out of hand, asserts that formal legal punishment has not been implemented properly. The costs of punishment are not salient enough to discourage criminal conduct. This is true at the levels of both sanction certainty (i.e., firms are unlikely to be caught when laws are violated) and severity (criminal sanctions often represent little more than the proverbial slap on the wrist for most corporations).

The risk of getting caught once a crime is perpetrated appears to be quite low for corporations (although it is difficult to estimate crime discovery probabilities accurately because few, if any, self-report data exist to establish such figures). Part of the discovery problem rests with offense complexity and victim awareness. Corporate criminal events are often complex affairs involving multiple interconnected actors over a long period of time. Moreover, because victimization is not obvious and direct effects are difficult to prove, the "reactive" element of enforcement (i.e., investigations precipitated by victim complaints) is compromised.[2]

A second problem affecting sanction certainty revolves around how corporate crimes are "policed" and who is responsible for enforcement efforts. Traditional policing techniques that enhance conventional crime discovery are unsuited for or are unable to penetrate the corporate setting (e.g., dragnets, undercover agents). Police are trained for conventional crime investigation and generally lack many of the investigatory skills necessary to follow the paper trail left by corporate criminals.[3] Other enforcement agencies are relatively uncoordinated in investigatory efforts across agencies and with local police or the FBI. Enforcement philosophies, goals, and practices tend to be diverse. Discretion affects which cases are dropped and which are pursued.[4] Prosecuted cases tend not to be the most complex,

---

Steve Tombs, "Hazards, Law and Class: Contextualizing the Regulation of Corporate Crime," *Social and Legal Studies* 6 (1997): 107–136; David R. Simon, *Elite Deviance*, 6th ed. (Boston: Allyn and Bacon, 1999). Others detail the difficulties that prosecutors have in meeting legal standards of evidence. See Michael Levi, "Equal before the Law?" *Crime, Law and Social Change* 24 (1996): 319–340; Michael L.Benson and Francis T. Cullen, *Combating Corporate Crime: Local Prosecutors at Work* (Boston: Northeastern University Press, 1998). The arguments presented here do not resolve this important debate.

[2] Albert J. Reiss Jr. and Albert D. Biderman, *Data Sources on White-Collar Law-Breaking* (Washington, D.C.: U.S. Department of Justice, 1980).

[3] Eliza Stotland "The Role of Law Enforcement in the Fight against White-Collar Crime," in H. Edelhertz and T. D. Overcast (eds.), *White-Collar Crime: An Agenda for Research* (Lexington, Mass.: Lexington Books, 1982), pp. 69–98.

[4] Sally S. Simpson, Anthony R. Harris, and Brian A. Mattson, "Measuring Corporate Crime," in M. B. Blankenship (ed.), *Understanding Corporate Criminality* (New York: Garland Publishing, 1993), pp. 115–140.

and offenders might be best described as the "little guys" – firms too small to fight the Justice Department effectively or to obfuscate a legal inquiry. In the environmental crimes area, for instance, only 1.6 percent of Fortune 500 companies have found themselves in court; "yet these 500 companies were responsible for $2.16 trillion of $3.954 trillion of non-farm business in the country in 1989."[5]

To some degree, the policing problem is a resource allocation problem. Yeager shows, for instance, that Occupational Safety and Health Administration investigations in the 1970s were conducted by four hundred agents who were responsible for regulating 4 million businesses.[6] It has been estimated that the Justice Department's antitrust budget is one-twentieth the advertising budget of the Proctor and Gamble Corporation.[7] These are some of the reasons why corporate crime is less likely to come to the attention of authorities. If resources are limited, however, deterrence advocates suggest that the government should focus its attention on cases that will bring the biggest deterrence "bang for the buck." Big cases with well-known concerns are more apt to fit this criteria. Data show, however, that these corporate violators are not the typical object of criminal sanctions.[8]

The case against sanction severity also can be easily documented. Once a case is brought into the system, the evidence suggests that the chances for harsh punishment are relatively rare. In fact, the literature is rich with examples of dropped cases, negotiated pleas, and paltry fines. Yeager's study of the enforcement efforts of the Environmental Protection Agency provides an excellent case in point. Between the years 1973 and 1978, EPA enforcement of industrial violations of the Clean Water Act in Region II (headquartered in New York City) resulted in taking no action at all (42.5 percent, 390 cases) or issuing a warning letter to violators (40.8 percent, 374 cases). The potential for more severe sanctions – administrative orders and civil and criminal referrals – constituted only 3.3 percent (30 cases) and .6 percent (5 cases) of the total enforcement response, respectively.[9]

Sanctions imposed in two of the largest price-fixing conspiracy cases uncovered by the Department of Justice are indicative of just how

---

[5] Robert W. Adler and Charles Lord, "Environmental Crimes: Raising the Stakes," *George Washington Law Review* 59 (1991): 796.

[6] Peter C. Yeager, *The Limits of the Law: The Public Regulation of Private Pollution* (Cambridge: Cambridge University Press, 1991), p. 37, n. 14.

[7] Mark J. Green, Beverly C. Moore Jr., and Bruce Wasserstein, *The Closed Enterprise System: Ralph Nader's Study Group Report in Antitrust Enforcement* (New York: Grossman, 1972), p. 122.

[8] "Sentence Rules Mainly Snag Small Firms," *Wall Street Journal*, August 28, 1995.

[9] Yeager, *The Limits of the Law*, p. 279.

inconsequential criminal fines can be. The thirteen defendants in the 1961 heavy electrical equipment price-fixing conspiracy received fines that averaged less than $105,000. In contrast, the firms' gross revenues averaged $657 million. A decade and a half later, nine firms convicted of price-fixing in the corrugated container industry received flat fines of $50,000 each – an equivalent of less than a $2.00 fine for someone earning $15,000 per year.[10] There are exceptions, of course. The largest antitrust fine ever was levied recently against Archer Daniels Midland Corporation – to the tune of $100 million.[11] Yet, these kinds of fines are rare.

More recent statistics show that 89 percent of 288 corporate offenders sentenced in federal criminal courts between 1984 and 1987 received fines averaging $53,974.[12] Sixteen percent of the sanctioned firms also were ordered to pay restitution. The average reimbursement was $239,987. Data from 1988 show similar patterns.[13] For firms sentenced in federal courts, the average criminal fine levied was $74,715 for environmental crimes; $253,437 for antitrust offenses; and $141,351 for other corporate offenses. Most fines were clustered toward the lower rather than higher ends of the dollar distribution. For instance, median fines of $12,500, $65,000, and $20,000 were levied for environmental, antitrust, and other corporate offenses, respectively. Data show that the average total fine for cases sentenced between November 1, 1991, and September 30, 1993, after sentencing guidelines were issued was $204,624 – up considerably from earlier years.[14] Caution must be taken with this figure, however, because that the U.S. Sentencing Commission data do not capture the universe of cases prosecuted pursuant to the guidelines.[15]

The body of empirical evidence suggests that it is profitable for firms to violate the law because the risk of discovery is low and the benefits of crime outweigh the relatively modest monetary costs of prosecution and guilty

[10] M. David Ermann and Richard J. Lundman, *Corporate and Organizational Deviance*, 2nd ed. (New York: Oxford University Press), p. 148.

[11] "Agribusiness Giant ADM to Pay $100 Million to Settle Price-Fixing Case," *Washington Post*, October 15, 1996.

[12] Mark A. Cohen, "Corporate Crime and Punishment: A Study of Social Harm and Sentencing Practice in the Federal Courts, 1984–1987," *American Criminal Law Review* 26 (1989): 610–611.

[13] Mark A. Cohen, "Environmental Crime and Punishment: Legal/Economic Theory and Empirical Evidence on Enforcement of Federal Environmental Statutes," *Journal of Criminal Law and Criminology* 82 (1992): 1079–1080.

[14] Nicole Leeper Piquero, "Impact of Mitigating and Aggravating Factors on the Sentencing of Organizations Convicted in Federal Courts, Post-1991 Guidelines" (Master's thesis, University of Maryland, College Park, 1998).

[15] Cindy R. Alexander, Jennifer Arlen, and Mark A. Cohen, "Regulating Corporate Criminal Sanctions: Evidence on the Effect of the U.S. Sentencing Guidelines" (unpublished manuscript, 1997).

findings. Low sanction severity coupled with low sanction certainty produce a relatively insignificant punishment threat.[16]

Criminal Law and Overkill. In some cases, the illegal acts committed by corporate offenders are quite simply unconscionable. For these crimes, criminal law, given its dual aims of deterrence and retribution, is the most appropriate vehicle to express society's outrage. The prosecution of Ford Motor Company, manufacturer of the infamously unsafe Pinto, for reckless homicide is a case in which criminal prosecution makes sense.[17] By building an automobile known to be unsafe in preproduction stages, failing to rectify the situation with known technology because of "cost considerations," and subsequently covering up to protect the firm from liability, Ford demonstrated morally offensive and blameworthy behavior – two important criteria for seeking criminal sanctions.

By contrast, however, many corporate violations are regulatory offenses – crimes that lack the moral offensiveness and blameworthiness associated with Ford's behavior. Regulatory offenses are not immoral in their own right but rather are illegal because they are prohibited by law – that is, *mala quia prohibita*.[18] Because there are no moral prohibitions against these acts, successful deterrence is purely a matter of effective legal sanctions. However, the success of legal sanctions depends on the extent to which society as a whole and potential offenders believe that such acts should be prohibited; deterrence depends on the perceived legitimacy of the law. To the extent that people feel that laws are illegitimate[19] or that the use of criminal law is excessive, the goals of deterrence will be undermined.[20] Rather than deterrence, defiance may result.[21]

Braithwaite argues that an overly punitive approach to corporate offending will result in lower rather than higher levels of compliance.[22]

---

[16] Critical criminologists argue that it is illogical within a capitalist society for the state to adopt a punitive corporate crime control policy, at least on a permanent basis. Punitiveness may be implemented during times of crisis when capital's hegemony and state legitimacy are challenged, but the state will ultimately revert back to more permissive relations when the crisis is averted.

[17] Russell Mokhiber, *Corporate Crime and Violence* (San Francisco: Sierra Club Books, 1988), pp. 373–382; Francis T. Cullen, William J. Maakestad, and Gray Cavender, *Corporate Crime under Attack: The Ford Pinto Case and Beyond* (Cincinnati: Anderson Publishing, 1987).

[18] Johannes Andenaes, *Punishment and Deterrence* (Ann Arbor: University of Michigan Press, 1974), p. 45.

[19] Tom R. Tyler, *Why People Obey the Law* (New Haven: Yale University Press, 1990).

[20] "Corporate Crime: Regulating Corporate Behavior through Criminal Sanctions," *Harvard Law Review* 92 (April 1979): 1369.

[21] Lawrence W. Sherman, "Defiance, Deterrence, and Irrelevance: A Theory of the Criminal Sanction," *Journal of Research in Crime and Delinquency* 30 (1993): 445–473.

[22] John Braithwaite, *To Punish or Persuade* (Albany, N.Y.: SUNY Press, 1985).

Indiscriminate use of punishment, he claims, will lead to obfuscation, coverups, alienation of firms from regulators, denial of wrongdoing, and system inefficiencies (because scarce resources are being used to pursue punitive instead of preventative strategies). In their evaluation of nursing home compliance in Australia, Makkai and Braithwaite found that compliance following inspections varied with the style of the inspection team. Compliance declined after visits by disrespectful teams and increased following inspections by respectful agents.[23]

Applicability of Due-Process Safeguards. The difficulties of applying criminal law to illegalities perpetrated by organizational entities (legally defined as juristic persons) instead of individuals have been discussed elsewhere at length.[24] When the corporate control process is criminalized, corporate entities are accorded all of the constitutional safeguards and protections that are granted to individual defendants.[25] These rights were conferred to individual defendants as a means of protecting persons against the potential abuses of state power. However, corporations neither qualify as weaker adversaries vis-à-vis the state nor do they "suffer" the same consequences as individuals upon conviction (i.e., deprivation of freedom or life). The protections that come to corporations through criminal processing affect both the likelihood that charges will be brought and the probability that punishment will be received. Moreover, although sanction celerity is not discussed here, criminal cases against corporate defendants are not apt to be swift either. In fact, obdurate companies will drag the process out, assuming (often correctly) that the state will judge the case as too costly to continue prosecution.[26]

It is exceedingly difficult to prove a corporation guilty of a criminal violation beyond a reasonable doubt.[27] Even though enforcement agents (e.g., local prosecutors) may believe that a criminal violation has occurred, the case will probably not end up in court or, if it does, will be too complex

---

[23] Toni Makkai and John Braithwaite, "Reintegrative Shaming and Compliance with Regulatory Standards," *Criminology* 32 (1994): 361–386.

[24] Christopher D. Stone, *Where the Law Ends* (New York: Harper and Row, 1975); John Collins Coffee, "'No Soul to Damn: No Body to Kick': An Unscandalized Inquiry into the Problem of Corporate Punishment," *Michigan Law Review* 79 (1980–1981): 386–459; "Corporate Crime."

[25] Gilbert Geis, "From Deuteronomy to Deniability: A Historical Perlustration on White-Collar Crime," *Justice Quarterly* 5 (1988): 17–18.

[26] Sometimes, politics will affect these decisions as well. For instance, the Reagan administration dropped a number of antitrust cases left pending from Carter's more proactive Justice Department.

[27] John Braithwaite and Gilbert Geis, "On Theory and Action for Corporate Crime Control," *Crime and Delinquency* 28 (April 1982): 292–314.

to result in a conviction.[28] Part of the problem rests with proving criminal intent and establishing culpability – requirements of a successful criminal prosecution. It is a challenge for the state to identify responsible parties (other than the firm itself), to target faulty policies or directives, and to counter employees' alternative explanations of the act(s).

These problems notwithstanding, some scholars still favor deterrent strategies claiming that conviction problems are more important to overcome than the difficulties associated with discovery and apprehension, partially because corporate offenders are easier to apprehend than regular offenders. "This difficulty [with convictions] rather than the low visibility of offenses...is the real stumbling block to effective corporate crime control."[29]

This kind of thinking creates several problems. First, in the empirical literature sanction certainty generally produces greater crime inhibition than the imposition of harsh punishments.[30] Second, if corporations are less likely than conventional criminals to elude apprehension once an illegal act is discovered, this possibility does not translate into either a greater likelihood that corporate offenses will be uncovered (sanction certainty) or that, if prosecuted, convictions will result (sanction severity).

Corporate organizations, and especially the large, multinational corporations that are the present focus of concern, will obviously have greater difficulty eluding enforcement authorities than, for instance, a burglar or mugger. However, whether this fact adds sufficiently to certainty of sanction to counterbalance the low values on the other response variables is open to question.

Consider, for instance, a corporation's decision to enter into a price-fixing arrangement. Will near certainty of apprehension effectively negate a low probability of detection ("rarely ever") coupled with a low probability of conviction ("almost always difficult") even if apprehended?[31]

Finally, we also need to consider whether increasing the level of punishment for corporate illegal acts would, in fact, produce greater corporate

---

[28] Ibid., p. 298.

[29] Ibid., p. 300.

[30] Simpson and Koper, however, find that sanction severity has a stronger inhibitive impact on firm recidivism than does sanction certainty. These findings may suggest that the effects of certainty and severity may vary depending on whether one is examining specific or general deterrence. However, the authors acknowledge that their measure of sanction certainty is a weak one. See Sally S. Simpson and Christopher S. Koper, "Deterring Corporate Crime" *Criminology* 30 (1992): 347–375.

[31] Charles A. Moore, "Taming the Giant Corporation? Some Cautionary Remarks on the Deterrability of Corporate Crime," *Crime and Delinquency* 33 (1987): 388.

crime deterrence. Instead of crime inhibition, strategies for avoiding harsh punishment could produce more crime or other undesirable outcomes. For instance, in order to avoid harsh sanctions, companies could become less cooperative and more evasive in their dealings with criminal justice representatives. In fact, a CYA (cover your ass) strategy may be a purely rational response to increased sanction severity. Judges and juries might be less willing to convict offenders if penalties are perceived to be excessive and evidence against defendants is insufficient, or they may be unwilling to levy maximum fines even if defendants are found guilty.[32] Furthermore, firms are more likely to pass sanction costs along to customers if fines and restitution pose a threat to firm profits or survival. In some cases, to avoid criminal penalties a company may file for bankruptcy protection (like Johns Manville and A. H. Robins),[33] move the firm to a more "hospitable" legal environment, or "dump" their banned products in other countries.[34] Thus, while it may be desirable to increase punishment for certain kinds of corporate crimes for reasons of proportionality or just desert,[35] *deterrence* may in fact be nullified if excessively severe sentences are imposed on corporate violators.

Organizational Structure Problems

The prospects for deterrence also are lessened by the features of corporations themselves. This position is somewhat ironic given that many feel the corporate entity is more readily deterrable than corporate personnel.

Corporations are future-oriented, concerned about their reputation, and quintessentially rational. Although most individuals do not possess the information to calculate rationally the probability of detection and punishment, corporations have information-gathering systems designed precisely for this purpose.[36]

On the face of it, this appears to be a reasonable assertion. But, in order for deterrence to work, companies must respond to these sanction probabilities in a rational way. The problem is that our image of corporate rationality is more caricature of the way individual managers make corporate decisions

---

[32] Adler and Lord, "Environmental Crimes: Raising the Stakes," p. 809.

[33] Celia Wells notes that laws developed to hold corporations accountable for their "acts" (e.g., juristic separation) may also provide firms the means to avoid criminal sanctions. "It is comparatively easy for a company to disappear, and the greater the deterrent impact of criminal penalties then also the greater the incentive to evade liability through some wizardly maneuvering under company laws designed for quite different purposes." Wells, *Corporations and Criminal Responsibility* (Oxford: Oxford University Press, 1993), p. 93.

[34] Moore, "Taming the Giant Corporation?" pp. 390–94.

[35] Kip Schlegel, *Just Deserts for Corporate Criminals* (Boston: Northeastern University Press, 1990).

[36] Braithwaite, *To Punish or Persuade*, p. 88.

than reality. Charles Moore, for instance, argues that the appraisal of corporations as more rational and more sensitive to sanction risk than individuals fails to account for the vast array of factors that affect corporate rationality and, by implication, corporate deterrence.[37]

The Problem with Corporate Rationality. Most models of corporate rationality assume management to be risk-averse[38] or risk-neutral.[39] Research has shown, however, that decision making in a collective operates differently than it would if each person were acting alone.[40] Groups are more risk-prone in their decision outcomes than are individuals. Therefore, factors that inhibit individuals from violating the law – or that make them risk-averse – may not be deterrents at the group level. Individual perceptions of sanction costs are filtered and adjusted through group dynamics. To the extent that many (if not most) corporate criminal decisions are arrived at collectively, a deterrence model is undermined.

In a similar vein, corporations are highly intricate entities within which managers and other employees interact, form attachments and working relationships, define goals and subunit goals, compete with one another for resources and power, and make business decisions. In short, organizations contain minicultures that affect decision processes and outcomes. A number of factors influence corporate decision processes, including "subcultural influences, [a firm's] position within national and international market structures, and the differential opportunity to employ criminal means as an alternative method of realizing profits, protecting or stabilizing markets, or other 'legitimate' corporate goals."[41]

The difficulty for deterrence, of course, is that these forces impinge on firms differently. Assessments of crime costs and benefits will be unique across and within corporate units. Within companies, illegality may be the product of criminogenic subunits. The fact that General Dynamics, for instance, is frequently charged with bid rigging suggests that managers within sales and marketing share a deviant subculture. Yet, other subunits within the company may be relatively crime-free.

Consequently, companies will not refrain from criminal activity simply because the law tells them not to and threatens them with punishment.

---

[37] Moore, "Taming the Giant Corporation?" see also Stone, *Where the Law Ends.*

[38] Kenneth G. Elzinga and William Breit, *The Antitrust Penalties: A Study in Law and Economics* (New Haven: Yale University Press, 1976).

[39] Richard Posner, *Antitrust Laws: An Economic Perspective* (Chicago: University of Chicago Press, 1976).

[40] John Collins Coffee Jr., "Corporate Crime and Punishment: A Non-Chicago View of the Economics of Criminal Sanctions," *American Criminal Law Review* 17 (1980): 433.

[41] Moore, "Taming the Giant Corporation?" p. 386.

In order to induce specific deterrence, our system of punishment must be sensitive to firm complexity and variability. Punishment, then, must also be variable. But, variable punishments erode the essential relationship between crime and punishment in the collective corporate conscience. By varying punishment in the specific case, we render general deterrent effects problematic.[42]

The Normalization of Deviance. Related to the corporate rationality problem are the ways that organizations can facilitate wrongdoing even when officers follow standard organizational practice or, indeed, formalized procedures. In the first case, organizational culture intervenes to establish parameters of acceptable and unacceptable conduct. While agents may understand that they are "technically" violating the law, the culture of the organization nullifies the significance of the illegality. Geis's General Electric price-fixers, for instance, reflected that, although they knew price-fixing was wrong, their acts did not – in their minds – constitute a criminal act.[43] A survey sent to business leaders not long after the General Electric case found that a full quarter of respondents agreed with that sentiment.[44] When illegality is a way of organizational life, as it was in the electrical equipment industry in the 1950s and the defense and securities industries of the 1980s, it is exceedingly difficult for law to penetrate the actor's definitions of right and wrong and affect cost-benefit calculations.[45]

A somewhat more complicated problem for deterrence theorists has to do with what Vaughan describes as deviance normalization. In her review of documents and interviews with key decision makers associated with the *Challenger* disaster, contrary to commonsense explanations that the explosion was due to amoral calculators at NASA succumbing to broader economic and political pressures, Vaughan found a rule-based decision – a decision that emerged from and reflected cultural imperatives of technology, production, secrecy, and risk assessment.

Prerational forces . . . shape worldview, normalizing signals of potential danger, resulting in mistakes with harmful human consequences. The *Challenger* launch is a story of how people who worked together developed patterns that

[42] Ibid., p. 383.
[43] Gilbert Geis, "White Collar Crime: The Heavy Electrical Equipment Antitrust Cases of 1961," in Marshall B. Clinard and Richard Quinney (eds.), *Criminal Behavior Systems: A Typology* (New York: Holt, Rinehart and Winston, 1967), pp. 139–151.
[44] Mark J. Green, Beverly C. Moore, and Bruce Wasserstein, *The Closed Enterprise System; Ralph Nader's Study Group Report on Antitrust Enforcement* (New York: Grossman, 1972).
[45] Gary E. Reed and Peter Cleary Yeager, "Organizational Offending and Neoclassical Criminology: Challenging the Reach of a General Theory of Crime," *Criminology* 34 (1996): 357–382.

blinded them to the consequences of their actions. It is not only about the development of norms but about the incremental expansion of normative boundaries: how small changes – new behaviors that were slight deviations from the normal course of events – gradually became the norm, providing a basis for accepting additional deviance. No rules were violated; there was not intent to do harm.[46]

Vaughan's analysis challenges the very foundation of deterrence-based corporate crime control by calling into question the assumed "rationality" of some kinds of corporate decisions.

Corporate Reincarnation. Regardless of personnel fluctuation and managerial changes, a company, through corporate reincarnation, can continue "on its elephantine way almost indifferent to its succession of riders."[47] Yet, the transition of organizational personnel across positions of responsibility and over time is consequential for successful deterrence. First, transition makes it difficult ex post facto to tie acts of illegality to specific personnel, especially when the gap between the occurrence of the act and official discovery is large. Additionally, however, it means that punishment effects are apt to be short-lived.[48] Although the corporation that commits an offense at one time is the same corporation that repeats the offense some years later, the people who occupy the boxes in its table of organization may be very different or, indeed, an entirely new set of people.[49]

It is not essential to the idea of deterrence, of course, that punishment be long-term. Nonetheless, for purposes of specific deterrence, punishment risks should remain salient over time. To the extent that these risks are experiential and specific to the person holding a particular organizational position, changes and shifts in organizational personnel can disrupt deterrent effects.

Criminal Penalties without the Sting. Some of the harshest penalties attached to violations of criminal law involve the loss of life (death penalty) and imprisonment. Neither of these outcomes can be imposed on corporations.

---

[46] Diane Vaughan, *The Challenge Launch Decision: Risky Technology, Culture, and Deviance at NASA* (Chicago: University of Chicago Press, 1996), p. 409.

[47] Kenneth E. Boulding, *The Organizational Revolution* (Chicago: Quadrangle, 1968), p. 139, cited in Brent Fisse and John Braithwaite, *The Impact of Publicity on Corporate Offenders* (Albany, N.Y.: SUNY Press, 1983), p. 227, n. 1.

[48] Fisse and Braithwaite, *The Impact of Publicity*, p. 227.

[49] Albert A. Cohen, "Criminal Actors: Natural Persons and Collectivities," in Melvin J. Lerner (ed.), *New Directions in the Study of Justice, Law, and Social Control*, Critical Issues in Social Justice Series (New York: Plenum Press, 1990), pp. 101–125.

There is even some debate as to whether firms can be stigmatized in the same way as individuals by the attachment of a criminal label. Unless profits are affected by the attachment of a criminal label (and little evidence exists that profits are severely tested by negative publicity)[50] and the stigma of criminality filters down to responsible parties in the corporate structure, there is little chance for deterrence.[51]

In sum, organizational deterrence may fail because of the way criminal law is implemented or how organizations respond to punishment; because of organizational complexities and vagaries; or because of problems with corporate rationality and reincarnation. These failures are associated with the organizational entity, but the empirical research demonstrates that sanctions also fail to deter individual managers from crime.

Criminal Law and Corporate Managers

Why are corporate managers relatively immune to formal sanction threats? Some of the same arguments offered to explain why criminal law fails to inhibit the organizational offender are equally relevant for managers.

System Implementation Failures

Criminal sanctions, even though they are potentially available for a variety of illegal acts including antitrust, unsafe workplace conditions, environmental pollution, as well as bribery, frauds, and conspiracies,[52] pose little direct threat to managers. As noted in the preceding section, it is far easier to target a corporation for criminal sanctioning than it is to identify and prosecute culpable parties within it. Moreover, when individuals are prosecuted, the jury is often unwilling to stigmatize, label, and punish managers for acts society does not view as immoral. Guilty verdicts are rare for corporate officers and punishment typically results in an insignificant fine. Instead, juries prefer to punish the corporation in order to "force the business to disgorge at least some of its ill-gained profits."[53]

---

[50] Corporations cannot feel the shame of a criminal conviction, but individual officers who act on behalf of the company realize that stigma can affect employee morale and the good name of the firm. See Fisse and Braithwaite, *The Impact of Publicity;* John Braithwaite, *Crime, Shame and Reintegration* (Cambridge: Cambridge University Press, 1989), pp. 124–151.

[51] "Corporate Crime," p. 1366.

[52] William E. Knepper and Dan A. Bailey, *Liability of Corporate Officers and Directors,* 4th ed. (Charlottesville, Va.: Michie Company, 1988), pp. 231–254.

[53] "Corporate Crime," p. 1367.

The nature of the illegal act is also apt to interfere with managerial perceptions of individual sanction threats. Recall from Chapter 1 that corporate crime is defined as conduct by a corporation or employees *acting on its behalf*, which is proscribed and punishable by law. Unlike conventional crime where most illegalities are motivated by individual needs, corporate managers mostly violate the law in order to pursue organizational ends. Hence, the relationship between perceived sanction threats and illegal conduct is disrupted as corporate criminals are apt to perceive the firm to be more directly responsible for the act and, consequently, subject to sanction threats.

Questions of Managerial Rationality

Like corporate actors, managerial rationality is more complex that typically assumed. In a recent study of organizational change and managerial decision making conducted by this author, top- and middle-level managers were asked to describe the kinds of decisions they make on the job and their decision processes. Responses demonstrate that decision processes take into account a number of factors and that these factors vary by decision type. For instance, when asked about the kinds of corporate decisions he or she typically made, managers distinguished strategic from routine and "quick response" corporate decisions.[54]

Strategic decisions fall more readily into the purely "rational" camp (and therefore more deterrable) because they are arrived at through a lengthy process of research, discussion, and cost-benefit analysis. The other two categories, routine and on-the-spot decisions, employ very different decision processes. In the case of routine decisions, little forethought is necessary. The manager simply "signs off," assuming that prior evaluation is embedded in the decision itself. On-the-spot decisions are those that confront managers in a nonroutine way. They typically require immediate action. Among corporate officials in my study, these decisions created the greatest degree of discomfort because decision makers have neither the luxury of time to assess and evaluate the strength and weaknesses of various lines of action nor can they assume that a particular decision will be appropriate because of its past functionality.

For on-the-spot decisions, managers are confronted with their own accountability and vulnerabilities. One top-level manager asked that I turn off my tape recorder – the only occasion when I was asked to do so – while

---

[54] Sally S. Simpson, unpublished research, Department of Criminology and Criminal Justice, University of Maryland, College Park, MD 20742.

he relayed that such decisions were reached "by the seat of the pants." Others spoke of using gut instinct, past experience, or a variety of formal or informal rules (e.g., financial considerations, legal, ethical, business plan, corporate culture, etc.) to assist them in the decision process.

Given these differences, strategic decisions are most amenable to deterrence as formal legal costs can easily be incorporated within the cost-benefit decision calculus. Routine decisions will be the least responsive to formal legal sanctions because they are the least likely to be assessed and evaluated.[55] Finally, to the extent that formal sanction threats can be incorporated into decision rules when managers confront unexpected and unfamiliar situations, there is some hope for deterrence. However, this may vary greatly from manager to manager depending on his or her taste for risk, knowledge level, prior experience, intellectual capacity, and so forth.

Perceived Legitimacy of the Law

Peter Yeager, in his recent book, suggests that corporate managers' beliefs about the legitimacy of law will vary depending on whether the law controls economic relations (such as antitrust law) or social relations (e.g., regulation of labor and environmental standards, discrimination in hiring and promotion, among others).[56] The former defines the limits of acceptable market behavior by corporations, rendering predictable and relatively stable economic relations in capitalist societies. Social regulation, however, restricts management autonomy and organizational behavior "at the point of production rather than simply in market relations, and can impose costly regulatory and liability requirements on companies."[57] Whereas managers are apt to view laws that regulate economic relations as necessary and beneficial (at least to a certain extent), Yeager argues that just the opposite is true of social regulation – when regulation creates illegalities out of what were formerly common business practices.

Yeager's analysis is relevant for deterrence in two ways. First, to the extent that managers perceive laws to be illegitimate or unnecessarily restrictive

---

[55] These decisions are the most like those that Vaughan studied in the *Challenger* disaster (Vaughan, *The Challenge Launch Decision*). It is implicitly assumed that these decisions are relatively risk-free because others in the firm at some earlier time assessed the costs and benefits to produce a policy or a standard operating procedure. See Sally S. Simpson, Raymond Paternoster, and Nicole Leeper Piquero, "Exploring the Micro-Macro Link in Corporate Crime Research," in Peter Bamberger (ed.), *Research in the Sociology of Organizations: Deviance in and of Organizations* (Greenwich, Conn.: JAI, 1998).

[56] Peter C. Yeager, *The Limits of Law: The Public Regulation of Private Pollution* (Cambridge: Cambridge University Press, 1991), pp. 8–10.

[57] Ibid., p. 9.

and costly, they are less likely to adhere to the letter of the law. Second, the success of criminal sanctions in constraining corporate deviance should vary by crime type. We would expect a stronger deterrent effect for economic-relations offenses and less of an effect for social-relations offenses.

Alternative Sources of Social Control

Perhaps the most important explanation for why managers are unde-terred by legal sanction threats is that other social control mechanisms are more powerful inhibitors of misconduct. If we limit our deterrence framework to the inhibitive effect of criminal law and its enforcement ("mere deterrence",)[58] then extralegal sources of legal compliance would include factors such as internalized norms and attachment to significant others, guilt, shame, and threats to valued goals. Grasmick and Bursik distinguish between these two types of sanctions as state-imposed costs (material deprivation via fines and imprisonment) and socially or self-imposed costs (depending on whether costs stem from the negative eval-uations of significant others or from individual violations of conscience).[59]

There are many reasons to believe that socially or self-imposed costs will be more influential over managers than those imposed by the state. Ironi-cally, the bases of these claims are similar to those advanced by deterrence adherents.

1. Corporate personnel are not committed to a deviant life-style. Most man-agers *are* committed to conventional activities and normative behaviors. Therefore, illegality simply will not be contemplated because of prosocial habits.
2. Engaging in crime would threaten meaningful commitments and attach-ments for corporate personnel. To the extent that managers are embed-ded in a valued social network based on ties with conventional others (e.g., peers, family, and friends), the discovery of unethical conduct can threaten these ties. If the opinions of friends and family matter to man-agers, then the accompanying threat to these relationships should have inhibitory effects. Additionally, negative assessments of a person's char-acter by significant others (such as a work supervisor) can affect desired career goals or life ambitions.

---

[58] Andenaes, *Punishment and Deterrence*, p. 35.
[59] Harold G. Grasmick and Robert J. Bursik Jr., "Conscience, Significant Others, and Rational Choice: Extending the Deterrence Model," *Law and Society Review* 24 (1990): 837–861.

3. Managers tend to see themselves as principled and responsible citizens. Violation of this self-image, through criminal participation, produces feelings of guilt and challenges one's self-esteem.

It is important to note that these negative or stigmatic effects can occur absent "official" reaction. Crime inhibition can stem from self-knowledge, confessionals to friends or family, or organizational (as opposed to formal legal) discovery. Social integration into conventional groups serves an important social control function beyond that of formal legal systems.

Conclusions

Criminal law is an ineffective and inefficient deterrent for corporate criminals. Some argue that criminal law is not well suited for use against corporate offenders, whereas others suggest that the problem is one of implementation, that is, the threat of criminal processing will not produce deterrent effects until criminal sanctions are more certain and severe. Another position, however, rejects the deterrence framework as theoretically and empirically unsound.

For all of the reasons discussed here, criminal law is apt to produce less than effective corporate deterrence. However, because the majority of corporate crime cases are legally administered outside of the criminal justice system, we cannot reject legal sanction threats absent a discussion of the potential deterrent effects of civil and regulatory sanction threats. In the next chapter, we review whether alternatives to criminal law – specifically "tort" law – can prevent and deter corporate offending.

CHAPTER FOUR

Corporate Deterrence and Civil Justice

BECAUSE legal responses to corporate offending involve multiple systems of law, the potential for crime inhibition may also be embedded in these alternative formal justice systems. In this chapter, we investigate how corporations and corporate officers experience the civil justice process and, in doing so, assess whether and under what conditions civil law may yield deterrent effects. In discussing corporate deterrence and civil law, I review the primary assumptions, goals, and normative rules of civil justice; compare the substantive and procedural requirements for case development and processing in the civil and criminal legal systems; and assess the deterrence capacities of civil law and, in particular, punitive civil sanctions.

Civil Law and Corporate Offending

Delineation of the legal duties of persons in relationship to one another comprises the body of civil law. In the United States, civil laws regulate family and business relations, contracts, and interpersonal disputes, among other relations.[1] In the study of corporate crime, businesses primarily come into the domain of civil law in one of two ways. Victims of corporate crime may seek compensation for injury by filing a complaint, or "tort action," in civil court. The so-called moving agent in these cases is the private citizen. Civil cases against corporations may also originate within the prosecutorial or administrative process as state or federal authorities (such as state attorneys general, the Department of Justice, the Environmental Protection Agency,

---

[1] Raymond J. Michalowski, *Order, Law, and Crime* (New York: Newbery Award Records, 1985).

or Securities and Exchange Commission) increasingly have the option of employing either civil or criminal means to pursue corporate violators.

In a strictly legal sense, the decision to process a case civilly or criminally is determined through substantive or procedural criteria. Substantive civil and criminal laws define what acts or omissions qualify for legal intervention while also setting penalties for specific violations. Definitions and descriptions of criminal acts (e.g., aggravated assault is defined as the unlawful intentional inflicting of serious bodily injury or death with a deadly or dangerous weapon) form the basis of substantive criminal law. Specifying the rights and mutual obligations of persons (e.g., drivers must exercise care when operating a motor vehicle) is the substance of civil law.[2]

Procedure, on the other hand, "sets the rules of decision making that determine whether a sanction should be applied in a particular instance."[3] Procedural rules guide how the state can legally proceed when a criminal case is brought against a corporation or corporate officer. In the same manner, civil procedure guides citizens or government authorities in seeking compensation when rights have been violated. Typically, civil law is invoked by private citizens while criminal cases are brought by the state, taking the role of complainant. Civil and criminal procedure also define the geographical jurisdiction of legal authority; the statute of limitations affecting when a complaint can be legally brought; the rules of investigation, discovery, and evidence; and the degree of certainty required for reaching a decision.[4]

Often, similar kinds of prohibited acts may be subject to either civil or criminal law. Assault, for example, may be pursued as a violation of criminal law or as a private tort claim wherein the victim seeks compensation from the offender for inflicted injuries. The case involving the murders of Nicole Brown Simpson and Ronald Goldman is perhaps the most famous recent example of criminal and civil charges stemming from the same incident.[5] In the case of corporate crime, civil or criminal prosecution is possible for many kinds of illegality, including environmental wrongdoing, anticompetitive acts, and financial frauds.[6]

[2] Howard Abandinsky, *Law and Justice,* 2nd ed. (Chicago: Nelson-Hall, 1991), p. 22.
[3] Kenneth Mann, "Procedure Rules and Information Control: Gaining Leverage over White-Collar Crime," in Kip Schlegel and David Weisburd (eds.), *White-Collar Crime Reconsidered* (Boston: Northeastern University Press, 1992), p. 334.
[4] Ibid., p. 334.
[5] See, e.g., *People of the State of California vs. Orenthal James Simpson* (Case No. BA09721); the wrongful-death suit of *Fredric Goldman and Kimberly Erin Goldman vs. Orenthal James Simpson* (Case No. SC036340); and the Complaint for Damages-Survival Action of *Louis H. Brown vs. Orenthal James Simpson* (Case No. SC036876).
[6] Frederick W. Addison III and Elizabeth E. Mack, "Creating an Environmental Ethic in Corporate America: The Big Stick of Jail Time," *Southwestern Law Journal* 44 (1991): 1427–1448.

Civil remedies (as opposed to criminal) are most likely sought when evidence surrounding a case is weak, because evidentiary requirements are more restrictive in criminal cases (where conviction requires evidence beyond reasonable doubt rather than a preponderance of evidence); or when the offense lacks clear culpability or blameworthiness. Criminal law is more appropriate for cases that offend the morality of the community, bringing forth a collective sense of outrage toward the offender and his or her act. Thus, criminal prosecution makes more sense in cases where responsibility is clear-cut and the actor is blameworthy. Some legal scholars believe that civil law is a more appropriate tool for addressing most corporate wrongs because illegal acts by organizations are perceived to be missing the necessary elements of moral culpability that accompany other kinds of criminal acts.[7]

Perhaps the most important mechanism of redress against corporate offenders in civil law is the tort claim. Both private parties and the government may bring suit against corporate offenders and the potential economic costs to firms from successful tort cases are great.

The Law of Torts

Tort claims may be divided into three types: intentional interference with others' interests, negligent interference with others' interests, and faultless interference with others' interests.[8] By bringing a tort action, the plaintiff seeks restoration to an undamaged state. Tort claims, then, are primarily restitutive.

A classic private tort case, as described by Christopher Stone,[9] has several important features. The injured party is aware that an injury has taken place; the victim knows who is responsible for the injury; the nature and extent of injuries are relatively straightforward and easy to assess; causality is technically easy to ascertain; and, if legal damages can be attributed to the responsible actor, *it is assumed that she or he will change that behavior in the future* (i.e., specific deterrence).

To fulfill these legal requirements, a simple tort case would be one in which "Smith, who is walking across the street, is accidentally but negligently

---

[7] "Corporate Crime: Regulating Corporate Behavior through Criminal Sanctions,"*Harvard Law Review* 92 (1979): 1127–1375.

[8] George W. Spiro, *The Legal Environment of Business* (Englewood Cliffs, N.J.: Prentice-Hall, 1989), p. 306.

[9] Christopher D. Stone, *Where the Law Ends* (New York: Harper and Row, 1975), p. 103 (emphasis added).

driven into by Jones. Smith falls, suffering internal injuries, and sues for damages."[10] The plaintiff, Smith, has suffered physical injuries that can be directly linked to the actions of Jones, the driver of the automobile. It is ascertained that Jones, who knew that the brakes on his automobile were faulty and failed to correct the situation, drove into Smith accidentally but negligently. Both the extent of Smith's injuries and their costs are relatively straightforward (health costs, loss of employment) and are easily causally ascertained (i.e., resulting from being hit by Jones's automobile). Suing Jones and recovering damages should, in this case, be easily achieved.

Victimizations by corporations, however, typically fail to follow such straightforward scenarios. Victims are often unaware that they have been injured (e.g., short weighing of consumer products, price-fixing, or employee exposure to carcinogens at work) and, if aware, may not be able to identify the responsible party because the chains of responsibility are convoluted. As a result of the indirect victimization, it is highly likely that most corporate crime victims will fail to seek any kind of redress for their injuries, civil or otherwise.

Among those who do seek compensation, however, tort claims can be expensive and time-consuming. Pitting modest resources and time constraints on the plaintiff's side against an often powerful, well-funded, well-counseled, and obstructive corporate defendant on the other mitigates the likelihood of successful recovery by the plaintiff.

Deterrence and Civil Sanctions

Data on civil litigation has been collected by the *Bureau of Justice Statistics*. A survey of state courts in seventy-five of the nation's largest counties found that of the 378,000 cases disposed in 1992, the majority involved individual plaintiffs filing claims against other individuals.[11] (In fact, 94 percent of all cases involved an individual plaintiff.) The type of defendant, however, varied by the kind of case filed (i.e., auto torts, product liability, malpractice medical, and so forth). Toxic substance and product liability cases most often involved a business defendant (96.3 and 93.2 percent, respectively), as did premises liability (74.8 percent) and nonmedical malpractice (53.4 percent).[12] The average processing time from filing to disposition for

---

[10] Ibid., p. 103.

[11] "Civil Justice Survey of State Courts, 1992," *Bureau of Justice Statistics Special Report* (Washington, D.C.: U.S. Department of Justice, April 1995).

[12] In medical malpractice cases, hospitals were the overwhelming recipients of litigation (71.8 percent); however the numbers are somewhat inflated because of the way multiple

all cases was 19.3 months. Auto tort cases took the least amount of time to disposition because, "compared to all other types, auto torts were the most likely to have an individual (rather than a business, hospital or government agency) as the defendant."[13] Very few cases actually went to trial (jury or bench) for disposition. Of the 3 percent that made it to trial, outcomes were about equally split in favor of the plaintiff and defendant. Although the data are limited, there is some evidence that a tort claim against an individual is more likely to result in a verdict for the plaintiff than if the defendant is an organization (business or hospital).[14] These data suggest that civil cases against corporations are rare events; that cases brought against firms are unlikely to be resolved by a jury; and that corporate defendants are likely to prevail.

Another study examined civil jurors' perceptions of corporate defendants and individual litigants. This research found that jurors scrutinized the potential motivation for why individual plaintiffs bring a case and penalize those "who did not meet high standards of credibility and behavior."[15] Plaintiffs must convince a jury that they have a "legitimate" case. Sometimes this requires evidence beyond the fact that a business is responsible for injuries. These results are contrary to common perceptions that juries are biased against corporate defendants (i.e., the "deep pockets" argument). In truth, tort actions against corporations result in successful jury awards in only half of the cases that make it to trial.[16]

Similarly, Diamond and Casper's study of how information is processed by juries shows that in complex cases (such as an antitrust case) jurists are much more active in sorting through information than typically assumed. They are not, as claimed by some, overwhelmed by expert testimony, and they tend to respond to judicial instructions – especially when the law is explained to them. This effect was clearly seen when jurists (advised that their award would be trebled but were not admonished to disregard this information) adjusted the award to plaintiffs downward to control for plaintiff "windfalls." A similar outcome occurred when jurors were told of treble

---

defendants were counted. For example, "a case involving a hospital defendant is categorized as a hospital even if there were also business, individual, or government defendants in the case." Ibid., p. 4.

[13] Ibid., p. 3.

[14] Ibid., p. 5.

[15] Valerie Hans and William Lofquist, "Jurors' Judgements of Business Liability in Tort Cases: Implications for the Litigation Explosion Debate," *Law and Society Review* 22 (1992): 95.

[16] Kevin M. Clermont and Theodore Eisenbert, "Trial by Jury or Judge: Transcending Empiricism" (paper presented at the annual meeting of the Law and Society Association, Amsterdam, the Netherlands, 1991); but see Hans and Lofquist, "Jurors' Judgements of Business Liability," p. 90, for higher trial win rates for plaintiffs.

66   CORPORATE CRIME, LAW, AND SOCIAL CONTROL

damages but were admonished to disregard the trebling effect in their deliberations (without an explanation). However, awards were significantly
higher when jurists were told why they should not adjust their awards even
though they may want to do so.[17]

When tort litigation against corporate offenders is successful, however, it
is assumed that the costs of the decision to the defendant will positively affect the future behavior of the corporate entity. Thus, successful tort claims
are believed to produce specific deterrent effects. Yet, this assumption has
mixed empirical support in the literature. A study of corporate deterrence
conducted by Simpson and Koper uncovered no evidence that civil actions
(including tort claims) against a group of corporate offenders significantly
deterred firms from further offending. In fact, just the opposite was true.
Bringing a case civilly significantly increased the likelihood that corporate offenders would reoffend![18] These findings are tempered somewhat by those
of Block and his colleagues who discovered a strong deterrent effect associated with class action suits, as well as results from a study of oil tanker spills
that showed spill size was negatively related to enforcement of the Water
Quality Improvement Act of 1970 (the act provides civil penalties for intentional spills resulting from negligence).[19] However, the Block study does
not find significant deterrent effects associated with civil suits in general,[20]
and the oil spill study only indirectly linked sanction imposition and severity to firm behavior. Instead, deterrent effects are inferred from a negative
relationship between spill frequency and the number of Coast Guard man-
hours per transfer. Finally, none of the studies examined whether individuals
within corporate entities were deterred by tort claims (as employees of the
firm or as corporate codefendants). Thus, at least at this point, the empirical data are too sketchy to provide much support on either side of the
deterrence debate.

Anecdotal evidence, however, suggests that civil sanctions, especially
those that are *punitive*, are economically consequential for corporate defendants. In fact, in some cases litigation may extract greater monetary costs
and result in greater behavioral change from corporations than would criminal prosecution for the same offense. For instance, Ford Motor Company

[17] Shari Seidman Diamond and Jonathan D. Casper, "Blindfolding the Jury to Verdict Consequences: Damages, Experts, and the Civil Jury," *Law and Society Review* 26 (1992): 553–554.
[18] Sally S. Simpson and Christopher S. Koper, "Deterring Corporate Crime," *Criminology*
30 (1992): 347–375.
[19] Dennis Epple and Michael Visscher, "Environmental Pollution: Modeling Occurrence,
Detection, and Deterrence," *Journal of Law and Economics* 27 (1984): 29–60.
[20] Michael Kent Block, Frederick Carl Nold, and Joseph Gregory Sidak, "The Deterrent Effects
of Antitrust Enforcement," *Journal of Political Economy* 89 (1981): 429–445.

decided to recall all 1.5 million Pinto automobiles after the firm lost a costly civil case in Santa Ana, California. A civil jury awarded Richard Grimshaw $2.8 million dollars, and the family of Lily Gray $659,680 in compensatory damages, due to the negligence Ford showed in producing and marketing a known hazardous product. The jury also imposed a $125 million dollar punitive damage award (which was later reduced on appeal). The rationale for imposing punitive damages rested in jurors' shared belief that Ford had willfully disregarded the safety of its consumers and that the company needed to be sent a message not to design cars in this way again.[21]

Ford is not alone. Asbestos, pharmaceutical, and oil tanker companies have also faced stiff compensatory and punitive damage awards. Manville, for instance, the largest asbestos manufacturer in the United States prior to filing for bankruptcy in 1982, was found liable for punitive damages by ten separate juries, averaging $616,000 per case. By 1984 an excess of twenty-five thousand civil suits were filed against various asbestos manufacturers, increasing by an average of five hundred cases per month over a year's time.[22] Pharmaceutical firms involved in the thalidomide disaster (just one of many cases in which drug companies have been subjected to civil suits) suffered serious consequences not from criminal sanctions but from civil actions that cost "hundreds of million dollars."[23]

Punitive civil damages add an important element to the mix of available sanctions for use against corporate offenders. They require the defendant to make monetary amends beyond that of the original wrong or injury, adding additional monetary costs to corporate violators. Awards may take the form of multiple damages (double or treble the amount of harm), civil money penalties, or forfeitures. Punitive sanctions in the civil legal context can be imposed when corporate behavior is intentional and causes harm to the public interest.[24]

In the vernacular of the deterrence tradition, punitive civil damages increase the severity of civil sanctions. An explicit purpose for the imposition of punitive damages is "social control" – that is, the belief that corporations will adjust their actions to avoid costly punitive sanctions in the future. In a sense, punitive damages allow private persons to serve a law enforcement function in that citizens are encouraged "to enforce societal norms through

[21] Russell Mokhiber, *Corporate Crime and Violence* (San Francisco: Sierra Club Books, 1988), pp. 378–379.

[22] Ibid., pp. 285–286.

[23] John Braithwaite, *Corporate Crime in the Pharmaceutical Industry* (Boston: Routledge & Kegan Paul, 1984), p. 107.

[24] Kenneth Mann, "Punitive Civil Sanctions: The Middleground between Criminal and Civil Law," *Yale Law Journal* 101 (1992): 1795–1873.

civil litigation, thereby supplementing enforcement through the criminal process."[25]

Middleground Jurisprudence

Because legal scholars disagree as to when or even if punitive damages should apply to civil wrongs,[26] we need to examine the rationale for punitive civil sanctions, the circumstances under which civil penalties are sought, and some contradictions produced by this legal hybrid. The resulting jurisprudence has been characterized by Kenneth Mann as "middleground" because it draws on both civil and criminal law paradigms.[27]

H. M. Hart notes a simple distinction between civil and criminal legal systems, "what distinguishes a criminal from a civil sanction . . . is the judgement of community condemnation which accompanies . . . its imposition."[28] According to Blackstone:

> The distinction of public wrongs from private, of crimes and misdemeanors from civil injuries, seems principally to consist in this: that private wrongs, or civil injuries, are an infringement or privation of the civil rights which belong to individuals, considered merely as individuals: public wrongs, or crimes and misdemeanors, are a breach and violation of the public rights and duties due to the whole community, considered as a community, in its social aggregate capacity. [29]

Blackstone goes on to suggest that while crimes, like civil wrongs, also may injure private individuals, they are "something more" – injurious to the society as a whole. The aggregate threat posed by these acts requires additional penalty beyond the restoration of the individual. Thus, crimes are distinct from private wrongs because they subject the offender to *punishment*.

---

[25] Richard C. Ausness, "Retribution and Deterrence: The Role of Punitive Damages in Products Liability Litigation," *Kentucky Law Journal* 74 (1985–1986): 1–25.

[26] Given the dramatic increase in the government's use of civil monetary penalties coupled with piecemeal legislation that has produced a dramatic expansion of collateral sanctions (e.g., revocation of the corporate charter, suspension, debarment), Yellen and Mayer suggest that criminal and civil sanctions must be better coordinated. See David Yellen and Carl J. Mayer, "Coordinating Sanctions for Corporate Misconduct: Civil or Criminal Punishment," *American Criminal Law Review* 29 (1992): 961.

[27] Mann, "Punitive Civil Sanctions," p. 1799.

[28] H. M. Hart, quoted in Steven Walt and William S. Laufer, "Corporate Criminal Liability and the Comparative Mix of Sanctions," in Kip Schlegel and David Weisburd (eds.), *White Collar Crime Reconsidered* (Boston: Northwestern University Press, 1992), p. 313.

[29] William Blackstone, *Commentaries on the Laws of England*, vol. 4, adapted by Robert Malcolm Kerr (Boston: Beacon Press, 1962), p. 5.

The contemporary debate surrounding the function of and intent of punitive civil sanctions acknowledges that the boundaries between substantive civil and criminal law have always been blurry; yet, legal scholars disagree as to whether the increasing use of punitive civil sanctions against white-collar offenders is a positive or negative development. John Collins Coffee Jr., a prominent critic of middleground sanctions, claims that tort law's primary function is to "force defendants to internalize the social costs that their conduct imposes on others"[30] – that is, to prevent social harm. In the case of corporations, the function of civil law is to "price" undesirable organizational behavior that occurs in the context of some socially desirable activity (i.e., pollution that inevitably results from industrial production). Because civil law cannot achieve the goal of no social harm (i.e., no pollution), the law is necessarily aspirational. To maximize the discretion and flexibility of judges who "make" civil law, the parameters or boundaries of the law are necessarily blurry.

Criminal law, according to Coffee, is punitive in nature and concerned with establishing the blameworthiness (guilty mind, or *mens rea*, and culpability) of the offender. Because of this trait, the rights of the accused are highly protected via a system of procedural barriers to conviction. Criminal law also seeks to publicly stigmatize and censure violators – that is, to punish them.

A problem with punitive civil sanctions is that punishment (a goal of criminal law) is meted out in civil proceedings that lack the procedural safeguards allocated under criminal prosecution.[31] While such paradigmatic encroachment raises important concerns about legal principles, procedures, and practice (e.g., appropriate domain, constitutional safeguards, the implications of punishment), our concern with corporate deterrence adds another slant to this discussion. Does the invasion of one type of law into the other affect the deterrence capabilities of either legal system?

Deterrence and Punitive Civil Sanctions

In Coffee's view, both civil and criminal law can deter; however, Coffee uses an economic definition of deterrence.[32] Civil law deters by imposing a price (or kind of tax) on acts that have positive social utility but impose negative externalities on others (e.g., the manufacture of pesticides – a socially necessary activity, but one that exposes workers to toxic substances).

---

[30] John Collins Coffee, "Paradigms Lost: The Blurring of the Criminal and Civil Law Models – And What Can Be Done about It," *Yale Law Journal* 101 (1992): 1878.
[31] Mann, "Punitive Civil Sanctions," p. 1798.
[32] Coffee, "Paradigms Lost."

"Excessive" sanctions brought under civil law may lead to "overdeterrence," or the reduction of otherwise productive activity to less than optimum levels.

Criminal law, on the other hand, deters by prohibiting and punishing conduct that lacks any social utility (e.g., homicide). Deterrence theory imposes no natural limit on the severity of punishment for *crime* as long as the harm to be deterred continues to exist. Limitations on punishment are more often set through a just-deserts philosophy.[33] For example, criminal sanctions are calibrated according to perceived social harm, relative seriousness of criminal acts, and degree of culpability.

Another way to think about the contrast between the purposes of civil and criminal law is to illustrate the difference between total and optimal deterrence. Again, Coffee's arguments are instructive.[34]

> The optimal amount of fraud is zero, but the same cannot be said for pollution, which is an inevitable byproduct of industrial society. On this basis, fraud is a natural candidate for criminal penalties, and nonfraudulent (i.e., negligent) pollution for civil penalties. In addition, there are also crimes where the gain or benefit to the criminal is wholly illicit (the obvious example is the crime of rape), and thus a mere "pricing" policy produces the morally objectionable result that the defendant can benefit. Hence, a total deterrence approach is necessary.

When punitive sanctions are added to civil law, however, these distinctions between civil and criminal legal paradigms are compromised. Civil law is encroaching on criminal legal territory at the same time that criminal law is extending its reach into civil areas. Coffee worries that within this kind of environment, criminal law is overextended and will lose some of its "nondeterrent function," including the moral education and socialization of the public (a function that some, e.g., Andeneas, do not view as necessarily distinct from the total deterrence process). Thus, Coffee wants to stop criminal encroachment into civil (or regulatory) areas.

This sentiment is shared by others. For example, Abraham Goldstein is less critical of punitive civil sanctions than is Coffee, but he does warn against "the helter skelter" of legal processes and sanctions.[35] He fears that "the stigma and sanctions associated with 'crime' will be imposed, in both civil and criminal processes, on persons who are not culpable in any widely

---

[33] See Franklin E. Zimring and Gordon J. Hawkins, *Deterrence: The Legal Threat in Crime Control* (Chicago: University of Chicago Press, 1973), pp. 37–42; and Franklin E. Zimring, "The Multiple Middlegrounds between Civil and Criminal Law," *Yale Law Journal* 101 (1992): 1902.

[34] Coffee, "Paradigms Lost," p. 1878, n. 6.

[35] Abraham S. Goldstein, "White-Collar Crime and Civil Sanctions," *Yale Law Journal* 101 (1992): 1895–1899.

accepted sense of that term" and that if such a thing occurs, "the 'crime' label will lose its incremental utility, the moral force of the criminal sanction will be dissipated, and many more people will suffer unjust treatment."[36]

Other critics raise concerns about the overreach of punitive damages beyond behaviors that are excessive, flagrant, and culpable to all civil cases. Ausness, for instance, questions whether punitive damages are being used as an "all-purpose substitute for compensatory damages" in product liability cases.[37] Similar challenges to the deterrence doctrine raise the following questions:

- Did the wrongdoer know the action was wrong and could she or he accurately assess the potential costs of wrongdoing (including punitive damages)?
- Can the firm pass on or insure against the receipt of punitive damages?
- Will the organization alter its conduct to avoid the imposition of punitive damages?
- Can the aims of punitive damages be more efficiently achieved through other means?[38]

A more favorable view of punitive civil sanctions and their deterrent capacities is offered by Mann, who supports encroachment of civil law into criminal legal areas, but only if the shift is accompanied by increased legal protections for defendants who face punitive sanctions.[39] Because this concern over procedure is an essential point, we need to examine more explicitly the procedural differences between civil and criminal processing.

Criminal processing occurs within the context of an adversarial relationship between the defendant and the state. Procedural protections emerged precisely because of the inequity between legal parties (with the state assumed to hold greater power) and because potential criminal penalties are presumed to be severe (e.g., loss of liberty via incarceration or life through capital execution). Thus, "paradigmatic criminal procedure requires more information than paradigmatic civil procedure because it puts a higher value on certainty before imposing sanctions."[40] If guilt and individual responsibility can be determined beyond a reasonable doubt, then the criminal process determines the appropriate punishment. Although there may be many justifications for the imposition of criminal sanctions (e.g., incapacitation, just

---

[36] Ibid., p. 1899.
[37] Ausness, "Retribution and Deterrence," p. 77.
[38] Ibid., pp. 81–92.
[39] Mann, "Punitive Civil Sanctions."
[40] Ibid., p. 1811.

deserts, restitution, and even rehabilitation), there is no question that the sanctions are punitive. And, at the heart of the deterrence argument is the assumption that it is fear of punishment that inhibits the likelihood of reoffending (in the case of the convicted party) and the occurrence of similar misconduct by others (general deterrence).

Punitive civil sanctions, on the other hand, have been defined by state courts as "remedial" in purpose, not punitive per se.[41] Such a definition, according to Mann, maintains a "legal fiction" that is seriously consequential for those subject to this form of sanction. By declaring punitive sanctions "nonpunitive" in function, the normal kinds of procedural safeguards allocated under the more punitive criminal legal system are bypassed. Paradoxically, a corporate defendant may find itself paying compensation in addition to a "remedial" sanction that sums to an amount greater than legally obtainable under the provisions of criminal law *based on evidence that would not support a criminal finding of guilt.*

This contrived view of the purpose of punitive sanctions raises both theoretical and empirical problems for the deterrence debate. By allocating a remedial purpose to sanctions "that courts did not want to define as punitive in the criminal sense, but that were clearly not simple compensatory damages,"[42] the courts attempt to distinguish punishment from deterrence. They fail to do so, however, by also claiming that the purpose of remedial civil sanctions is prospective deterrence (social control). How can remedial sanctions have a deterrent effect unless they impose some sort of punishment? Noting this contradiction, Mann argues that, "in the case of monetary sanctions, deterrence is achieved through punishment. It is the pain of having to pay a large fine that deters similar actions in the future."[43]

Not unlike the corporations and others subject to nonpunitive punitive civil sanctions, the author finds herself in an ironic position – that of trying to assess the deterrence capacities of civil law that ostensibly does not punish yet seeks social control.[44] Philosophical subtleties aside, however, there are

[41] Ibid., p. 1813. For a recent review of Eighth and Fourteenth Amendment challenges to the application of punitive sanctions, see Ed Stevens and Brian K. Payne, "Applying Deterrence Theory in the Context of Corporate Wrongdoing: Limitations on Punitive Damages," *Journal of Criminal Justice* 27(1999): 195–207.

[42] Mann, "Punitive Civil Sanctions," p. 1829.

[43] Ibid., p. 1839.

[44] The resolution of the problem lies not in the traditional deterrence literature, but in a rational-choice view of corporation decision making. Civil sanctions, whether remunerative or punitive, impose economic costs on corporations. From a rational-choice perspective, corporations will adjust their actions based on the perceived (or assessed) costs and benefits of a particular line of action. If the anticipated illegal act is perceived by corporate decision makers to be more costly than beneficial, then the choice of crime over noncrime will be

some important arguments to evaluate regarding whether civil law can deter corporate misconduct.

Can Civil Law Deter Corporate Crime?

Arguments in Favor

Argument 1. Relative to criminal law, sanction imposition will be more certain under civil law. This argument is based in several points. First, unlike criminal prosecution of corporate offenders, civil processing eases the procedural safeguards for defendants, making it easier to achieve a verdict against the corporation. Positive outcomes are also more apt to occur in light of recent reforms in civil investigatory powers. The Department of Justice and other regulatory agencies now have greater authority in some cases to demand documents and to compel production of information from defendants merely based on suspicion that the law is being violated.[45]

Finally, the moving agent in civil cases is more inclusive. Both individuals (as private parties) and the state can bring tort claims against corporate defendants. When the political climate does not favor formal intervention by the state (as in the case of environmental enforcement during the Buford years, i.e., the early 1980s), civil suits by mobilized citizens and political interest groups are likely to multiply. Yeager's study of environmental enforcement discovered that "stunted federal enforcement and high rates of noncompliance with the water pollution laws generated *private enforcement* at a level not before seen in the history of American regulatory law."[46] For instance, prior to 1983, only 41 notices to sue and lawsuits were brought by citizens under the water law. However, between 1983 and mid-1984, 195 notices and suits by citizens (many organized by a coalition of national environmental groups) were filed.

When the state is actively involved in enforcement efforts, it can, through class action suits, bring together numerous plaintiffs whose cases may be too insignificant to justify litigation as individuals, but who, as collectivities, may seek remuneration as part of an aggregate. The fact that this process has been eased somewhat (since the Supreme Court amended Rule 23 of the Federal Rules of Civil Procedure) has both increased the number of persons

---

inhibited. Given, however, that we wish to address the deterrence capacities of civil law from a traditional deterrence position (in which fear of sanction is the primary behavioral control mechanism), rational-choice theory is superfluous to our discussion.

[45] See, e.g., *Morton v. U.S.*, 338 U.S. 632, 1950, p. 642.

[46] Peter C. Yeager, *The Limits of Law: The Public Regulation of Private Pollution* (Cambridge: Cambridge University Press, 1991), p. 320 (emphasis in original).

who qualify for inclusion as plaintiffs in class actions suits and, in some types of corporate crime, the use of *parens patriae* (cases in which the state attorney general sues on behalf of a group of victimized consumers) class action suits for deterrence purposes.[47] Since 1989 it is even possible for individuals (or groups of individuals) within some states to seek remuneration for "indirect" financial losses, such as those that result from antitrust violations.[48]

For these reasons, more cases of corporate misconduct will be brought into the civil legal system and the likelihood of corporate sanctioning is increased relative to criminal prosecution. Thus, greater corporate deterrence is achieved through civil than through criminal processing.

Argument 2. Relative to criminal law, under civil law the imposition of sanction will be more severe. Civil legal processing of corporate crime cases can extract more severe economic costs from corporate defendants than comparable criminal prosecution. Civil sanctions are capable of levying three kinds of distinct costs against corporate defendants: they compensate victims for their injuries; civil sanctions can incorporate enforcement costs adding additional disincentive to offenders (e.g., plaintiff attorneys fees, court costs, etc.); and punitive sanctions can add multiplicative costs beyond the original injury. Consequently, civil sanctions impose more severe financial punishments on corporations increasing the likelihood of deterrence.

Argument 3. The primary goal of criminal law is retribution *and* deterrence (social control). Using criminal law against behaviors that are not morally blameworthy or to impose sanctions absent fault (i.e., behaviors more appropriately controlled civilly) lessens the fairness and efficiency of both legal systems.[49] Moreover, the chances of overdeterrence (reducing positively valued corporate activities by overpunishment) and underdeterrence (lessening the stigmatic and educative power of criminal law by overuse and inappropriate use) are lessened when civil and criminal procedures and sanctions are kept relatively distinct.[50] Given these negatives associated with criminal prosecution of corporate wrongdoing, civil law is left as the more appropriate intervention system.

[47] See, e.g., Michael Kent Bloc, Frederick Carl Nold, and Joseph Gregory Sidak, "The Deterrent Effect of Antitrust Enforcement," *Journal of Political Economy* 89 (1981): 441, n. 34.

[48] Marshall B. Clinard, *Corporate Corruption* (New York: Praeger, 1990), p. 181.

[49] "Corporate Crime: Regulating Corporate Behavior through Criminal Sanctions," *Harvard Law Review* 92 (April 1979): 1369.

[50] Coffee, "Paradigms Lost"; and Goldstein, "White-Collar Crime and Civil Sanctions."

Argument 4. Civil law is a more appropriate mechanism than criminal law for holding supervisors and top managers accountable for their own actions as well as those of their subordinates. "Strict liability civil sanctions are more attractive than strict liability criminal sanctions, since on the corporate level the former can effect the same degree of deterrence as the latter, and on the individual level, imposing the stigma of criminality upon those who may not be culpable sacrifices fairness."[51]

This argument assumes that responsibility for illegal acts that occur within an organizational context is difficult if not impossible to unravel. Crime in organizations is typically "serially produced" (i.e., involving multiconnected actors who are interdependent within the organization but not necessarily equally culpable).[52] Consequently, while it may be generally agreed that managers and supervisors should be held accountable for the actions of their subordinates and for illegalities that occur "on their watch," it is generally less accepted that corporate officers be criminally prosecuted for these acts *unless* it is possible to ascertain specific managers' actual participation, culpability, and blameworthiness.

Argument 5. Absent theory that imputes fault to the organizational entity and that justifies criminal punishment, civil law is a more appropriate tool in which to impose a tax on corporate wrongdoing while avoiding the problem of applying constitutional safeguards to nonpersons (i.e., artificial entities) required in criminal prosecutions.[53] Advocates suggest that deterrence will be achieved if the fine imposed is marginally greater than the benefit achieved by the illegal act *under a condition of high sanction certainty.* Therefore, if American Steel Corporation violates EPA standards, saving $100 million dollars per year, the optimal fine to achieve deterrence would be, say, $110 million per year (multiplied by the number of years during which the firm violated the standards).

Advocates of the use of civil sanctions to achieve corporate deterrence believe that civil processes are a more appropriate and efficient tool to control the behavior of corporations. Yet, there are several reasons to believe that civil sanctions are not the panacea envisioned by civil-law adherents.

---

[51] "Corporate Crime," p. 1370.
[52] Sally S. Simpson, Anthony R. Harris, and Brian Mattson, "Measuring Corporate Crime," in Michael Blankenship (ed.), *Understanding Corporate Criminality* (New York: Garland, 1993), p. 115–140.
[53] "Corporate Crime," p. 1369.

Arguments Against

Argument 1. Many of the same arguments made previously about the failure of criminal law to deter corporate crime are equally apt here. For instance, victimizations are not likely to come to the attention of or be recognized as violations by victims or government authorities. Consequently, many corporate misbehaviors escape notice. To maximize deterrence, some have suggested modifying sanction severity to adjust for a lack of sanction certainty. That is, if the punishment risk is 25 percent (a one in four chance of getting caught) and the expected gain from the illicit act is $1 million, then the appropriate sanction would be $4 million (the gain multiplied by the number of times a company avoided detection).[54]

Critics of this approach, however, question the legal system's ability to estimate and implement escalated cash penalties in addition to the potential costs (or negative externalities) imposed on the public by these sanctions.[55] In the first place, estimates of risk apprehension lack any sort of empirical validity. There are no empirical data to document or give reasonable estimates on how much corporate offending occurs absent detection. Consequently, our estimates of sanction risk are merely theoretical.

Second, multiplicative sanctions are limited by corporate financial resources, and these bounds may be surprisingly low.[56] When sanctions are imposed that are beyond the offender's means to pay, the sanction is unreasonable (absent alternative sanctions such as community service or flexible payments) and risks company bankruptcy – a negative externality for workers, shareholders, and affected communities.

Third, courts and juries may be uncooperative, failing to find firms responsible for injuries, disregarding multiplicative sanctions, or nullifying earlier awards through the appeals process. Finally, the legal and behavioral differences between definitions of corporate violations will affect perceptual assessments of sanction risk. For example, legal authorities merely need to discover a price-fixing conspiracy to establish de facto that a violation has occurred. Other corporate offenses require some element of intent, such as "willfully" disregarding the health and safety of workers. Thus, the corporate (and individual) sanctions necessary to inhibit illegality are likely to vary by offense type. A complicating factor, however, is that risks are also apt to vary by the structural location of the individual manager because she or he will

---

[54] Richard A. Posner, *Economic Analysis of Law*, 2nd ed. (Boston: Little Brown, 1977), p. 167.
[55] John Collins Coffee Jr., " 'No Soul to Damn, No Body to Kick': An Unscandalized Inquiry into the Problem of Corporate Punishment," *Michigan Law Review* 79 (1980): 389, n. 11.
[56] Ibid., n. 13.

experience the threat of corporate sanctions vis-à-vis her or his own risks differently.[57]

> For the middle-level official the question is not whether the behavior is too risky to be in the interests of the corporation from a cost/benefit standpoint. Rather, it is which risk is greater – the criminal conviction of the company or his own dismissal for failure to meet targets set by an unsympathetically demanding senior management. Because the conviction of the corporation falls only indirectly on the middle manager, it can seldom exceed the penalty that dismissal or demotion means to him.[58]

Argument 2. Another argument against civil corporate deterrence revolves around whether individual managers will be held liable for their participation in or responsibility for corporate misconduct. Although it has been argued that civil law may be more suitable than criminal law for holding top managers, officers, and supervisors accountable for the actions of their subordinates, studies suggest that individuals are rarely targeted by civil or any other kind of law. For instance, between 1974 and 1976, in a study of the illegal activities of over five hundred large U.S. corporations, Clinard and Yeager found that in less than 2 percent of all enforcement actions was a corporate manager held responsible for the deeds of his or her corporation.[59] It may well be that even though top-level managers can be held legally liable for failure to discharge proper oversight, plaintiffs and courts are reluctant to do so. Pragmatically, the company is apt to have deeper pockets than any individual employee.

Additionally, given that corporate crime emerges as a result of managers pursuing corporate and not personal interests, assessing the firm for liability (wherein firms are forced to disgorge illicit profits) *should* deter as efficiently as individual liability.[60] Even among those who believe that individual factors may affect corporate decision making (e.g., to enhance his or her own position – gain prestige, promotion, peer esteem – or to use that position to violate a law that he or she believes is unjust), it is agreed that determining an appropriate civil fine to achieve efficient deterrence for these nonmonetary rewards is extremely difficult.[61] In these cases, criminal prosecution would be more appropriate.

---

[57] See, e.g., Derek B. Cornish and Ronald V. Clarke, *The Reasoning Criminal: Rational Choice Perspectives on Offending* (New York: Springer-Verlag, 1986).

[58] Coffee, "No Soul to Damn," p. 399.

[59] Marshall B. Clinard and Peter C. Yeager, *Corporate Crime* (New York: Free Press, 1980), p. 272.

[60] See, e.g., Posner, *Economic Analysis of Law* and "*Corporate Crime.*"

[61] "Corporate Crime," p. 1372, n. 36.

Conclusions

Some theoretical and anecdotal empirical evidence suggests that civil justice processes may offer more efficient corporate deterrence than the imposition of criminal legal sanctions. This conclusion is based in two primary points: sanction certainty and severity (at least monetarily) are potentially greater under civil than criminal law; and overdeterrence and underdeterrence are possible negative results stemming from the extension of criminal law into civil areas. (However, to the extent that punitive damages are part and parcel of civil sanctions, overdeterrence is also apt to occur in the civil arena.)

Even with these potential benefits, however, the actual risks of discovery and the imposition of civil sanctions are, by all accounts, rare. Thus, like criminal legal deterrence, implementation failure affects how successfully the civil justice can achieve corporate social control. Moreover, civil violations do not carry the same kinds of stigmatic costs associated with criminality. Acts that lack moral culpability and blameworthiness are unlikely to provoke informal sanction risks for most corporate managers.

CHAPTER FIVE

Corporate Deterrence and Regulatory Justice

THE PRIMARY responsibility for corporate crime control in the United States resides in regulatory agencies. These agencies are involved in all aspects of administrative justice from law making and administration to adjudication and sentencing.[1] In examining the goals, strategies, and accomplishments of regulatory justice, I address similar issues and concerns raised in earlier chapters, such as whether legal processing of corporate criminals through administrative law and its remedies (e.g., investigation, processing, and sanctioning) promotes deterrence. In this vein, it is important to note that the goal of regulation is not punishment per se, but rather to produce business behavior that adheres to rules or standards.[2] Although this may appear to be a fine distinction, it is not an inconsequential one from a deterrence perspective that assumes law-abiding behavior to stem from the *fear* of punishment. At issue, then, is whether nonpunitive compliance systems are capable of yielding deterrent effects.

As part of this overall review of regulatory justice, I highlight particular challenges to deterrence that coincide with three distinct periods of regulatory activity in the United States; assess current deterrence arguments, both theoretical and empirical; compare assumptions embedded in punitive (deterrence) versus compliance (persuasion) strategies; and consider

---

[1] Nancy Frank and Michael Lombness, *Controlling Corporate Illegality: The Regulatory Justice System* (Cincinnati: Anderson Publishing, 1988), pp. 24–25.

[2] Albert J. Reiss Jr. and Albert D. Biderman, *Data Sources on White-Collar Law-Breaking* (Washington, D.C.: U.S. Department of Justice, National Institute of Justice, 1980), p. 131.

whether these approaches to corporate crime control are oppositional[3] or complimentary in nature.[4]

Business Regulation in the United States

Regulation is defined as "state-imposed limitation on the discretion that may be exercised by individuals or organizations, which is supported by the threat of sanction."[5] From this definition, it is clear that the regulation of business activity has been a feature of society since the inception of the state.[6] Geis, in his "historic perlustration" of white-collar crime law, demonstrates that illegal market practices have been officially defined as crimes in Western societies for at least five hundred years and that the origins of these laws can be traced to Judeo-Christian admonitions.[7] Even laws that appear to be creations of modern society such as pollution statutes can be found on record in fourteenth-century England.[8]

First- and Second-Wave Regulation

In the United States, historians recognize three stages of regulation.[9] The first wave, coinciding with the Progressive Era (1890–1920), emerged in the context of unfettered economic competition and rising concerns about new health hazards and the relationship between unsanitary conditions and disease.[10] Important new statutes including the Sherman Antitrust Act, the Food and Drug Act, and the Federal Trade Commission Act created federal agencies to contain the more pernicious of business excesses and to gain control over the nation's banking and transportation infrastructure (via the

---

[3] Albert Reiss, "Selecting Strategies of Social Control over Organizational Life," in Keith Hawkins and John M. Thomas (eds.), *Enforcing Regulation* (Boston: Kluwer-Nijoff, 1984), pp. 23–35.

[4] John Braithwaite, *To Punish or Persuade: Enforcement of Coal Mine Safety* (Albany, N.Y.: SUNY Press, 1985), p. 100.

[5] Alan Stone, *Regulation and Its Alternatives* (Washington, D.C.: Congressional Quarterly Press, 1982), p. 11.

[6] Neal Shover, Donald A. Clelland, and John Lynxwiler, *Enforcement or Negotiation: Constructing a Regulatory Bureaucracy* (Albany, N.Y.: SUNY Press, 1986), p. 2.

[7] Gilbert Geis, "From Deuteronomy to Deniability: A Historical Perlustration on White-Collar Crime," *Justice Quarterly* 5 (1988): 9.

[8] Peter Cleary Yeager, *The Limits of Law: The Public Regulation of Private Pollution* (Cambridge: Cambridge University Press, 1990), p. 53.

[9] Protective legislation against food tampering and other market practices is evident in colonial law. See, e.g., Eugene Bardach and Robert A. Kagan, *Going by the Book* (Philadelphia: Temple University Press, 1982), p. 8.

[10] Ibid.

Interstate Commerce Commission, the Federal Reserve Board, and other banking and transportation agencies).[11]

Regulatory activity during this first wave was justified by perceptions that laissez-faire capitalism had produced less competitive markets because of acquisitive and uncontrollable monopolies.[12] But, for the most part, laws were relatively lenient and some, like the Sherman Act, often were directed against "enemies" of business instead of businesses themselves.[13] The desire to restrict markets, however, waned in the 1920s. Mandatory controls gradually gave way to voluntary limitations. The interim years between the first and second waves of regulation were not overtly hostile to past regulatory efforts (indeed, some of the acts passed earlier became even more comprehensive during this time), but no significant pieces of new legislation were produced during this period either.[14]

The Great Depression brought an abrupt end to the economic volunteerism of the earlier decade. Commerce was blamed for the dire economic situation in which the country was mired. Business was viewed as "an erratic and irresponsible force requiring strict social discipline"[15] by lawmakers, and President Roosevelt's New Deal emphasized the need for government to exert greater control over the economy. To achieve these aims, Congress passed the Securities Act of 1933 and, as part of the National Industrial Recovery Act, geared legislation toward stimulating the economy through direct government intervention (e.g., attacking unemployment, stabilizing prices, and abolishing destructive competition). Between 1933 and 1939, many new regulatory agencies were created, including the Federal Communications Commission, the Securities and Exchange Commission, the Federal Deposit Insurance Corporation, the National Labor Relations Board, and the Civil Aeronautics Board. While the primary function of these agencies was to regulate financial and business practices, they also served to legitimate government, finance, and business in the eyes of the public whose faith in capitalism and the state had been severely tested during the 1930s.[16]

[11] Stone, *Regulation*, p. 31.
[12] Historian Gabriel Kolko in *The Triumph of Conservatism* (New York: Free Press, 1963) offers a different interpretation of regulation during the early twentieth century, arguing that the kind of regulation and political intervention that occurred during this period reflected business control over politics rather than vice versa.
[13] Frank Pearce, *Crimes of the Powerful* (London: Pluto, 1976).
[14] Stone, *Regulation*, p. 30.
[15] Arthur M. Schlesinger Jr., *The Coming of the New Deal* (Boston: Houghton Mifflin, 1959), p. 444; see also Roberta S. Karmel, *Regulation by Prosecution: The Securities and Exchange Commission vs. Corporate America* (New York: Simon and Schuster, 1982), p. 39.
[16] Frank and Lombness, *Controlling Corporate Illegality*, p. 2.

Although many industries and products tended to become safer as a consequence of government intervention during the first and second regulatory waves, agencies created during these periods were criticized for failing to do enough. Journalists and social reformers could identify numerous cases of lax enforcement or areas in which the government totally ignored (i.e., failed to regulate) dangerous substances and business practices.[17]

World War II stimulated the economy into a long period of sustained growth. Unparalleled economic prosperity brought about a decline in business controls and it was not until the late 1960s that regulatory activity reasserted itself. Although this last wave of regulation coincided with the first serious economic recession since World War II (1967–1968), government intervention efforts during the "Great Society" took a decidedly different turn.

In the 1960s, regulation shifted toward "new-style" social agendas[18] with an emphasis on controlling the human costs of production. Concurrent with this aim was the establishment of regulatory agencies that would be less vulnerable to corruption and undue corporate influence. A number of new statutes were enacted by Congress to regulate health and safety (primarily geared toward protecting consumers and employees), employment practices (to thwart discrimination against minorities and women), and environmental protection (to regulate water and air quality, toxic substances, and so forth). The Environmental Protection Agency, the Office of Surface Mining, the Equal Employment Opportunities Commission, the Occupational Safety and Health Administration, and the Consumer Product Safety Commission emerged out of these statutes.[19]

Third-Wave Regulation

The third wave of regulatory activity, with its new emphasis on the social costs of production and past regulatory failures, brought its own unique challenges to deterrence. Ironically, some of the most significant challenges stem from the adoption of explicit legalistic enforcement practices.[20] Legislators, in assessing past failures, thought that controls over discretion and implementation of formalistic procedures would enhance prevention and

---

[17] Bardach and Kagan, *Going by the Book*, p. 45.

[18] William Lilly III and James C. Miller III, "The New 'Social Regulation,'" *Public Interest* 47 (1977): 49–61; Shover et al., *Enforcement or Negotiation*, pp. 2–3; and Yeager, *The Limits of Law*, pp. 24–25.

[19] Bardach and Kagan, *Going by the Book*, pp. 43–44.

[20] Shover et al., *Enforcement or Negotiation*, pp. 75–79.

deterrence while avoiding excessive business influence over the regulatory process. Yet critics claim that just the opposite result occurred.[21]

Four identifiable impediments to deterrence are argued to stem from legalistic enforcement: universal rules are applied to cases in which the standards are irrelevant; investigators exclusively focus on legal wrongdoing (which may be trivial) and often ignore other potentially serious problems because they are not "in the regs"; documentation and record keeping are overemphasized while informal cooperation and voluntary disclosure are underused as remedies; and firms adopt a tit-for-tat strategy, responding to enforcement legalism with their own brand of legalistic challenges.[22] All of these outcomes erode deterrence because, even though sanction threat is salient, respect for the law and regulatory agents is undermined.

These impediments constitute *procedural* problems that interfere with deterrent outcomes; yet, as noted, substantive challenges to deterrence also emerged with the shift in regulatory focus – that is, away from economic regulation toward new-style social interventions. The primary basis of new-style social regulation is an assumption that business is financially and technologically capable of preventing the social harms associated with production but refuses to assume responsibility because of "an insufficiently restrained profit motive."[23] Business, on the other hand, has opposed social regulation primarily because the government is dictating reforms that force firms to absorb production costs that had in the past been borne primarily by third parties. Thus, the substantive challenge to deterrence rests in competing notions of who should assume responsibility for "negative externalities" (i.e., the unintended consequences of business activity for third parties).

Resistance to social legislation has brought together firms, trade associations, and sympathetic lobbyists whose aim is to challenge the content of administrative law. In some cases statutes have been amended to lessen the breadth of the law (Occupational Safety and Health Act) whereas in others the basis on which rules were created has been replaced by cost-benefit analysis (i.e., a shift from social consciousness toward what is economically feasible from the perspective of business).[24] This concerted effort to challenge laws or change the criterion upon which rules are enacted clearly

[21] Toni Makkai and John Braithwaite, "Reintegrative Shaming and Compliance with Regulatory Standards," *Criminology* 32 (1994): 361–386.

[22] Bardach and Kagan, *Going by the Book.*

[23] Ibid., p. 13.

[24] A case in point is the operation of the National Highway and Traffic Safety Administration. See, e.g., Jerry L. Mashaw and David L. Harfst, *The Struggle for Auto Safety* (Cambridge, Mass.: Harvard University Press, 1990); Bridget M. Hutter, "Regulation: Standard Setting and Enforcement," *Law and Society Review* 27 (1993): 233–248.

defeats the goals of deterrence, while also subverting the law and the legal process.

Governmental regulation of business has waxed and waned in this country, varying as social, economic, and political conditions change.[25] As a consequence of these influences, regulatory enforcement has been inconsistent and unpredictable, characteristics that interfere with punishment certainty and severity. Similarly, distinct types of regulation and regulatory styles (punitive versus conciliatory) also affect corporate deterrence by creating cultures of resistance among the regulated.

The Deterrent Capacity of Administrative Law

Theoretical and Empirical Justifications

Studies of regulation emerge from distinct theoretical and political positions regarding the desirability and ability of government to "intervene" and control business activity. Such theoretical views of the regulatory process are important to help us understand how corporate crime deterrence is apt to operate. As Reiss and Biderman are quick to point out, general theoretical frameworks and special theories of social control (such as deterrence) "underlie much of the rhetoric and practice of law enforcement and regulatory practice" and are thus useful tools to appraise how regulation works and to what end.[26]

In their book, *Enforcement or Negotiation*, Shover, Clelland, and Lynxwiler summarize the basic assumptions of these different viewpoints, contrasting pluralist and elitist, consensus and conflict, and liberal and Marxist positions.[27] These theoretical camps are consolidated into conservative, liberal, and radical perspectives. Arguably, consolidation oversimplifies the complexity and elegance of these arguments. However, given that theories of regulation are not of primary interest here (while deterrence is), simplification allows us to capture the ideas without becoming lost in the detail.[28]

Regulatory observers address two important and interrelated issues: whether regulation of business is desirable, and whether government

---

[25] See also Ross E. Cheit, *Setting Safety Standards: Regulation in the Public and Private Sectors* (Berkeley: University of California Press, 1990).

[26] Reiss and Biderman, *Data Sources on White-Collar Crime Law-Breaking*, p. 107.

[27] Shover et al., *Enforcement or Negotiation*, p. 3.

[28] These theoretical views have also been summarized and categorized as radical, reactionary, and reformist. See, e.g., Michael S. Lewis-Beck and John R. Alford, "Can Government Regulate Safety? The Coal Mine Example," *American Political Science Review* 74 (1980): 746–747.

control of business is effective. On the issue of desirability, conservatives view most government intercession as generally unsound, unnecessary, and ultimately deleterious. Liberals, on the other hand, hold a more positive view of government control, believing that the state plays an important role in rectifying harms and protecting citizens' rights. The radical position on this issue is more equivocal. Government intervention in a capitalist society is mere "mystification" as it serves to legitimate property rights and protect class interests. In socialist societies, however, the state (the dictatorship of the proletariat) represents worker interests and protects against the disruptive effects of the final vestiges of capitalism. Radicals, conservatives, and liberals often search for concrete examples that support their respective cases, creating what Shover and associates characterize as "false polarizations"[29] that is, accenting differences between positions that may actually share a similar logic. The trichotomy is often a false one.

On the issue of whether government can effectively control business, opinions fall along a continuum with left radicals and right conservatives weighing in on the same side and liberals inching their way toward the center. Neither conservatives nor radicals suppose that government can successfully control business, but the explanations for failure are quite different. Conservatives tend to believe that laissez-faire capitalism will correct economic deficiencies and that less government (i.e., deregulation) makes for a more efficient system. They are quick to claim that the government is incapable of regulating behaviors that business itself cannot control. A perfect example of this position is drawn from the area of mining safety regulation. Conservatives believe that "laws cannot significantly affect mine safety because they fail to touch on the two principal causes of mining accidents: the inherent dangers in the activity of mining coal and the carelessness of the miners."[30] Similar arguments are made about automobile safety (i.e., the problem lies with the driver and driving conditions), pollution control (pollution is a natural byproduct of industrial production), and so forth.

Radicals, on the other hand, adhere to the position that the government is captured by class concerns and that laws which purport to regulate merely obfuscate the underlying corporate interests.[31] Assuming that corporate capture is a fact that produces inefficient regulation, the radical position is reinforced whenever an accident or disaster prompts attention to a particular failing of regulatory law. If regulation were effective, the argument

[29] Shover et al., *Enforcement or Negotiation*, p. 3.
[30] Lewis-Beck and Alford, "Can Government Regulate Safety?" p. 747.
[31] Pearce, *Crimes of the Powerful.*

goes, no accidents would have occurred. Ergo, when accidents do occur, regulatory activity is proved to be merely symbolic.

Closer to the center of the spectrum are liberals who profess the need for government intervention while, at the same time, acknowledging that regulatory capture can occur. Liberals are more apt to argue, however, that the state responds to a cacophony of special interests. Consequently, regulatory policy reflects compromise and negotiation between interest groups. This position is also known as pluralism. Successful regulation, from the liberal standpoint, is that which induces companies to do what would not normally be in their own best economic interests, and the best way to achieve this aim is through *legalistic enforcement* (strict, rigid, universalistic) of the law.

The issue of corporate capture is an important one for deterrence advocates. How can corporations fear punishment and adjust behavior accordingly if administrative law is essentially controlled by corporate interests? The answer, it seems, is that deterrence will fail under these conditions. Yet, this position is not universal. Arguments that some forms of agency capture are desirable and actually enhance the attainment of regulatory goals are gaining ground.[32]

Agency Capture

Although an extensive set of studies has been conducted on the issue of regulatory capture,[33] it is not uncommon for studies of the same agency to reach contradictory conclusions as to whether or to what extent capture has occurred. Samuel Huntington and W. Z. Ripley, for instance, in separate studies drew entirely different conclusions about whose interests were protected by the Interstate Commerce Commission. Huntington concluded that commission decisions consistently favored railroad interests over those of motor carriers (a much more diverse group), whereas Ripley claimed to have evidence of just the opposite pattern of favoritism.[34]

---

[32] Ian Ayres and John Braithwaite, "Tripartism: Regulatory Capture and Empowerment," *Law and Social Inquiry* 16 (1991): 435–496.

[33] John P. Plumlee and Kenneth J. Meier, "Capture and Rigidity in Regulatory Administration: An Empirical Assessment," in J. W. May and A. B. Wildavsky (eds.), *The Policy Cycle* (Beverly Hills, Calif.: Sage, 1978), pp. 215–34; Peter Freitag, "The Myth of Corporate Capture: Regulatory Commissions in the United States," *Social Problems* 30 (1983): 480–491. Andrew Szasz, "Industrial Resistance to Occupational Safety and Health Legislation: 1971–1871," *Social Problems* 32 (1984): 102–116. Jack High and Clayton A. Coppin, "Wiley and the Whiskey Industry: Strategic Behavior in the Passage of the Pure Food Act," *Business History Review* 62 (1988): 286–230.

[34] Stone, *Regulation*, p. 230; Samuel Huntington, "The Marasmus of the ICC," *Yale Law Journal* 61 (April 1952): 467–509; William Z. Ripley, *Railroads: Rates and Regulation* (New York: Longman, 1913), p. 118.

Contradictory findings may be related to methodological differences between studies. For instance, studies tend to operationalize the concept of capture in quite different ways. The concept has been defined vaguely (e.g., "the policies pursued generally coincide with the preference previously expressed by those being regulated"),[35] allowing great flexibility in confirmatory evidence, as well as more restrictively – for example, there is little economic disruption of the regulated industry (i.e., firm profits are unaffected by regulatory policy); regulations are minimal, lenient, and acceptable to industry; enforcement of the law is lenient;[36] and a high degree of personnel interchange occurs between regulated firms and the agencies designed to regulate them.[37] Consequently, one study of a particular agency may find that regulations do not disrupt firm profits in regulated industries, a finding that suggests capture, whereas another may find few instances in which agency-business personnel overlap – evidence of a lack of capture.

In some cases, whether or not data "prove" capture is a matter of opinion. Shover et al. acknowledge that data from their research on the Office of Surface Mining can be interpreted as offering support for both "special interest theory – instrumentalist control of an agency by a regulated fraction of capital" and "the relative autonomy of [administrative] law."[38]

Freitag, in his study of the "revolving door" thesis (i.e., agencies recruit business leaders who, after their appointment, return to the corporate sector), concludes that "corporate dominance of the commissions has been overestimated."[39] His research traces the background of commissioners representing the "Big Seven" (Interstate Commerce Commission, Federal Trade Commission, Federal Communications Commission, Securities and Exchange Commission, National Labor Relations Board, Civil Aeronautics Board, and Federal Power Commission) federal regulatory commissions between 1887 and 1975 to assess the extent to which commissioners are drawn from or move to corporate positions in the years surrounding their regulatory appointment. Finding that most commissioners did not hold positions in the industry they were regulating prior to their appointment and that, when overlaps did occur (both prior to and after the commission appointment), few commissioners were "corporate elites or superlawyers" (i.e.,

---

[35] James E. Anderson, "The Public Utility Commission of Texas: A Case of Capture or Rapture?" *Policy Studies Review* 1 (1982): 484.

[36] Paul Sabatier, "Social Movements and Regulatory Agencies: Toward a More Adequate – and Less Pessimistic – Theory of 'Clientele Capture,'" *Policy Sciences* 6 (1975): 301–342.

[37] Freitag, "The Myth of Corporate Capture," p. 480.

[38] Shover et al., *Enforcement or Negotiation*, p. 156.

[39] Freitag, "The Myth of Corporate Capture," p. 480.

an officer or director of a major U.S. corporation), Freitag concludes that "'the foxes have not taken over the hen house.'"[40]

A closer look at Freitag's data, however, can lead to a different – or at least more cautious – conclusion. For instance, Freitag's data show that less than 50 percent of all regulators are drawn from or return to the *regulated* industries. Yet, his data also demonstrate the close postappointment link between regulators, business, and a career in corporate law. Whereas only 32 percent of the commissioners are drawn into agency service from these positions, more than 60 percent are recruited into these environments after tenure. The data also reveal that the degree of personnel overlap varies significantly across regulatory agencies (i.e., the Securities and Exchange Commission shows the greatest personnel exchange while the Federal Power Commission shows the least) and over time – although the time trend is not unidirectional. Thus, some agencies may be more vulnerable to capture than others; capture may operate in more of an indirect manner through ex-commissioner expertise and advice to firms; and agencies may be vulnerable to capture at different historical times, perhaps reflecting political or social influences that are not measured in Freitag's analysis.

Variations over time in agency vulnerability to political and business in-fluences are evident in many historical or case studies.[41] The Occupational Safety and Health Administration (OSHA) has been the object of much recent investigation.[42] It is debatable as to whether the initial legislation signed into law by President Richard Nixon (the Occupational Safety and Health Act of 1970) and its early implementation truly protected labor, yet scholars concur that the agency gained strength through the 1970s only to be eviscerated by the Reagan administration's efforts to deregulate the economy.

Other studies of agency capture document similar political pressures and changing fortunes.[43] This author's interviews with a former attorney at the Federal Trade Commission, coupled with other sources,[44] substantiate how

[40] Ibid., p. 489.

[41] Susan Shapiro, *Wayward Capitalists: Target of the Securities and Exchange Commission* (New Haven: Yale University Press, 1984); Cheit, *Setting Safety Standards*; Mashaw and Harfst, *The Struggle for Auto Safety*; Lewis-Beck and Alford, "Can Government Regulate Safety?"

[42] Szasz, "Industrial Resistance"; see also Kitty Calavita, "The Demise of the Occupational Safety and Health Administration: A Case Study in Symbolic Action," *Social Problems* 30 (1983): 437–448.

[43] Shover et al., *Enforcement or Negotiation*, pp. 149–156, document how the Office of Surface Mining was affected by Reagan's election and the subsequent appointment of James Watt as secretary of the interior.

[44] Robert A. Katzmann, *Regulatory Bureaucracy: The Federal Trade Commission and Antitrust Policy* (Cambridge, Mass.: MIT Press, 1980), pp. 134–179.

distinct political influences affect agency directives and enforcement practices from one administration to another. The Federal Trade Commission was considerably strengthened under Presidents Ford and Carter, whose administrations encouraged more proactive enforcement of cases. Under the Reagan administration, however, a policy of less intervention – especially in merger and predatory pricing cases – became the norm.[45] This position is clearly seen in the comments of former Federal Trade Commission chairman Daniel Oliver who wrote in a note to former president Reagan, "I am sometimes asked, 'why would a deregulator be put in charge of a regulatory agency?' I answer, 'only people who know how dangerous guns are should be allowed to play with a gun.' "[46]

Although it may be difficult to determine whether a given agency is captured or not,[47] there is no denying that corporate deterrence will be affected by the possibility of capture. If corporations come to believe that administrative law is malleable and subject to business influences, then the fear of punishment is mitigated.

The extent to which the deterrent capacity of regulatory law is negatively affected by capture, however, is a matter of considerable debate. Although the obvious position on this issue is that corporate capture always sacrifices the deterrent capacity of the law, Ayres and Braithwaite, using game theory, show how certain kinds of agency capture can actually enhance regulatory effectiveness.[48] Specifically, they demonstrate that capture causes agencies to care about the welfare of regulated firms. This outcome is positive under the following conditions: companies defect from cooperating with regulators; the agency defects from cooperation as a consequence; and mutual defection results in joint cooperation. This outcome reinforces a cooperative strategy, and corporate deterrence is enhanced.

Following this same logic, the most pernicious kind of capture occurs when joint cooperation between the firm and agency shifts to a firm defect–agency cooperate equilibrium model. Regulatory inefficiencies are produced under this scenario because firms are rewarded for noncompliance and there is no resulting benefit to the agency or society at large.

Theoretical models of regulatory capture such as the economic one proposed by Ayres and Braithwaite are useful analytical tools, but the authors themselves suggest that the model is analytically limited and that more

---

[45] *Business Week,* June 19, 1989, p. 70.

[46] *FTC News,* May 16, 1989.

[47] Frank and Lombness, *Controlling Corporate Illegality,* p. 118, claim that the problem is "frankly, insoluble."

[48] Ayres and Braithwaite, "Tripartism," pp. 457–459.

empirical research is needed to flesh out the circumstances under which departure from cooperation occurs as well as the consequences of departure for both the firm and regulatory agency. Studies of regulatory deterrence can provide some insight into the situations and circumstances under which firms depart from regulations, consider the costs and benefits of compliance (from the perspective of the firm), and identify whether regulatory policies achieve goals that may be distinct from deterrence per se.

Administrative Law and Deterrence

Most empirical studies of regulatory deterrence do not directly measure the relationship between punishment and criminality. Instead, studies tend to examine how regulatory shifts or new pieces of legislation are related to some tangible indicator of legislative success – for example, a decline in industrial accidents or pollution levels, racial or gender integration of firms, more competitive prices. This focus is understandable given the intent behind much regulatory legislation. For instance, the Occupational Safety and Health Administration's goal is to attain safety and health in the workplace. Obviously this task can be achieved through various means, one of which is certain and severe punishment. Unfortunately, many studies that employ these indicators of legislative success do not discriminate (or even measure) fear of punishment (specific or general) from other factors that can produce these outcomes. This implies that deterrence is at work absent actual evidence that the lessening of accidents or lowering of pollution levels stems from sanction fear. Results from these studies are equivocal.

Some find little relationship between inspections and injury rates,[49] but critics claim these data are flawed or fail to assess long-term as opposed to short-term enforcement effects.[50] Lewis-Beck and Alford, in their research on mine safety legislation, show that statutes passed by the government in 1941 and 1969 had the effect of reducing mining accidents over the long term. The authors argue that, in contrast to other mine safety bills that were merely "symbolic" (e.g., the legislation of 1952), these laws provided

---

[49] See, e.g., David P. McCaffrey, "An Assessment of OSHA's Recent Effects on Injury Rates," *Journal of Human Resources* 18 (1983): 131–146; Robert S. Smith, "The Impact of OSHA Inspections on Manufacturing Injury Rates," *Journal of Human Resources* 14 (1979): 145–170; W. Kip Viscusi, "The Impact of Occupational Safety and Health Regulation," *Bell Journal of Economics* 10 (1979): 117–140.

[50] Wayne B. Gray and John T. Scholz, "Does Regulatory Enforcement Work? A Panel Analysis of OSHA Enforcement," *Law and Society Review* 27 (1993): 177–213. See also Viscusi's reexamination of OSHA enforcement after the mid 1970s; W. Kip Viscusi, "The Impact of Occupational Safety and Health Regulation, 1973–1983," *Rand Journal of Economics* 17 (1986): 567–580.

"comprehensive, detailed, and mandatory [legal] provisions" along with "vigorous" enforcement.[51] However, there is no measure of illegal behavior in their equations – no indicator of sanction certainty or severity. Instead, the OSHA yearly budget is used as a proxy for commitment to mine safety and then is contrasted to shifts in the fatality rate during similar time periods. When there is a correspondence between high budgets and lower fatality rates, this evidence is appropriated to show deterrence effects.

Other studies of regulatory enforcement incorporate the number or rate of inspections or citations as deterrence variables (reasonable indicators of detection certainty or sanction certainty or severity), but typically capture deterrence variables only as part of an independent set of variables. The dependent variable fails to measure firm-, plant-, or industry-level compliance. Additionally, researchers claim that by varying the level of analysis (i.e., firm- or plant-level data versus industry-level data), the studies can differentiate specific from general deterrence effects.[52] But unless firm compliance is measured instead of approximated by injury or accident rates, this avowal is dubious, especially in light of evidence showing that compliance is only weakly related to injury rates.[53]

One way to get around these criticisms is to incorporate a more flexible model of deterrence than that used throughout this work and in most of the extant criminological literature. This tactic is implemented by Gray and Scholz, who study the relationship between OSHA enforcement (measured as inspections, penalties, and penalty amounts) and plant injuries at 6,842 manufacturing sites between 1979 and 1985. Rather than measuring deterrence as the reduction of violations of a specific statute, they employ a *behavioral* model of deterrence that incorporates the following hypotheses about how firms respond to safety and sanction risk:[54]

1. Firms monitor their injury experience and, when unexpected changes occur, enact corrective measures to return injuries to an acceptable level.
2. Firms monitor the enforcement activities of OSHA that are relevant for their own experiences and respond when perceived enforcement risk increases (i.e., general deterrence is achieved).
3. Firms lower injury rates when sanctions are levied against them (i.e., specific deterrence is achieved).

[51] Lewis-Beck and Alford, "Can Government Regulate Safety," p. 755.
[52] Gray and Scholz, "Does Regulatory Enforcement Work?"
[53] Ann Bartel and Lacy Glenn Thomas, "Direct and Indirect Effects of Regulation: A New Look at OSHA's Impact," *Journal of Law and Economics* 28 (1985): 1–25.
[54] John T. Scholz and Wayne B. Gray, "OSHA Enforcement and Workplace Injuries: A Behavioral Approach to Risk Assessment," *Journal of Risk and Uncertainty* 3 (1990): 284.

4. Firms monitor two dimensions of expected penalty (likelihood and amount) separately, responding more to the former than the latter.

This behavioral model of deterrence, borrowed from a behavioral model of the firm,[55] incorporates elements of organizational (i.e., managerial) learning, conflict resolution, short-run reaction to change in the environment, and organizational problem solving. Gray and Scholz suggest that businesses respond to enforcement practices, that they learn from their mistakes, and that they take action to address salient operational and managerial deficiencies.

Using this broader definition of deterrence, Gray and Scholz show that OSHA penalties brought about a 22 percent reduction in plant injuries in the years immediately following penalty imposition, clearly demonstrating – at least according to their *behavioral* definition of deterrence – a deterrent effect.

> Managerial attention does indeed respond to regulatory enforcement actions. Inspections imposing a penalty focus managerial attention on safety issues, thereby reducing injury rates in inspected firms to a greater extent than could be explained if firms simply abated the cited violations.[56]

Studies that use a more traditional definition of deterrence than that employed by Gray and Scholz (i.e., explicitly link the threat of punishment or the receipt of punishment to offending at either the firm or industry level) offer a less optimistic view of regulatory justice and deterrence. For instance, Simpson and Koper follow thirty-eight basic manufacturing firms over fifty-five years of business activity to assess the likelihood of future antitrust offending if companies had been subjected to either civil, criminal, and regulatory law for prior anticompetitive acts.[57] In contrasting the specific deterrence effects of the three types of legal processing, they find that regulatory justice fails to significantly inhibit future reoffending by firms. Importantly, however, regulatory processing has more of a negative, albeit insignificant, effect on recidivism than other justice systems. They find that civil and criminal prosecution tends to *increase* the chances that a firm will reoffend. In the case of criminal processing, this effect is significant.

As noted in earlier chapters, a salient problem with corporate deterrence research lies in the difficulty of capturing the perceptual processes of the

---

[55] Richard Cyert and James G. March, *A Behavioral Theory of the Firm* (Englewood Cliffs, N.J.: Prentice-Hall, 1963).

[56] Gray and Scholz, "Does Regulatory Enforcement Work?" p. 182.

[57] Sally S. Simpson and Christophers Koper, "Deterring Corporate Crime," *Criminology* 30 (1992): 201–209.

executives and managers who actually make organizational decisions. Gray and Scholz and Simpson and Koper try to avoid this problem by arguing that adjustments in organizational outcomes that temporally occur after legal changes or the application of punishment *signify* managerial learning and a change in management priorities. This assumption, however, is never subjected to empirical verification.

In their study of nursing home compliance in Australia – where almost all detection and sanction is conducted through regulatory law – Braithwaite and Makkai use a perceptual deterrence model to tease out factors that influence the compliance decisions of nursing-home executives. Their research demonstrates a small deterrent effect for *detection* certainty; however, neither *sanction* certainty nor severity appears to affect compliance decisions.[58] This finding seems to suggest that fear of formal punishment does not drive executive decisions to offend or not to offend. Rather, consequences related to detection – perhaps costs to reputation, embarrassment, guilt, and other informal costs – may affect managerial choices.

It seems fair to conclude from this theoretical and empirical review that the further one moves from the specific decisions of managers and traditional definitions of deterrence, the greater the evidence supporting regulatory deterrence. More restrictive models of deterrence (including perceptual deterrence) and tests that measure actual compliance rather than other regulatory goals, however, tend to reject deterrence arguments.

It also seems fair, nonetheless, to conclude that regulatory justice has demonstrated some success in achieving goals of safer workplaces and consumer products, lower pollution levels, more efficient markets, and so forth. If these ends are not achieved through traditional deterrence or if we cannot determine *whether* these ends have been achieved through punishment,[59] what can account for these successes?

Regulatory law brings with it certain advantages unavailable through other legal systems. It has both the capacity to persuade through cooperation and the capacity to punish corporate wrongdoers. This dualistic purpose is not viewed in a positive light by those who claim that cooperation weakens deterrence. However, others assume that punishment and persuasion are not separate aims but parts of an overall enforcement strategy that

[58] John Braithwaite and Toni Makkai, "Testing an Expected Utility Model of Corporate Deterrence," *Law and Society Review* 25 (1991): 7–40.
[59] John Braithwaite argues that it is impossible to ferret out from aggregate data whether it is the punitive aspect of law that saves lives or whether it is the persuasive pressure put on managers by inspectors that lowers fatalities and saves lives. See Braithwaite, *To Punish or Persuade*, pp. 84–86.

maximizes both crime prevention and deterrence.[60] Critics of regulatory deterrence tend to separate legal systems by strategy (i.e., the purpose of criminal law is to punish, the purpose of regulatory law is to prevent harm). Advocates of regulatory deterrence tend to accept the belief that one system of law can simultaneously pursue both strategies.

Punishment or Persuasion

Separate Systems, Separate Strategies

Prosecutorial (deterrent) and cooperative strategies are based in a different set of assumptions about the impetus toward crime and, consequently, the amount and type of social control deemed necessary to inhibit or prevent illegality. Deterrence approaches assume a more pessimistic view of human motivation and the need for punitive social controls over deleterious desires. Corporate decision makers are viewed as rational actors who weigh the benefits of noncompliance against the probability and costs of punishment. The firm is conceived as an "immoral calculator" motivated solely by profits.[61] Failure to comply with the law occurs when the anticipated benefits of crime are large in relation to the likelihood and severity of punishment. From this viewpoint, regulatory agencies must be aggressive police officers whose primary function is to identify and punish deviants, as only the fear of punishment keeps the potential criminal on the straight and narrow.[62]

This model of deterrence is quite limited and simplistic both in terms of how managers and firms are envisioned as well as in its conception of crime causation. Noncompliance occurs for many reasons, only some of which are economic. Two important reasons for noncompliance include disagreement with or ignorance of the law (the firm as "political citizen" or as "organizationally incompetent").[63] Under these conditions, the punitive response to noncompliance dictated by the deterrence model can backfire.

Alternatively, compliance models assume decision makers are amenable to good faith negotiation and are willing to follow the advice of regulators.[64]

---

[60] Ibid.; Brent Fisse and Peter A. French, *Corrigible Corporations and Unruly Law* (San Antonio, Tex.: Trinity University Press, 1985); Ayres and Braithwaite, "Tripartism."

[61] Francis T. Cullen, William J. Maakestad, and Gray Cavender, *Corporate Crime under Attack* (Cincinnati: Anderson Publishing, 1987), p. 350, argue that this "rational" manager is typically viewed as "oversocialized" by the conditions of organizational life and turned into a profit-seeking sociopath.

[62] Robert A. Kagan and John T. Scholz, "The Criminality of the Corporation and Regulatory Enforcement Strategies," in K. Hawkins and John Thomas (eds.), *Enforcing Regulation* (Boston: Kluwer-Nijhoff, 1984).

[63] Ibid.

[64] Braithwaite, *To Punish or Persuade*, p. 118.

The tactics of persuasion, not punishment, form the primary basis of control. Successful persuasion depends on shared understandings and interpretations between regulators and the regulated. "What is at issue is not the condemnation of an act, but the negotiation of an agreed practice. It matters greatly not just that the offender committed the act and knew what he was doing, but also how he constructed his action."[65]

The primary goal of corporate regulation is not to punish but to ensure legal compliance by corporations. Compliance systems seek to prevent harm by disseminating knowledge about the risks of misconduct and extant regulatory standards; by ensuring that businesses are competent to operate and to act in a socially responsible manner; and by creating cooperative relationships with the regulated. Although regulatory justice is not without sanctioning power, the primary goal of the administrative strategy is prevention. When offenses do occur and punishment is deemed necessary, the compliance model breaks down.[66] "Punitive" sanctions, absent due-process protections, tend by legal necessity to be weak and ineffective deterrents.

The separate systems perspective views regulatory and punitive justice systems as necessarily distinct. Deterrence should be achieved through criminal law and compliance through regulatory law. Albert Reiss summarizes this position:

> *Compliance* and *deterrence* forms of law enforcement have different objectives. The principle objective of a compliance law enforcement system is to secure conformity with law by means insuring compliance or by taking action to prevent potential law violations without the necessity to detect, process, and penalize violators. The principle objective of deterrent law enforcement systems is to secure conformity with law by detecting violations of law, determining who is responsible for their violation, and penalizing violators to deter violations in the future, either by those who are punished or by those who might do so were violators not punished.[67]

Same System, Complementary Strategies

In direct contradiction to the different system, different strategy approach just articulated, compliance and deterrence goals can be seen as complementary. Managers and firms are assumed to be both rational and moral – that is,

[65] Michael Clarke, *Business Crime: Its Nature and Control* (New York: St. Martin's Press, 1990), p. 225.

[66] See, e.g., Michael Clarke's disussion, "Prosecutorial and Administrative Strategies to Control Business Crime: Private and Public Roles," in Clifford D. Shearing and Philip C. Stenning (eds.), *Private Policing*, vol. 23 (Beverly Hills, Calif.: Sage, 1987), pp. 266–292.

[67] Reiss, "Selecting Strategies."

guided by both self-interest and ethical considerations.[68] Consequently, our legal systems need the flexibility to persuade when appropriate and punish when necessary. This strategy need not be limited to distinct legal systems. If separate systems do exist, however, responses to wrongdoing should not operate in a mutually exclusive manner. Instead, persuasion and punishment by one system should interact with how another legal system responds to firm illegality.[69]

The clearest statement of this position is the "benign big gun" regulatory strategy. Regulatory (and even criminal justice) responses to wrongdoing are seen as organized within a pyramid structure. Persuasion and cooperation strategies, which are the most flexible and used most often, compose the bottom layers of the pyramid (the "benign" part of the intervention strategy). Punitive responses, which are more hidden and used less often, are clustered near the top of the structure (the "big gun" part of the intervention strategy).[70]

The big-gun perspective assumes that managers have a will to comply with the law and that persuasion should be the first response to wrongdoing. It also assumes that managers who have been warned and who refuse to cooperate with regulators (i.e., firms that deviate from cooperation) may respond better to punitive strategies. Yet, using the big gun first absent the attempt to create cooperation with managers, rather than producing deterrence, can amplify deviance through the "organized culture of resistance," described by Bardach and Kagan earlier in this chapter.

It is difficult to criticize the big-gun strategy from a deterrence perspective because the approach does not explicitly distinguish criminal from regulatory punitive responses. Yet, the fact that regulatory punishments in general tend to lack ferocity (because of due-process concerns) needs to be more carefully considered by big-gun advocates. If, as deterrence theorists argue, it is both certainty and severity of punishment that deters managers and firms, then regulatory justice must incorporate more severe punishments into its arsenal. Further, the conception of legal systems as interactive fails to take into account the reason for justice system separation in the first place. Criminal complaints tend to be more serious cases or at least cases that represent more egregious and flagrant violation of law. Yet, if the firm is a first-time offender or if the act was not carefully calculated, regardless of

---

[68] Amitai Etzioni, *The Moral Dimension* (New York: Free Press, 1988).
[69] Ian Ayres and John Braithwaite, *Responsive Regulation: Transcending the Deregulation Debate* (New York: Oxford University Press, 1992).
[70] Ibid., pp. 19–53.

the consequences, the big-gun perspective might advocate relatively benign intervention for these offenses.

Conclusions

The jury on regulatory deterrence, it seems, is still out. If we take a strict definition of deterrence (mere deterrence in Andenaes's terms), then the threat of regulatory sanction and the subsequent fear that derives from this threat are relatively minuscule. Reactive enforcement, small budgets and staff, agency capture, few punitive options, and so forth mitigate the likelihood that firm illegality will be discovered (certainty) and harshly sanctioned (severity).

Compelling and not easily dismissable evidence, however, suggests that administrative enforcement may inhibit recidivism (specific deterrence) while also accomplishing other regulatory goals – for example, reduce accidents, increase product safety, reduce pollution levels. Regulatory agencies may inhibit firms from reoffending simply because of their capacity to observe and monitor past offenders continually (something criminal and civil laws do not do – at least as far as corporations are concerned). Thus, detection certainty is increased for firms that have already come into contact with an administrative agency, and this may offer a deterrent effect.

Yet the cooperative nature of regulation (legalistic enforcement notwithstanding), with its dual emphasis on morality and rationality, may be the more important source of corporate control in the long run. In a sense, cooperative strategies build on the idea that most companies and corporate executives will, when given the chance (and in some cases, a push), do the right thing – not because they fear the formal legal sanction, but because they fear disapproval, rejection, feelings of guilt, shame, or embarrassment, and the loss of future opportunities that accompany the commitment and potential discovery of an illegal act by significant others.

In the next chapter, we build on the idea of informal control and corporate self-regulation. Punishment may not be an effective deterrent for corporations and managers under most circumstances, but constructing systems of compliance that tie into informal sanction threats are potentially much more effective sources of corporate crime prevention.

CHAPTER SIX

Cooperative Models of Corporate Compliance: Alternatives to Criminalization

SUBJECTING corporations and corporate managers to greater and harsher criminal law will not produce the kind of deterrent effect that is generally assumed. In fact, our review suggests that criminalization may even backfire by producing hostility and resistence to law within firms.[1] Recall that one of the key assumptions of a deterrence argument is that fear of punishment is what produces law-abiding behavior. If companies (or, more accurately, their personnel) do not fear, fail to consider, discount, or disparage formal legal sanctions, deterrence will not be achieved. Yet advocates of criminalization suggest that deterrence fails because of implementation deficiencies.

> The fact that increasing the number and severity of criminal laws has not provided better control over corporate crime is explained by focusing on insufficient utilization. If criminal sanctions were to be deployed regularly, if corporations knew that their chances of escaping criminal conviction were slight, if fines commensurate with the size of the firm and the profitability of the crime were imposed, if jail sentences were given, if these procedures were coupled with more enforcement personnel and more punitive laws, backed by civil and administrative remedies where appropriate, then *criminalization and deterrence would be effective.*[2]

As this quotation illustrates, deterrence defenders recommend ratcheting up the amount of punishment instead of reconsidering how best to

---

[1] For a recent summary, see Peter N. Grabosky, "Counterproductive Regulation," *International Journal of the Sociology of Law* 23 (1995): 347–369.

[2] Laureen Snider, "Cooperative Models and Corporate Crime: Panacea or Cop-Out?" *Crime and Delinquency* 36 (1990): 375–376 (emphasis added).

achieve corporate compliance. It has been difficult for policy makers, politicians, and the general public to step out of the "deterrence trap" – a step that is necessary to consider *seriously* alternative methods of crime control. The shortsightedness of such a position is summarized by Grabosky, who suggests that bad policy results from bad science.

> Those policy entrepreneurs who are enamoured of a certain paradigm, such as rational choice or deterrence theory, may discover that not all targets of regulation are "utility maximizers." . . . The threat of punishment may *invite* offending. . . . Recall how the identical stimulus can elicit compliance from some individuals and provoke defiance on the part of others.[3]

Others have also rejected a purely punitive model in favor of more comprehensive approaches to corporate crime control.[4] Marshall Clinard, Peter Yeager, Jurg Gerber, Jack Coffee, and Christopher Stone (among others)[5] have considered revoking corporate charters, changing the composition and character of corporate boards, limiting firm size, imposing equity fines, product or firm boycotts, self-regulation, and shaming as control strategies. (Clinard generally discards these approaches in favor of criminalization.)[6]

Perhaps the most systematic investigation of crime control alternatives, however, is found in Braithwaite's work. Relying on almost two decades of empirical investigation, Braithwaite and his associates have developed four interrelated strategies or schemes to achieve corporate compliance with law and ethical standards. The elements of his models include self-regulation, informal social control, a pyramid of enforcement, and cooperative regulation (the latter two were briefly discussed in Chapter 5). Known as "cooperative models,"[7] the strategies are based in the assumption that compliance will be best achieved – at least initially – through a strategy of cooperation rather than adversarial relations.

---

[3] Grabosky, "Counterproductive Regulation," p. 356.

[4] In lieu of calls for stronger enforcement and stiffer penalties, conservatives promote the idea of deregulation and a return to market control. This recommendation, like the simpleminded calls for criminalization, fails to recognize the complexity of corporate offending and the need for multipronged social control efforts.

[5] See, e.g., John C. Coffee Jr., "Beyond the Shut-Eyed Sentry: Toward a Theoretical View of Corporate Misconduct and an Effective Legal Response," *Virginia Law Review* 63 (1977): 1099–1278; Christopher Stone, *Where the Law Ends* (New York: Harper and Row, 1975); Marshall B. Clinard and Peter C. Yeager, *Corporate Crime* (New York: Free Press, 1980); Marshall Clinard, *Corporate Corruption* (New York: Praeger, 1990); Jurg Gerber, "Enforced Self-Regulation in the Infant Formula Industry," *Social Justice* 17 (1990): 98–112.

[6] Clinard, *Corporate Corruption*.

[7] Ibid., pp. 378–380.

In this chapter, cooperative models provide a point of contrast to a strategy of control based in criminalization and deterrence. Consequently, the key elements of Braithwaite's strategies are revealed and critiqued.[8]

Enforced Self-Regulation

The concept of enforced self-regulation was developed in response to problems associated with government regulation of businesses and the recognition that a significant percentage of businesses will not voluntarily self-regulate.[9] Enforced self-regulation combines the benefits of voluntary self-regulation with the coercive power of the state. Businesses are in a much better position to police themselves than is the state. Inspections will be more regular and in-depth. Internal auditors will be better informed about business practices and the potential for misconduct (organizational "hot spots"). Compliance teams will be better trained with more resources and greater investigative powers at their disposal than external regulators.[10] Self-regulation also avoids excessive governmental intrusion into business, which may create "delay, red tape, costs, and stultification of innovation."[11]

Even with these benefits, some firms will not self-regulate without external pressure. While many companies will prioritize ethical conduct over profit maximization (i.e., obey the law because it is the morally right thing to do), others will act in an economically self-interested manner.[12] In other words, they will do the right thing only when forced to do so. With an eye toward these latter firms, Braithwaite suggests a model that couples the virtues of self-regulation with the monitoring and sanctioning capabilities of the state.

Enforced self-regulation incorporates the following components:[13]

1. Each firm is required to put together a set of rules (or standards) that are relevant to its transaction contingencies.

---

[8] John Braithwaite, "Enforced Self-Regulation: A New Strategy for Corporate Crime Control," *Michigan Law Review* 80 (1982): 1466–1507. John Braithwaite and Brett Fisse, "Asbestos and Health: A Case of Informal Social Control," *Australian-New Zealand Journal of Criminology* 16 (1983): 67–80. John Braithwaite, *To Punish or Persuade: Enforcement of Coal Mine Safety* (Albany, N.Y.: SUNY Press, 1985); John Braithwaite and Brent Fisse, "Self-Regulation and the Control of Corporate Crime," in Clifford D. Shearing and Phillip C. Stenning (eds.), *Private Policing* (Newbury Park, Calif.: Sage, 1987), pp. 221–246; Ian Ayres and John Braithwaite, *Responsive Regulation: Transcending the Deregulation Debate* (New York: Oxford University Press, 1992).

[9] Braithwaite, "Enforced Self-Regulation," p. 1470.

[10] Ibid., pp. 1467–1469.

[11] Ibid., p. 1470.

[12] Braithwaite and Fisse, "Self-Regulation and the Control of Corporate Crime," pp. 221–224.

[13] Braithwaite, "Enforced Self-Regulation," pp. 1470–1473.

2. Internally developed rules will be evaluated and approved by relevant regulatory agencies.
3. Third parties will have the opportunity to comment on the proposed rules.
4. Compliance responsibilities and costs will be assumed by the firm.
5. Rule violations will be punishable by law.
6. A compliance officer must report to relevant regulatory agencies whenever management overrules compliance group directives; neglecting this duty may result in the criminal prosecution of the officer.
7. Prosecutorial resources will be directed toward firms that systematically and irresponsibly disregard compliance group recommendations.

Obviously, in order for enforced self-regulation to operate efficiently, firms must have an effective internal compliance system. Braithwaite is careful to acknowledge that each firm's compliance structure and operation will vary according to the unique "contingencies facing that firm."[14] However, based on their interviews with over two hundred executives within fifty corporations, Braithwaite and Fisse suggest that effective internal compliance systems generally have the following five characteristics:[15]

1. Compliance personnel are granted intraorganizational influence and top management support.
2. Compliance accountability is clearly articulated and rests with line managers.
3. Compliance is monitored and deviations are reported to responsible personnel.
4. Compliance problems are effectively communicated to persons who can do something about them.
5. There is adequate compliance training and supervision (especially by front-line supervisors).

Applications

The ideas of enforced self-regulation figure prominently in the carrot-and-stick approach built into the U.S. Sentencing Commission Guidelines for Organizational Sanctions.[16] For instance, culpability scores (and thus sentence severity) for organizational defendants may be reduced by up to three

---

[14] Ibid., p. 1470.
[15] Braithwaite and Fisse, "Self-Regulation and the Control of Corporate Crime," p. 225.
[16] U.S. Sentencing Commission, *Guidelines Manual* (Washington, D.C.: U.S. Government Printing Office, 1991), chap. 8.

points if the offending firm has a "reasonable" compliance program. While this definition will vary by firm, generally the guidelines designate reasonableness in a manner similar to that of Braithwaite and Fisse. If an offending firm lacks an effective compliance program and has fifty or more employees, the sentencing guidelines require that the court shall order a term of probation.[17] A condition of probation may dictate that the sentenced firm "develop and submit to the court a program to prevent and detect violations of law, including a schedule for implementation."[18]

While the "carrot" of the sentencing guidelines is to offer more lenient treatment to "responsible corporate citizens" at sentencing to avoid the "stick" of harsh criminal penalties, some legal scholars support the notion that firms should be able to point to clear and concise compliance programs as a defense (a modified due-diligence defense) against vicarious corporate criminal and civil liability. A successful defense might hinge on whether the compliance program was of long duration; whether it was clearly specified to employees and well integrated into the corporate culture; and whether it was sensitive to organizational hot spots, implemented by top management, well enforced, and periodically reviewed and updated.[19] If a corporation demonstrates due diligence by a preponderance of the evidence (i.e., the firm meets the necessary elements of a reasonably diligent compliance program), it should be entitled to acquittal for criminal and civil liability.

From practitioners and defense attorneys to the U.S. Sentencing Commission, it is clear that corporate self-regulation is an idea whose time has come. The "enforced" part of Braithwaite's concept of enforced self-regulation, however, is still a bit sketchy. Apart from a few examples that Braithwaite cites (e.g., civil aviation and some EPA activities),[20] the Insider Trading and Securities Fraud Enforcement Act (which requires firms to put together policies and procedures to "prevent the misuse of . . . material, nonpublic, information"),[21] and court required compliance programs as a condition

---

[17] Ibid., §8 (D) (1.1).
[18] Ibid., §8 (D) (1.4) (c.1), p. 96.
[19] Harvy L. Pitt and Karl A. Groskaufmanis, "Minimizing Corporate Civil and Criminal Liability: A Second Look at Corporate Codes of Conduct," *Georgetown Law Journal* 78 (1990): 1573; Charles J. Walsh and Alissa Pyrich, "Corporate Compliance Programs as a Defense to Criminal Liability: Can a Corporation Save Its Soul?" *Rutgers Law Review* 47 (1995): 605, 618, 685–686. See also Kevin B. Huff, "The Role of Corporate Compliance Programs in Determining Corporate Criminal Liability: A Suggested Approach," *Columbia Law Review* 96 (1996): 1252–1298.
[20] Braithwaite, "Enforced Self-Regulation"; see also Gerber, "Enforced Self-Regulation in the Infant Formula Industry."
[21] Nancy Reichman, "Insider Trading," in Michael Tonry and Albert J. Reiss Jr. (eds.), *Beyond the Law: Crime in Complex Organizations*, Crime and Justice Series, vol. 18 (Chicago: University of Chicago Press, 1993), p. 88.

of corporate probation, privately written rules that are publicly ratified and punishable by law are relatively rare. More generally, firms are *encouraged*, not required, to develop relevant and effective compliance programs and to self-police. Incentives are then attached to corporate self-policing and self-reporting. For instance, firms with compliance programs that self-report may receive more lenient sentencing considerations,[22] or the avenue through which redress is sought may shift from criminal processing toward less stigmatic and punitive civil or administrative proceedings.[23]

Problems

By far, the most common criticism of firm self-regulation is that it leaves the fox in charge of the henhouse. Clinard argues that the bottom-line mentality that governs most corporate decision making is bound to defeat the aims of self-regulation. "Enforced self-regulation ... might well result in the cooptation of the regulatory process by business, with corporations writing the rules in such a way that they would actually help them to circumvent the very purpose of the regulation."[24]

As evidence, Clinard cites studies that demonstrate how ethics codes are overly broad and tend to lack enforcement provisions. Mathews, for instance, studied 202 corporate codes of ethics and found that few contained specific penalties for violations and almost none mentioned reprimands, demotions, or fines.[25] Similarly, Reichman found no regulations that established the minimum criteria for Chinese wall construction within securities firms, even though the Insider Trading and Securities Fraud Enforcement Act of 1988 and the National Association of Securities Dealers advocate the creation of these protective devices within firms to architecturally separate "information collection and analysis from its sale, trade, or both."[26]

Like Clinard, Reichman doubts the success of self-regulatory practices because "the motives and enabling structures for insider trading" are unchanged.[27] Even retired Fortune 500 middle managers doubt that industry (and, by extension, corporate) rules could be effectively enforced in

---

[22] Huff, "The Role of Corporate Compliance Programs."

[23] Collene C. Murnane, "Criminal Sanctions for Deterrence Are a Needed Weapon, but Self-Initiated Auditing Is Even Better: Keeping the Environment Clean and Responsible Corporate Officers Out of Jail," *Ohio State Law Journal* 55 (1994): 1181–1206.

[24] Clinard, *Corporate Corruption*, p. 162. See also Braithwaite, "Enforced Self-Regulation," pp. 1492–1493.

[25] M. Cash Mathews, *Strategic Intervention in Organizations: Resolving Ethical Dilemmas in Corporations* (Newbury Park, Calif.: Sage, 1988).

[26] Reichman, "Insider Trading," p. 88.

[27] Ibid., p. 89.

the face of unethical behavior by top managers within industries and the "greed and unethical practices of some corporations."[28]

Somewhat of a different direction is taken by Snider, who is also critical of enforced self-regulation and other "cooperative" models of regulation. Reform models, like those advocated by Braithwaite, are based in plural-ist theories that ignore the essential role of capital in pressuring the state to protect the production and accumulation of capital. The state, caught between capitalist needs and interests and pressures to maintain its own le-gitimacy, will pass reform efforts that will be anemic at best.[29] Snider believes that cooperation will not work because the same corporate power that has "invitiated" efforts to criminalize corporate illegality has an equally delete-rious impact on cooperative measures.[30]

Another challenge for enforced self-regulation stems from the interde-pendency and autonomy of internal regulatory systems, especially within large and complex organizations. In Vaughan's review of the space shuttle *Challenger* disaster, for instance, she highlights how the regulatory effective-ness at NASA was limited by "structurally engendered weaknesses."[31] Using incident-related documents, congressional hearings, presidential commis-sion documents, and personal interviews to analyze NASA's safety regulatory system, Vaughan reveals how the autonomy of NASA's safety teams affected the discovery, monitoring, and investigation of safety problems at NASA and within other contracting agencies. Intraorganizational interdependence of NASA's safety teams on NASA itself also compromised the safety process (i.e., the "regulatory authority, resources, and time" spent on safety issues were internal to the regulated organization).[32]

Structural problems associated with enforced self-regulation are even more salient for the control of multinational firms. Current legal systems lack the jurisdiction as well as the resources to enforce self-regulation. Which nation's codes and standards would one expect the firm to follow? Although there are informal means available that can shame multinational firms into acting responsibly (e.g., boycotts and bad publicity), these forces are

---

[28] Marshall B. Clinard, *Corporate Ethics and Crime* (Beverly Hills, Calif.: Sage, 1983) p. 153.

[29] Laureen Snider, "The Regulatory Dance: Understanding Reform Processes in Corporate Crime," *International Journal of the Sociology of Law* 19 (1991): 209–236.

[30] Ibid., p. 380.

[31] Vaughan makes similar points about external regulators and the organizational relationships between internal and external regulators. Diane Vaughan, "Autonomy, Interdependence, and Social Control: NASA and the Space Shuttle Challenger," *Administrative Science Quarterly* 35 (1990): 230. Braithwaite ("Enforced Self-Regulation," pp. 1497–1500) generally agrees that independence is difficult for compliance auditors, but he suggests that dependence does not equate with impotence.

[32] Vaughan, "Autonomy, Interdependence, and Social Control," p. 231.

inchoate until mobilized by a crisis.[33] Braithwaite and Drahos believe that successful global regulation is possible but it depends on intersections of powerful actors (states, nongovernment organizations, corporations, mass publics) who utilize multiple mechanisms (e.g., coercion, self-regulation) to achieve regulatory principles.[34]

Agency relationships (whereby individuals or organizations are empowered to act on another's behalf) are a key feature of white-collar crime.[35] By their very nature (i.e., based in trust), agency relationships are difficult to police, especially when they occur within large, complex, and diffuse organizations. Shapiro suggests that policing difficulties arise for both private and public police. As a consequence of policing failures, agents attempt to minimize the opportunities for trust abuse through alternative means such as subjecting prospective employees to "honesty" testing or restructuring organizational opportunities.

Shapiro challenges Braithwaite's assertion that private policing of corporate crime will be more effective than policing by the state. In fact, she suggests that public and private police are more similar than dissimilar.

> Public police are no different from private ones in the considerable variation in the efficacy and trustworthiness of their social control initiatives – the vigilance of policing, degree of access to the loci of trustee misdeeds, ability to anticipate abuse, timeliness of intervention, capacity to restore or compensate victimized principals, deterrent threat, and so forth – and in the level of acceptable risk to which these policing standards aspire.[36]

She does, however, argue that public policing has advantages over private policing during times of crisis (such as during the savings-and-loan frauds of the 1980s). The government has more resources than private police; thus, it can create a sense of stability and unlimited resources (an important characteristic, say, during a bank run). Additionally, the government is seen as more independent and disinterested than private social control. For these reasons "public police are uniquely positioned to renegotiate the level of acceptable risk, to offer disinterested social control, and thereby to restore trust."[37]

---

[33] Gerber believes that enforced self-regulation (publicity and boycotts) worked quite well in getting Nestle to reconsider marketing infant formula to lesser developed countries; see, e.g., Gerber, "Enforced Self-Regulation in the Infant Formula Industry."

[34] John Braithwaite and Peter Drahos, *Global Business Regulation* (Cambridge: Cambridge University Press, 2000).

[35] Susan Shapiro, "Policing Trust," in Clifford D. Shearing and Phillip C. Stenning (eds.), *Private Policing* (Newbury Park, Calif.: Sage, 1987), pp. 195–220.

[36] Ibid., p. 214.

[37] Ibid., p. 215.

A last set of criticisms directed toward enforced self-regulation suggest that there are hidden economic, legal, and moral costs associated with the strategy. Regulatory costs are bound to go up as agency rule-making oversight responsibilities increase. Firm costs will go up as well with greater time spent on paperwork and waiting for rules to be approved or modified.[38]

Less tangible but nonetheless significant are the real or potential legal and moral costs associated with enforced self-regulation. Because illegal acts uncovered during internal audits can be used in legal proceedings, the incentives for firms to self-report are mitigated by the threat that prosecutors may use audits to prove knowledge in criminal cases or that the information may be sought via subpoena and discovery in civil cases.[39] Western jurisprudence also may have difficulty accommodating the public enforcement of privately written rules.[40] For instance, there are some due-process concerns that private regulation results in regulation by competitor.[41] Lastly, the particularistic rules that emerge from enforced self-regulation may threaten the universal legitimacy of law. If law is viewed as particular (based in circumstance and not applicable to all), the morality that is embodied in a universal code of proscribed behavior is weakened. Law will lose its legitimacy and compliance will be compromised."[42]

Most of the deficiencies with enforced self-regulation identified here are acknowledged and discussed by Braithwaite, but he generally concludes that the promise of self-regulation in conjunction with oversight by the justice system can overcome these obstacles.[43] One reason for Braithwaite's optimism is that he believes strongly in the power of informal social controls to maintain prosocial behavior or to shame those who deviate back into conformity.

Informal Social Control

A key part of corporate compliance rests in the operation of informal social control. The majority of us act in a law-abiding manner because to do otherwise would violate personal values and collective sensibilities. Our consciences would be pricked by acting in a manner contrary to our own beliefs and values. Significant others would be disappointed in us if they were to learn of our acts. We would feel a sense of shame and embarrassment

[38] Braithwaite, "Enforced Self-Regulations," pp. 1490–1493.
[39] Murnane, "Criminal Sanctions for Deterrence."
[40] Braithwaite, "Enforced Self-Regulation," pp. 1493–1494.
[41] See, e.g., "Rethinking Regulation: Negotiation as an Alternative to Traditional Rulemaking," *Harvard Law Review* 94 (1981): 1871.
[42] Tom R. Tyler, *Why People Obey the Law* (New Haven: Yale University Press, 1990), p. 26.
[43] Braithwaite, "Enforced Self-Regulation."

knowing that we had done something wrong – regardless of whether our acts were discovered or not.[44] In sum, informal social control exerts more power over human behavior than does formal social control and, in the case of corporate crime, it may be even more relevant in the crime control equation than it is for street criminals.

Braithwaite and Fisse define informal social control as "behavioral restraint by means other than those formally directed by a court or administrative agency."[45] There are many sources of informal control, but Braithwaite and Fisse primarily investigate how adverse publicity and stigma operate to control illegal conduct by corporations. Publicity may be levied informally (i.e., generated by sources external to the legal system) and formally (i.e., as part of a legal sentence).[46]

Adverse Publicity and Stigma

In a case study analysis (using publicly available sources such as news accounts and nonstructured interviews with corporate personnel), Fisse and Braithwaite examine the impact of adverse publicity on seventeen transnational corporations.[47] Results from their study suggest that managers (especially top executives) and firms comply with the law because they fear the deleterious consequences of adverse publicity. Firms that have suffered public humiliation are likely to take steps to insure that it does not happen again.

Although public humiliation was cited as an inhibitor of misconduct in the in-depth interviews that I conducted with business executives in 1989, it did not play as prominent a role as it did in Braithwaite and Fisse's case studies – perhaps because the question asked of them was more general (i.e., do managers use a cost-benefit calculation when confronting ethical dilemmas?).[48] In response to my inquiry, two administrators felt that their company was much more sensitive to public perceptions of misconduct than it had been in the past. One manager suggested that negative publicity hurts

---

[44] Fisse and Braithwaite, *The Impact of Publicity*, pp. 246–247. John Braithwaite, *Crime, Shame, and Reintegration* (Cambridge: Cambridge University Press, 1989), pp. 144–145.

[45] Braithwaite and Fisse, "Asbestos and Health," p. 67.

[46] Fisse and Braithwaite, *The Impact of Publicity*. See also Braithwaite and Fisse, "Asbestos and Health."

[47] See also Braithwaite and Fisse's review, "Asbestos and Health," of how the worldwide asbestos and health scare affected James Hardie, an Australian multinational corporation that manufactured numerous asbestos products. Fisse and Braithwaite, *The Impact of Publicity*.

[48] The interviews took place within three Fortune 500 companies. Fifty-nine managers (including the CEO at one company, numerous executive vice presidents, supervisors, and entry-level managers) responded to my questions about unethical conduct. Sally S. Simpson, "Corporate-Crime Deterrence and Corporate-Control Policies: Views from the Inside," in Kip Schlegel and David Weisburd (eds.), *White-Collar Crime Reconsidered* (Boston: Northeastern University Press, 1992), pp. 289–308.

the firm's competitive position. He felt that "unethical decisions ultimately come back to hurt the company. It isn't worth it. Ever!" A corporate attorney employed by the same company (which, in the 1970s, had a very public product safety failure) mentioned that negative publicity comes back to haunt the company. "Everyone knows what happens when you cross the line. We don't need any more examples."

The negative consequences of adverse publicity are not merely pecuniary (although the financial costs of negative publicity may be considerable). Because there is intrinsic value associated with having a positive reputation and feeling good about oneself and the company for whom one works, the stigma that results from an infamous case of misconduct is difficult for a firm to shake. Employee morale is negatively affected and customer confidence tends to be hard to restore.

Informal social control may originate from consumer movements (such as boycotts),[49] investigative journalism (journalists Jack Anderson, Les Whitten, and Mark Dowie exposed the defects in the Ford Pinto),[50] enforcement actions or official inquiries (e.g., an enforcement agency may generate publicity about a questionable product or Congress may launch an investigation, usually after a problem has come to light).[51] Disclosures of problems by corporations (whether mandatory or voluntary) may also result in negative publicity, but how disclosures are greeted usually depends on how the issue (or incident) was handled by the firm and the spin put on the disclosures by the media, legal authorities, activists, and other communication agents.

Formal Publicity

As stated in chapter 8 (D)(1.4) of the U.S. Sentencing Commission Guidelines for Organizational Sentencing, the court may impose formal publicity as a condition of probation.

> The court may order the organization, at its expense and in the format and media specified by the court, to publicize the nature of the offense

[49] N. Craig Smith, *Morality and the Market: Consumer Pressure for Corporate Accountability* (New York: Routledge, 1990); Gerber, "Enforced Self-Regulation in the Infant Formula Industry."

[50] Jack Anderson and Les Whitten, "Auto Maker Shuns Safer Gas Tank," *Washington Post*, December 30, 1976, p. B7; Mark Dowie, "Pinto Madness," *Mother Jones* 2 (September–October, 1977): 18–32.

[51] Fisse and Braithwaite, *The Impact of Publicity*, pp. 260–272. Vaughan utilizes reports from a presidential commission and a bipartisan investigation by the U.S. House of Representatives Committee on Science and Technology to assess how the decision to launch the *Challenger* occurred in spite of knowledge at NASA and Morton Thiokol that the O-rings were potentially defective given launch weather conditions. Diane Vaughan, *The Challenger Launch Decision: Risky Technology, Culture, and Deviance at NASA* (Chicago: University of Chicago Press, 1995).

committed, the fact of the conviction, the nature of the punishment imposed, and the steps that will be taken to prevent the recurrence of similar offenses.[52]

The guidelines provide an example of how the court may impose formal publicity as part of criminal punishment, but formal publicity can enter into administrative and civil proceedings as well. Regulatory agencies have ordered companies to announce when they have participated in illegal acts and to encourage potential victims to come forward. Fisse and Braithwaite, for instance, describe how the National Labor Relations Board ordered J. P. Stevens to notify employees via mail and workplace bulletin boards about antiunion violations. Firms that have used deceptive advertising to mislead the public have been forced by the Federal Trade Commission to address publicly product misperceptions.[53] Firms may also be required to use the media and/or mail to notify claimants of their potential standing in class action suits.

Targets of Social Control

The informal control of corporate crime at the individual level works primarily through the organizational compliance system. Internal compliance programs are the means through which company standards are communicated and from which rewards and punishments emanate. When normative (prosocial) standards are internalized by employees, most will abide by the rules because it is the right thing to do. To do otherwise is to risk threats to conscience or potential discovery of the violation. The latter carries with it reputational losses and, quite possibly, organizationally imposed sanctions (such as a less desirable work assignment, demotion, or dismissal). As noted earlier, these kinds of "informal" sanctions are particularly salient for potential offenders and offer a potent source of crime inhibition for any crime control strategy.[54]

When the conscience fails and the illicit deed is done, publicity directed toward responsible parties within the firm and the negative reaction to the miscreant (and the act) by significant others fosters shaming. Braithwaite argues that systems that shame but reintegrate employees who stray from

---

[52] U.S. Sentencing Commission, *Guidelines Manual*, p. 95.

[53] Fisse and Braithwaite, *The Impact of Publicity*, pp. 286–287.

[54] Harold Grasmick and Robert J. Bursik Jr., "Conscience, Significant Others, and Rational Choice: Extending the Deterrence Model," *Law and Society Review* 24 (1990): 837–861. See also Raymond Paternoster, "The Deterrent Effect of the Perceived Certainty and Severity of Punishment," *Justice Quarterly* 4 (1990): 173–217, for a review of deterrence studies.

social responsibility are better at controlling illegal conduct than programs that are overly punitive or lenient. Positive reinforcement of prosocial behavior will produce more ethical conduct than social disapproval of unethical actions.[55]

Informal controls also may operate at the organizational level. A recent issue of the *Washington Post*, for instance, carried the following front-page headline, "ADM to Pay $100 Million to Settle Price-Fixing Case: Agribusiness Giant Will Plead Guilty after 4-Year Probe."[56] The Archer Daniels Midland case illustrates how publicity highlighting the illegal or unethical acts of the firm can be a powerful tool to effect changes in how a company conducts its business.[57] In this case, the negative publicity has led some of the firm's institutional investors to request the resignation of ADM founder and current CEO, Dwayne Andreas (a well-known lobbyist on behalf of agricultural interests and donor to both Republican and Democratic parties), and to seek restructuring of the board of directors to include more outsiders. As part of damage control, experts have advised ADM to take action against the top executives upon whose watch the price-fixing conspiracy took place.[58]

> The only way the company can truly repair its image after more than a year of high-profile charges and bad publicity would be for Dwayne Andreas and his top lieutenant, James Randall, 71, to resign. To put a good face on the move, it could be attributed to the ages of the two men, who are well past traditional retirement ages for executives.

Like the firms studied by Fisse and Braithwaite, the financial costs to Archer Daniels Midland resulting from the settlement itself are relatively insignificant. The fine of $100 million, while the largest criminal antitrust fine ever, barely makes a dent in ADM's $13.3 billion in sales during 1996. ADM's stock rebounded one day after the deal was announced, closing at a fifty-two-week high.[59] Clearly, the financial considerations, while no doubt salient, are less troubling to investors and other stakeholders than is the damage to the corporate giant's good name.

Given that both individuals and organizations may be targets of publicity (whether formal or informal), it is reasonable to wonder whether one is a more effective target for shaming than the other. This question has

---

[55] Braithwaite, *Crime, Shame, and Reintegration*, p. 135.
[56] *Washington Post*, October 15, 1996, p. A1.
[57] Fisse and Braithwaite, *The Impact of Publicity*.
[58] "Agribusiness Giant ADM to Pay $100 Million to Settle Price-Fixing Case," *Washington Post*, October 15, 1996, p. A7.
[59] Ibid.

generated a great deal of discussion, but no clear-cut conclusion. A number of issues are at the heart of the controversy. (1) Why should a corporation, which is a lifeless object, be subject to shaming that it cannot feel? As entities with "no soul to damn and no body to kick,"[60] businesses are incapable of feeling shame and embarrassment. (2) Why should "innocent" stockholders, employees, and other shareholders be held accountable for the actions of individual managers? Sarah B. Teslik, executive director of the Council of Institutional Investors and one of Archer Daniels Midland's stockholders, has stated plainly that her clients resent having to absorb the $100 million dollar fine levied against the firm for price-fixing. "We have a situation where *we* [the shareholders] pay the government and the wrongdoers don't suffer.... What's so disturbing about corporate crime is that the individuals [responsible] don't pay."[61] (3) Can the corporate facade be penetrated in order to identify persons responsible for the corporate misbehavior? If some firms have corporate personnel designated as senior vice-president "responsible for going to jail" when something goes wrong,[62] it makes more sense to publicize firm wrongdoing than to highlight the misdeeds of an individual manager or two.

The arguments that frame these questions are very similar to those that were addressed in earlier chapters. In this case, rather than pondering whether to levy punishment on the firm or individual managers, the question revolves around publicity and stigma. Braithwaite concludes that both targets are appropriate, effective, and mutually reinforcing. "If one fails at shaming the responsible individuals, there is still the opportunity to secure compliance by shaming the collectivity. The shamed collectivity can not only pass on this shame by sanctioning guilty individuals after the event, it can also activate internal controls proactively to prevent future crimes before they occur."[63]

Reinforcing or reciprocal systems of social control are a recurrent theme in Braithwaite's work. The imagery of a pyramid is evoked when he discusses how informal and formal controls build upon one another. "Just as shaming is needed when conscience fails, punishment is needed when offenders are beyond being shamed."[64]

---

[60] John C. Coffee " 'No Soul to Damn, No Body to Kick': An Unscandalized Inquiry into the Problem of Corporate Punishment," *Michigan Law Riview* 79 (1980): 386–359.

[61] *Washington Post*, October 15, 1996, p. A1 (emphasis in original).

[62] John Braithwaite, *Corporate Crime in the Pharmaceutical Industry* (London: Routledge and Kegan Paul, 1984).

[63] Braithwaite, *Crime*, pp. 126–127.

[64] Ibid., p. 75.

Enforcement Pyramid

As noted in Chapter 5, the main idea of Braithwaite's enforcement pyramid is that formal legal sanctions are punitive elements within a broader crime control strategy. Because law is the most commanding and intrusive form of social control, it should be the intervention of last resort (and, thus, located at the tip of the enforcement pyramid). The first line of defense against corporate criminals is informal control – socialization into ethical conduct and belief in the morality of the law. Firms that deviate from compliance should first be persuaded to conform. Persuasion is based in the idea that corporations, when given the chance, will generally do the "right" thing. Because persuasion is a less commanding and intrusive form of social control, it is located at the base of the pyramid and should be used first and retried often before resorting to more punitive interventions. Legal interventions (the most formal and punitive controls) are interventions of last resort (when persuasion or informal strategies of control fail) or a mechanism to ensure regulatory cooperation.[65]

In direct contrast to those who suggest that deterrence and compliance crime control strategies are contrary to one another, Braithwaite's pyramid incorporates both.[66] "Increasingly, within both scholarly and regulatory communities there is a feeling that the regulatory agencies that do best at achieving their goals are those that strike some sort of sophisticated balance between the two models. The crucial question has become: When to punish; when to persuade?"[67] To answer this question, Ayres and Braithwaite use game theory to predict winners and losers under conditions of regulatory cooperation and conflict between regulators and firms.

Tit-for-Tat Regulatory Philosophy

Scholz was one of the first to challenge the idea that deterrence and compliance strategies of crime control are antithetical to one another. In an article published in 1984, Scholz first contrasted the key elements of a deterrence (or rule-oriented) strategy with those of compliance and then, using game theory, explained how the two strategies were related.[68] Although the differences between the strategies have been noted previously in this work, it is useful to review the underlying assumptions of the models.

---

[65] Braithwaite, *To Punish or Persuade*; Ayres and Braithwaite, *Responsive Regulation*.

[66] The polarization between deterrence and compliance is characterized as "crude" by Ayres and Braithwaite (ibid., p. 21).

[67] Ibid.

[68] John T. Scholz, "Cooperation, Deterrence, and the Ecology of Regulatory Enforcement," *Law and Society Review* 18 (1984): 179–224.

The goal of deterrence is to seek compliance through coercion. The primary means through which this is accomplished is to identify and punish rule violators. A deterrence strategy assumes a rational actor[69] who will weigh the costs and benefits of crime relative to those of compliance. Deterrence will be achieved when amoral actors have a high likelihood of crime detection and maximal sanctioning.

A cooperative strategy, on the other hand, assumes that most actors are willing to obey legitimate rules. The approach assumes that full enforcement of the law is not possible or desirable. Thus, when violations do occur, regulators should take a more particular approach to rule enforcement. Persuasion and reasonable enforcement are advocated for known violators instead of maximum punishment.

Each of these strategies may be used by regulators but which is used and against whom depends on whether the firm is "good" or "bad." The good firm is the one that generally obeys the law and acts like a responsible citizen. This firm deserves the benefit of the doubt when violations are suspected.

> Technical violations are overlooked if trivial, and legitimate reasons for noncompliance are accepted when warranted by circumstances. More serious violations are noted, but generous abatement periods are granted and reasonable attempts to correct the situation will forestall prosecution. When prosecution is necessary, fines are likely to be minimal, congruent with the good intentions of the firm.[70]

Bad firms, however, are those that have established themselves as uncooperative and unmoved by persuasion. They are the habitual offenders, the hardened criminals, the recidivists. These firms qualify for punitive deterrent strategies.[71]

The dilemma for regulators, as Braithwaite has noted, is determining which strategy is appropriate under what conditions to maximize compliance. Punishing every offender is inefficient and potentially counterproductive. Failure to punish some offenders, however, has its own costs.

> Policymakers who believe that the 100 criminal cases they know about should be investigated and prosecuted with an eye to criminal sanctions set themselves an impossible goal in the domain of complex corporate crime. Policymakers who believe that there are better ways of dealing with 99 out of 100

---

[69] Rationality is assumed to be "bounded" or limited by individual characteristics and particular circumstances or situations (e.g., access to information). Herbert Simon, *Models of Man* (New York: John Wiley, 1957).

[70] Scholz, "Cooperation," pp. 182–183.

[71] Ibid., p. 182.

corporate crimes than taking them to court leave themselves with a superior capacity to concentrate their enforcement resources on the 1 case in 100 that they think is best handled by a criminal prosecution.[72]

To demonstrate the symbiosis between cooperation and punishment, Sholtz highlights Chester Bowles's observations when he served in the Office of Price Administration during World War II. Bowles estimated that approximately 20 percent of firms would comply with rules at all times. About 5 percent would be incorrigible all the time. The vast majority of companies (around 75 percent) would comply, *but only if they knew that the slackers were going to receive their just deserts.* According to this view, punishment is essential if cooperative strategies are to succeed.[73]

Firm and agency relations are not static onetime encounters. Instead, regulation is a dynamic and changeable process between regulator and regulatee. Because relationships are ongoing, a tit-for-tat (TFT) strategy may maximize regulatory efficiency and compliance.[74] The TFT strategy, simply stated, is to cooperate until your partner defects. In the upcoming round, adopt the strategy that your partner did last. For example, let's assume that a company was suspected of releasing toxins into the river near one of its manufacturing plants. When notified of the government's suspicions, the firm launched an internal inquiry and fully cooperated with regulators during their investigation. The next time that regulators have dealings with this company, a cooperative strategy will be assumed. If, however, the firm had tried to evade legal authorities (destroyed evidence, protected responsible managers, fought government access to records, and so forth), the next time around the agency would adopt a vengeful deterrence strategy.[75]

If Bowles is accurate in his percentage estimates, the TFT strategy could yield as high as 95 percent compliance (20 percent that always comply and 75 percent that will do so if the 5 percent are punished for their transgressions). But the success of TFT depends on two features of the enforcement pyramid: the variety or range of sanctions and regulatory styles available to agents, and

---

[72] John Braithwaite, "Transnational Regulation of the Pharmaceutical Industry," in Gilbert Geis and Paul Jesilow (eds.), *White-Collar Crime*, Annals of the American Academy of Political and Social Science, vol. 525 (Newbury Park, Calif.: Sage, 1993), pp. 12–31.

[73] Ibid., p. 184.

[74] Under experimental conditions, John Axelrod has demonstrated that the tit-for-tat tactic is an extremely effective tool to maximize cooperation between players who have ongoing encounters. For a summary of his research, see John Axelrod, *The Evolution of Cooperation* (New York: Basic Books, 1984).

[75] Braithwaite's enforcement pyramid differs somewhat in that cooperative strategies should be retried often before resorting to vengeful deterrence.

the punitiveness of the most severe sanction.[76] Coupling the TFT strategy with these regulatory features constitutes the previously defined "benign big gun" style of regulation. Using Theodore Roosevelt's foreign-policy analogy to "walk softly and carry a big stick," Ayres and Braithwaite suggest that "the bigger and the more various are the sticks, the greater the success regulators will achieve by speaking softly."[77]

Game theory scenarios are somewhat limited, however, because the models are untested in the real world (experimental studies do not simulate the real world) and because self-interest (such as costs, trade-offs, and pay-offs) dominates the elements of the model while other explanatory variables (e.g., trust, ignorance, normative commitments) are excluded.[78]

Conclusions

This chapter confirms that there has been little systematic investigation of corporate deterrence. Deterrence is assumed to work only for corporations and their managers (or it is assumed that deterrence would work if the justice system operated properly). Cooperative models, which have developed out of case studies and have expanded via game theory modeling (and experiments), also lack systematic empirical exploration. To address some of these empirical deficiencies, the next chapter draws from recent research that assesses the link between some presumed causes of corporate offending and strategies for crime inhibition, including punitive and other legal sanctions, organizational compliance programs, and informal sanction threats.[79]

---

[76] Ayres and Braithwaite, *Responsive Regulation*, p. 40.

[77] Ibid., p. 19.

[78] See Scholz, "Cooperation," p. 222; Ayres and Braithwaite, *Responsive Regulation*.

[79] Recent publications from this study include Raymond Paternoster and Sally S. Simpson, "Sanction Threats and Appeals to Morality: Testing a Rational Choice Model of Corporate Crime," *Law and Society Review* 30 (1996): 549–583; Lori A. Elis and Sally S. Simpson, "Informal Sanction Threats and Corporate Crime: Additive versus Multiplicative Models," *Journal of Research in Crime and Delinquency* 32 (1995): 399–424.

CHAPTER SEVEN

Criminalization versus Cooperation:
An Empirical Test

MOST ASSESSMENTS of corporate crime control policies, especially criminalization strategies, lack an empirical base. Deterrence is only presumed to work. Managers are assumed to fear criminal sanctions and hence will be more apt to adhere to the law if threatened with criminal prosecution. Firms will be less willing to commit crimes if criminal sanctions are likely. Yet the same criticism can be made of cooperative models.

The aim of this chapter is to bring additional evidence to bear on the question of corporate crime control. Why do corporations obey the law? How do deterrence (or criminalization) and compliance (or cooperative) strategies of corporate crime control fare in the world of managerial decision making? Data drawn from two factorial surveys (instruments that combine experimentally manipulated summaries with survey techniques) administered to MBA students and executives will be used to answer these questions along with others that have emerged from the preceding chapters. For instance:

- Does the salience of formal sanction threats vary by the degree to which managers are committed to crime?
- Do managers perceive sanction threats differently by sanction source (e.g., criminal, civil, or regulatory) and target (individual versus manger)?
- Do sanctions that are perceived as unfair produce more rather than less crime (i.e., is there a defiance effect)?
- How do formal and informal sanction threats compare in their prohibitory effects?

Study One

Vignette Construction

In 1993 and 1994 a factorial survey was developed to explore the link between the causes of corporate crime and potential control strategies.[1] The survey contained four hypothetical scenarios that described managers participating in different types of corporate offending including price-fixing, violation of emission standards, bribery, and sales fraud.[2] Each vignette was followed by a set of questions that directly related to the situation described in the scenario. Respondents were instructed to imagine that they were the manager in each vignette and to answer the questions accordingly. One question asked how likely it was (on a scale from 0 to 100 percent) that the respondent would act as the manager did in the vignette. Because the manager violated the law in all scenarios, this question measured the offending proclivity of the respondent under a similar set of conditions.

Scenarios were created by drawing on the corporate crime causation and control literatures. Ten categories (or dimensions) were constructed to capture concepts or variables thought to influence a manager's decision to commit corporate crime. Within specific categories (such as firm size), different levels (e.g., small, medium, large) were randomly assigned to each vignette. Thus, while every vignette was constructed from the same dimensions, different dimension levels were contained within each scenario.

Dimensions reflect characteristics of the manager, the firm or industry, and sources of social control (informal versus formal). Specific categories included:

1. The benefits of noncompliance for the manager.
2. Managerial location in the corporate hierarchy.
3. Managerial tenure at the firm.
4. Managerial authority.
5. The benefits of noncompliance for the firm.
6. Economic pressures on the firm.
7. Environmental constraints.

[1] See Raymond Paternoster and Sally Simpson, "A Rational Choice Theory of Corporate Crime," in Ronald V. Clarke and Marcus Felson (eds.), *Routine Activity Theory and Rational Choice: Advances in Criminological Theory*, vol. 5 (New Brunswick, N.J.: Transaction Press, 1993), pp. 37–58.

[2] With modifications, these examples are taken from Raymond Paternoster and Sally Simpson, "Testing a Rational Choice Model of Corporate Crime," *Law and Society Review* 30 (1996): 580–581.

8. External sources of compliance (formal justice systems).
9. Internal sources of compliance (self-regulation).
10. Crime types.

Because the primary goal of this work is to empirically assess corporate deterrence and cooperative models of regulation, some dimensions are more important than others. Recall that deterrence theorists prioritize the salience of criminal sanction certainty and severity over other sources of crime control. Seven levels of formal control were randomly assigned across vignettes.

1. An employee was recently caught and criminally sanctioned for a similar act.
2. An employee was recently sued and fined for a similar act.
3. The firm was recently criminally sanctioned for a similar act.
4. The firm was recently sued and fined for a similar act.
5. The firm was recently inspected and cited for a similar act.
6. An employee recently was acquitted of any wrongdoing for a similar act.
7. The firm recently was acquitted of any wrongdoing for a similar act.

If deterrence theorists are correct, criminal prosecutions (which carry the greatest stigmatic and punitive effects) should have a significantly greater inhibitory impact on offending decisions than any of the other levels. As the different levels described here imply, it is also possible to assess whether criminal sanctions directed toward the responsible manager or those directed toward the firm differ significantly from one another in their crime inhibition effects.

The research also examines how different levels of intraorganizational control (or self-regulation) may affect a manager's offending intentions. In the previous chapter, compliance programs were differentiated by a number of distinct elements. The vignette items were designed to capture some of these differences. For instance, the self-regulation dimension varied degrees of control from minimal (mandatory ethics training) to more intensive (a hotline in which illegal acts could be anonymously reported to management; internally implemented audits and inspections at random intervals). Included as well was an indication of how the corporation responded once illegality was discovered (an employee was recently fired after being caught engaging in a similar act). Lastly, the self-regulation dimension included threats to an effective compliance system that are situated in cultural supports for misconduct (e.g., the act is a common practice within the firm; the act is a common practice within the industry).

Based on our earlier discussions of cooperative models (reviewed in Chapter 6), internal compliance programs should exert a more powerful influence on offending decisions than the threat of formal legal sanctions (i.e., external compliance). Extensive compliance programs should be more effective at inhibiting misconduct than those that are rudimentary. Accordingly, we would expect randomized audits and anonymous hotlines to supplement significantly the inhibitory effect of mandatory ethics training. Moreover, programs that contain a disciplinary mechanism (i.e., an employee was fired) should also be more effective than those that merely introduce the employee to an ethics code. Finally, when deviance is reinforced within the corporate culture, it is likely that compliance programs will be undermined.

The self-regulation literature promotes the idea that top managers set the ethical tone and standards for the rest of the organization. One of our dimensions captures whether the manager depicted in the scenarios was "ordered" by a supervisor to violate the law versus having made the decision to violate the law himself or herself. Because the former suggests that top management (or at least one's direct supervisor) is not adverse to violating the law in order to achieve a desired goal, offending proclivities among respondents should increase when this item appears.

In order to get a sense of how the scenarios are constructed using different dimension levels, four examples of the different crime scenarios are depicted here.[3]

Price-Fixing. J. Jones, a low-level manager who has been with Steelcorp for years, is ordered by a supervisor to meet with competitors to discuss product pricing for the next year. It has been suggested to J. that the act will save the company a large amount of money. Steelcorp is a medium-sized company, currently experiencing growing sales and revenues in an industry that is losing ground to foreign competitors. J. thinks that the act increases the likelihood that J. will be positively noticed by top management, but also knows that an employee was recently fired after being caught for a similar act, and that the firm was recently sued and fined for a similar act. J. decides to meet with competitors to discuss product pricing for the next year.

Sales Fraud. J. Smith, a low-level manager who has been with *Steelcorp* for years, decides to order employees to inflate sales statistics in the firm's financial accounts that can be accounted for in anticipated sales in the

---

[3] Survey questions and responses broken down by crime type are reported in Appendix A.

following quarter. It has been suggested to J. that the act will save the company a small amount of money. Steelcorp is a small company, currently experiencing growing sales and revenues in an industry that is economically healthy. J. thinks that the act increases the likelihood of peer admiration, but also knows that the firm has a hotline in which such acts can be anonymously reported to management, and that an employee was recently sued and fined for a similar act.

Violation of Environmental Standards. J. Johnson, an upper-level manager recently hired by Steelcorp, decides to order employees to release into the air emissions that fail to meet EPA standards. It has been suggested to J. that this action gives the firm an opportunity to challenge legally the application or substance of the law. Steelcorp is a medium-sized company, currently experiencing growing sales and revenues in an industry that is economically deteriorating. J. thinks that the act increases the likelihood of promotion, but also knows that the firm has internally implemented audits and inspections at random intervals, and that the firm was recently inspected and cited for a similar act.

Bribery. J. Bradley, a middle-level manager recently hired by Steelcorp, is ordered by a supervisor to comply with a supplier's request to make a cash payment for the supplier's personal use. It has been suggested to J. that the act will increase the positive reputation of the firm. Steelcorp is a large company, currently experiencing declining sales and revenues in an industry that is economically healthy. J. thinks that the act increases the likelihood of peer admiration and knows that the act is a common practice in the firm, but that an employee was recently sued and fined for a similar act. J. decides to comply with the supplier's request to make a cash payment for the supplier's personal use.

Factorial Survey

Questions. Each vignette is followed by a set of questions that refer back to the scenario just read. Respondents are asked to assess the costs and benefits of the depicted crime for themselves and for the company. Measured costs include the perceived threat of formal (criminal, civil, and regulatory) and informal sanctions (discovery, shame, social censure). Benefits include the perceived likelihood of career advancement and the degree to which engaging in an illicit act would be thrilling or exciting for the respondent.

(These costs and benefits are in addition to those manipulated in the vignettes themselves.)

As previously stated, deterrence theorists anticipate that respondents will be less likely to offend when the risk of formal legal sanctions (certainty and severity) is perceived to be great. On the other hand, Braithwaite's enforcement pyramid would lead us to expect that formal legal sanctions will be most salient to those not amenable to persuasion (i.e., persons with little stake in conformity and uncommitted to prosocial behavior).

The factorial survey is uniquely suited to address some of the controversial questions surrounding corporate crime control. Formal and informal systems of social control can be compared and contrasted with an eye toward effective compliance. Within systems of control, it is possible to examine which type of sanction or program has the greatest effect on offending decisions. (For instance, are criminal, civil, or regulatory interventions more inhibitory of corporate crime? Do audits and hotlines enhance compliance beyond mandatory ethics training?) The data also allow us to assess which sanction target is more salient for managers – the firm or themselves? Lastly, we can examine whether adverse publicity (directed toward the manager and/or the firm) inhibits offending intentions independent of formal sanction threats.

Administration. The factorial survey was administered in three locations to first-year MBA students. At one university, all students in first-semester marketing were given the survey (approximately 200 students total). At the other two schools, students in smaller and more specialized MBA classes were asked to participate (roughly 75 students in each location). In addition to the student sample, a small group of managers attending an intensive executive education program at a fourth university were administered the survey (N = 40).

Respondents were asked to place their completed questionnaires in an envelope provided with the survey instrument and to mail it back to the researchers using U.S. or campus mail. At one school, they also had the option of delivering the envelope to a sealed box in the MBA office. The questionnaires were introduced at an extremely busy time for many students and, although the instrument could be completed in twenty minutes, its lengthy appearance was daunting. The survey completion rate suffered as a consequence. Only one-fourth of the surveys administered were returned (96 total, 84 from MBA students and 12 from executives). Statistical analysis revealed few differences between the MBA student and executive responses to the questions.[4] Therefore, the two groups were pooled for further analysis.

Because each participant read and responded to four different (and randomly constructed) scenarios, our total sample size is 384 (96 × 4). The final sample was reduced somewhat by three missing cases on the dependent variable (i.e., intentions to offend) and by dropping scenarios that were deemed "unrealistic" by respondents (N = 320). There were no significant demographic differences between students who participated in the survey and those who did not.[5] Moreover, missing data were randomly distributed across persons.

Respondent Characteristics. As shown in Appendix B (study 1), respondents were primarily males, but a fair number of females were also represented in the sample. Most respondents were white (85 percent) and U.S. citizens (82 percent). Their average age was twenty-eight. While it can be argued that students generally are a poor substitute for a group of managers, the MBA respondents in this sample averaged almost five years of business experience prior to attending graduate school. Thus, it was not a stretch for them to understand the business environment or to place themselves in the corporate crime scenarios described in the survey.

On the question of how likely (on a scale of 0 to 100 percent) respondents were to act as the manager did in the scenario, 66 percent indicated a nonzero probability that they would offend. The average probability, however, was low (around 20 percent). Thus, while respondents indicated that they were inclined to offend (i.e., there is a predisposition to commit corporate crime), very few found the situations so compelling that they were willing to commit themselves 100 percent to the criminal act.

Across all four offense types, only 4 percent of the respondents were unwilling to violate the law in any of the scenarios. In fact, 81 percent indicated that they would offend some of the time while 15 percent might be classified as criminally committed (i.e., willing to violate the law more than 50 percent of the time). In this latter group, however, only one scored above 50 percent offending likelihood for all scenarios. From these breakdowns, we can conclude that in this sample of respondents that few were "criminally committed" (i.e., always willing to contemplate crime); a small number were unwilling to consider offending across a wide array of circumstances; and

---

[4] The only significant difference found between the two groups was that the executives estimated formal legal sanctions to be more personally costly than did the students.
[5] This analysis was conducted only at the largest administration site.

Table 7.1. *Study One: Perceived Sanction Certainty and Severity by Source and Target (mean perceived risk and consequence)*

	Target	
Source	Individual	Company
Certainty		
Criminal	4.28	4.83**
Civil	3.70	5.13***
Regulatory	4.63	5.70***
Severity		
Criminal	9.51	8.18***
Civil	9.22	7.88***
Regulatory	NA	7.39

Notes: Mean differences (two-tailed test): **significant at .01;   ***significant at .001.

most were marginally committed to corporate offending – depending on the circumstances and assessments of cost-benefit.

Perceived Certainty and Severity of Formal Sanctions

Perceptions of formal sanction certainty and severity vary depending on sanction source and target. As shown in Table 7.1, it is clear that the organization was perceived to be at greater risk for official discovery and investigation or prosecution (certainty) than was the "responsible" manager. Respondents also reported that regulatory interventions were more likely than either civil or criminal proceedings. Overall, managers perceived the risk of sanctions to be modest for themselves (around 40–50 percent) and a bit higher for firms (50–60 percent).

Perceptions were reversed when sanction severity was considered. Here respondents felt that the costs associated with criminal prosecution and civil litigation would weigh more heavily on them than on the company.[6] Not surprisingly, respondents felt that being arrested and going to jail were more costly for them than being sued (i.e., the stigmatic costs were assessed to be more of a problem than the financial costs). However, all of the sanctions

---

[6] Because individuals tend not to be the subject of regulatory sanction, respondents were not asked to assess the severity of this intervention for themselves.

were generally rated high in terms of consequence (averaging between 7 and 9.5 on a 0–10 scale). Finally, it is interesting that the sanction threat managers thought most likely (regulatory investigation) was also the intervention least feared (at least when the company was the sanction target).

Respondents' estimates probably overstate the actual risks associated with the crimes described in the scenarios, but because perceptual deterrence suggests that subjective risk is more important than objective and given that the consequences were perceived to be dire (especially for the manager), one would expect that the decision to offend would take sanction threats into account.

Statistical Analysis

Data were analyzed in several ways. First, exploratory analyses using ordinary least squares (OLS) regression were run to assess the impact of our independent variables on respondent offending intentions. Second, given that 34 percent of the time offending estimates were coded zero (i.e., the respondent chose not to act like the manager depicted in the vignette), we recoded offending decisions into a binary 0,1 variable. In this coding scheme, the dependent variable is treated as a discrete decision-to commit the offense or not. Logistic regression analyses were performed to assess which factors (if any) affected the choice to offend. These results did not differ substantively from the OLS results. Finally, because respondents read and responded to four vignettes within each survey, analyses were conducted to test for correlated error terms across observations using a random-effects model. Error terms indicated that there were significant correlations and therefore results are reported using generalized least squares random-effects estimates.[7]

Vignette Analysis

Table 7.2 depicts data on the vignette items and the question of criminalization and deterrence. In the first equation, "criminal sanctions directed toward responsible managers" is excluded from the analysis and treated as the reference category for the other "formal" legal outcomes. In the second equation, "criminal sanctions directed toward the firm" is the excluded reference category. The results show no support for the argument that criminal

---

[7] See Paternoster and Simpson, "Testing a Rational Choice Model," pp. 565–566, for a more detailed description of these models.

sanctions (directed either at the manager or the firm) are more inhibitory of offending than other formal legal sanctions. None of the other levels of formal control (i.e., civil or regulatory sanctions) differs significantly from the excluded category except one: the acquittal of an employee (EMPACQ). When scenarios contained this measure of formal control, offending intentions significantly increased relative to the individual being criminally sanctioned (model 1) or the firm being criminally sanctioned (model 2).

These findings suggest that, once other factors are included in the analysis, managers do not prioritize one form of legal intervention over another. Civil and regulatory sanctions appear to be similar to criminal investigations and punishments in their prohibitory effects – at least so far as managers' own offending intentions are concerned. Results also indicate that managers do not adjust their behaviors based on information about sanction targets, that is, the individual or the company. Respondents were swayed, however, by information that conveyed a lower probability of formal processing. When the scenario depicted that an employee had been acquitted of wrongdoing in a similar situation, respondents' probabilities of acting like the depicted manager (i.e., meeting with competitors to fix prices, violating EPA standards, paying a bribe, or "cooking the books") increased significantly.

For the self-regulation variables depicted in Table 7.2, findings generally conformed to expectations. Anonymous hotlines and employee dismissals lowered offending levels beyond the prohibitive effect of mandatory ethics training (the deleted category). Random audits did not add significantly to crime inhibition, but the direction of the effect is as one would predict – negative. Thus, the additional layers of self-regulation beyond ethics codes and training appeared to add additional protection against crime. These self-regulatory systems were somewhat compromised, however, when an illegal act was common within the *firm*.[8] Information suggesting that the act was a common practice at the *industry* level was less salient to managers' decision processes.

The vignette data depicted in Table 7.2 highlighted other important factors related to offending proclivities among respondents. As expected, scenarios that depicted managers "ordered by supervisors" to violate the law (ORDERED) produced higher offending levels among respondents than depictions of managers who decided to violate the law themselves (excluded

---

[8] When self-regulation variables are analyzed separately and crime types are controlled, COMFIRM has a significant and positive impact on offending intentions. See Paternoster and Simpson, "Testing a Rational Choice Model," p. 567.

Table 7.2. *Study One: Random-Effects Regression Model of Offending Intentions on Vignette Items (Rho = 0.23, R^2 = 0.15)*

	Individual Sanction Target		Firm Sanction Target	
	b	(t)	b	(t)
Formal Control				
Firm Recently Criminally Sanctioned (FIRMCRIM)	.139	.26	−.139	−.26
Employee Recently Sued (EMSUED)	.165	.31	.026	.06
Firm Recently Cited (FIRMCITE)	−.077	−.14	−.216	−.44
Firm Recently Sued & Fined (FIRMSUED)	−.015	−.03	−.154	−.36
Employee Recently Acquitted (EMPACQ)	1.076	2.04*	.937	2.05*
Firm Recently Acquitted (FIRMACQ)	.637	1.02	.497	.86
Self-Regulation				
Employee Hotline (HOTLINE)	−.872	−1.89[+]	−.872	−1.89[+]
Random Audits (AUDITS)	−.530	−1.14	−.530	−1.14
Employee Recently Fired (EMFIRED)	−.844	−1.87[+]	−.844	−1.87[+]
Act Is Common within Firm (COMFIRM)	.579	1.20	.579	1.20
Act Is Common within Industry (INDUSTRY)	−.021	−.04	−.021	−.04
Manager Location				
Lower-Level Manager (LOW)	.374	1.18	.374	1.18
Upper-Level Manager (UPPER)	.346	1.08	.346	1.08
Manager Tenure				
Employed for Years (YEARS)	−.160	−.62	−.160	−.62
Manager Power				
Ordered (ORDERED)	.748	2.80**	.748	2.80**
Firm Size				
Small Company (SMALL)	−.408	−1.11	−.408	−1.11
Medium-Sized Company (MEDIUM)	−.053	−.18	−.053	−.18
Firm Pressures				
Firm Experiencing Growing Sales (GROWSALE)	.232	.89	.232	.89
Firm Benefits				
Save Firm Large Amount of Money (SAVELG)	1.099	2.39*	1.099	2.39*
Increase Firm Revenues (REVENUE)	.886	1.86[+]	.886	1.86[+]
Increase Positive Reputation of Firm (POSREP)	1.122	2.23*	1.122	2.23*

Table 7.2. *(cont.)*

	Individual Sanction Target		Firm Sanction Target	
	b	(t)	b	(t)
Improve Employee Morale (MORALE)	.717	1.45	.717	1.45
Change Status of Law (LAW)	1.363	2.53**	1.363	2.53**
Manager Benefits				
Increases Likelihood of Promotion (PROMOTE)	.026	.08	.026	.08
Impress Top Management (MANAGE)	.093	.30	.093	.30
Environment Constraints				
Industry Economically Deteriorating (ECDET)	.063	.19	.063	.19
Industry Losing Ground to Foreign Competitors (FOREIGN)	.812	2.24*	.812	2.24*
CONSTANT	.537		.676	

Notes: $^+$significant at .10; *significant at .05; **significant at .01.

category). Crime benefits also factored into manager's decision making. The benefits that mattered most were organizational. If the criminal act was likely to increase revenue, save the firm a large amount of money, improve employee morale, or enhance the firm's reputation (relative to more modest financial gains), offending intentions increased. The perceived legitimacy of law also was an important factor related to corporate offending. When vignettes depicted managers as challenging the application or substance of the law (LAW) by their illegal act, respondents' own criminal behavior increased. This finding suggests that managers calculate the long-term "legal" benefits of one short-term violation. In other words, if breaking the law once can lead to more efficient law (from the standpoint of the manager or his or her company), then the costs of potentially going to court once may be worthwhile.

Finally, relative to an economically healthy industry (the excluded category), offending probabilities increased when foreign competitors successfully move into domestic markets (FOREIGN). This finding is interesting because the more common explanation for corporate crime at the market or industry level is profit squeeze brought about by a deteriorating industry.[9] Yet, as is evident in Table 7.2, the measure of industry economic deterioration (ECDET) had no significant impact on intentions (relative to a "healthy" industry). Apparently, more is going on than pure economic determinism. It is possible that managers rationalized corporate criminal acts because they believe that foreign competitors fail to play by the rules. "If they are not playing fair," managers may reason, "why should we?" Illegal acts that benefit one's firm may level the playing field. Another possible interpretation is that ethnocentric managers were incapable of viewing foreign successes in domestic markets dispassionately. The popularity among business leaders of Sun Tzu's *The Art of War* (written in China more than two thousand years ago) suggests that some executives view commerce as "war." Foreign competitors[10] are "the enemy," and "all warfare is based on deception."

It is noteworthy that indicators of personal benefits for managers (promotion, positive attention by top management, or peer admiration) had no effect on respondent offending intentions. These results do not necessarily rule out the possibility that personal factors may weigh heavily in corporate crime decisions (as additional evidence will reveal). Results may indicate, however, that the personal factors salient to depicted vignette managers were not those that matter to respondents.

Effect Coding of Dimensions

Although analysis of the vignette levels has allowed us to examine how distinct levels within dimensions impact offending decisions relative to one another, we do not know which dimensions had the biggest impact on offending judgments. Using effect coding, however, it is possible to treat each dimension as a single variable in a regression equation. The standardized regression coefficients approximate the amount of variance in the dependent variable accounted for by each dimension.[11]

In Table 7.3, offending intentions were regressed on the effect coded dimensions. The most powerful predictors of offending decisions were the

---

[9] See, e.g., Sally S. Simpson, "The Decomposition of Antitrust: Testing a Multi-Level Longitudinal Model of Profit Squeeze," *American Sociological Review* 51 (1986): 859–875.

[10] Sun Tzu, *The Art of War* (Oxford: Oxford University Press, 1963), p. 66.

[11] We have created a quantitative "scale" for each dimension (e.g., formal control, managerial position, self-regulation) from the unstandardized coefficients of the individual vignette items listed in Table 7.1. The deleted category for each dimension is also included in the scale by coding it as equivalent to the constant; see Peter H. Rossi and Andy B. Anderson, "The Factorial Survey Approach: An Introduction," in Peter H. Rossi and Steven L. Nock (eds.), *Measuring Social Judgments* (Beverly Hills, Calif.: Sage, 1982), pp. 15–67.

Table 7.3. *Study One: Random-Effects Models with Behavioral*
Intentions Regressed on Effect Coded Vignette Dimensions
(Rho = 0.26, R^2 = 0.17)

	b	Beta	T-ratio
Crime type	1.00	.14	3.09**
Firm benefits	1.00	.14	2.97**
Firm pressures	0.98	.12	2.39*
Self-regulation	1.00	.17	4.28***
Manager power	1.00	.17	3.38***
Manager benefits	0.88	.01	0.25
Manager position	0.99	.09	1.80
Manager tenure	1.04	.03	0.66
Formal control	0.99	.15	3.03**
Firm size	0.97	.05	1.08
External pressures on firm	1.00	.02	0.50
CONSTANT	−10.06		

Notes: *significant at .05;   **significant at .01;   ***significant at .001.

dimensions of self-regulation and managerial power (betas = .17). Collectively, then, variables measuring internal compliance and authority structures affected corporate-crime decision making more than any other set of variables.

The dimensions of formal legal sanctions (formal control, beta = .15), firm-level benefits (beta = .14), crime types (beta = .14), and firm pressures (beta = .12) showed similar contributions to the variation in offending decisions. While respondents did not discriminate between criminal, civil, or regulatory interventions, the effect coded data show that offending decisions were influenced by collective measures of formal legal sanctions. We cannot assess from these results whether formal sanctions were taken into account by managers because they were punitive (the deterrence argument) or because they enhanced self-regulation (the enforcement pyramid). What is clear from the effect coded vignette data is that both factors mattered.

Decisions were also affected by assessments of whether the firm was likely to benefit from the decision. This finding is in contrast to the insignificant impact of personal benefit in the equation (manager benefits, beta = .01). As discussed in Chapter 1, corporate crime has been distinguished from other kinds of white-collar offending precisely along this cutting point; corporate offending is conducted to benefit the firm, whereas other organizational white-collar crimes are perpetrated to benefit the individual (e.g., embezzlement).

Because respondents assessed whether illegality would benefit the firm, it should not be surprising that managers also took into account environmental circumstances that can affect a firm's ability to achieve its goals (firm pressures). Finally, offending decisions also depended on the type of crime depicted in the scenario. Preliminary analyses in which offending decisions were regressed on EPA violations, price-fixing, sales fraud, and bribery showed that there was greater opprobrium associated with environmental crimes among the respondents in this sample than with the financial crimes described in the scenarios.[12] Thus, as rational-choice theorists would predict, the perceived costs and benefits of crime appear to vary by crime type.[13]

In sum, the effect coded data more strongly support the "cooperative" strategies of crime control based in effective self-regulation and persuasion, but punitive strategies also find some support in this analysis (although one cannot disentangle the influence of criminal sanctions from other formal sanction threats). In the next section, we combine significant vignette variables with measures of offending costs and benefits from the survey part of the questionnaire (i.e., the questions that follow the vignettes). The survey questions are particularly important for our purposes because respondents were asked to estimate the probability (or certainty) of official discovery (arrest, criminal prosecution, lawsuit, or regulatory investigation) for *themselves* (assuming that they committed the illegal act depicted in the scenario) *and* how much of a problem it would be for them should discovery result in arrest, jail, losing a lawsuit, or a regulatory citation. Formal sanctions were differentiated by type and individual versus corporate target.

It is important to recognize that the survey questions tap something different than do the measures of formal sanction threats rotated within the vignettes. Specifically, the vignette items convey information about what has happened to the firm or other managers in the past. The survey questions ask respondents to speculate about their own sanction risks should they commit the illegal act.

---

[12] Further analysis showed that, with control variables added, the significant differences between crime types disappeared.

[13] R. V. Clarke and D. B. Cornish, "Modeling Offenders' Decisions: A Framework for Policy and Research," in M. Tonry and N. Morris (eds.), *Crime and Justice: An Annual Review of Research*, vol. 6 (Chicago: University of Chicago Press, 1985), p. 163.

The survey questions also solicit probability estimates for informal sanction certainty and severity. For instance, respondents were told to assume that the illegal act depicted in the scenario was *not officially discovered.* They were then asked to estimate the probability that the crime would become known *informally.* Presuming that it did become known informally, they were asked to gauge how likely it would be that attachment, commitment, and stigmatic costs would result. For instance, how likely was it that: (a) they would be dismissed from their job; (b) they would lose the respect of business associates; (c) they would lose the respect of their family; and (d) they would jeopardize any future job prospects? Next, respondents were asked how much of a problem it would be for them if items (a) through (d) actually did occur (sanction severity).

Finally, regarding the potential importance that self-shaming may play in the offending decision, the survey asked respondents whether they would feel any personal guilt if they were to commit the described act (yes/no) and to estimate the degree of shame severity. In addition to measures of personal shame, the survey also inquired about firm-level reputational damage (i.e., how likely it was it that the act would damage the reputation of the firm and would respondents feel badly [yes/no] if this occurred?).

The self-regulation literature leads us to expect that respondent's perceptions of whether the depicted act is morally wrong should affect offending intentions. Moral rules narrow the range of behavioral possibilities because rules define the realm of acceptable conduct.[14] Thus, if our respondents perceive price-fixing, bribery, pollution, and sales fraud as morally wrong, offending intentions should decrease. Moreover, this variable should render formal sanction threats superfluous. That is to say, among respondents who find the acts morally repugnant, the threat of legal sanctions should have little effect on offending propensities.

In Table 7.4, two GLS regression models are reported. In the first equation, we examined how offending intentions were affected by respondent's perceptions of personal benefits, formal sanction threats and costs, act immorality, shame, and potential firm reputational damage should they act as the manager did in the vignette.[15] In the second equation, significant items from the vignette analysis were forwarded along with an aggregate indicator of respondent perceptions of informal sanction costs and

---

[14] Amitai Etzioni, *The Moral Dimension: Toward a New Economics* (New York: Free Press, 1988).

[15] Perceptions of formal sanction threats are calculated by multiplying the perceived certainty of the sanction type (such as criminal processing of the manager) by its perceived severity.

consequences.[16] A cooperative model would predict that informal sanction risk should inhibit offending, but persons who perceive greater personal benefit from the illegal act (measured as career advancement and thrills or excitement) should report higher offending intentions.

Full Models

The results in equation 1 show (Table 7.4) that offending decisions were strongly influenced by normative considerations (e.g., morality, shame) *and* the perception that the crime would either bring tangible career benefits or prove exciting to commit. When respondents thought that the act depicted in the scenario was highly immoral, offending intentions were reduced significantly. Similarly, intentions were significantly reduced among those who believe that they would feel badly (shame) if they committed the illegal act. It is also apparent that decisions were influenced by the potential for negative publicity and how discovery could affect the good name of the company. When respondents believed that engaging in the illegal act might tarnish a firm's reputation, offending propensities decreased.

Criminal sanctions directed toward the manager also had a marginal inhibitory effect on offending, in sharp contrast to the insignificant influence of other legal sanctions. Regulatory and civil interventions appeared totally irrelevant to offending considerations, as did criminal sanctions directed against the company.[17] For this group of managers, shame, morality, and fear of being arrested and maybe going to jail were the most salient crime inhibitors. These results changed, however, when the model was more fully specified.

In the second equation, items from the vignette dimensions that were consistently predictive of offending inclinations were added. (COMFIRM – the act is common in the firm – was included because in other exploratory

---

[16] Like formal sanction threats, this measure is an aggregate indicator of the likelihood and consequence of informal discovery. Respondents were asked to assess how likely the act would be discovered informally; and, given discovery, how likely the respondent would be dismissed, jeopardize future job prospects, or lose the respect of friends, business associates, and family. They are also asked to evaluate how costly each of the outcomes would be for them. Each of these possibilities is included in our measure. Informal sanctions = (discovery × dismissal × dismissal cost) + (discovery × job × job cost) + (discovery × friends × friends cost) + (discovery × associates × associates cost) + (discovery × family × family costs).

[17] The positive signs on the civil sanction coefficients are counterintuitive but not unique to this study. In their study of corporate crime recidivism, Simpson and Koper found that companies subject to civil interventions were significantly *more* likely to reoffend than other firms in the sample. See Sally S. Simpson and Christopher S. Koper, "Deterring Corporate Crime," *Criminology* 30 (1992): 360.

Table 7.4. *Study One: Random-Effects Regression Model of Offending Intentions on Formal Sanction Threats, Shame, and Morality*

	b	(t)
Equation 1 (Rho = 0.16, R^2 = 0.34)		
Criminal Sanction against Individual (CRIMINAL)	−.007	−1.85[+]
Criminal Sanction against Firm (CRIMFRM)	−.004	−.68
Civil Sanction against Individual (CIVIL)	.003	.66
Civil Sanction against Firm (CIVILFRM)	.009	1.43
Regulatory Sanction against Firm (REGFIRM)	−.004	−.70
How Morally Wrong Is Offense (MORAL)	−.216	−3.98***
Sense of Shame (SHAME)	−1.229	−3.49***
Tarnish Reputation of Firm (FIRMREP)	−.142	−2.09*
Guilt If Tarnished Firm Reputation (FIRMREPSS)	−.131	−.40
Career Advancement plus Thrill (BENEFIT)	.128	4.39***
CONSTANT	5.470	
Equation 2[a] (Rho = 0.24, R^2 = 0.40)		
How Morally Wrong Is Offense (MORAL)	−.209	−3.91***
Sense of Shame (SHAME)	−1.056	−3.04**
Career Advancement plus Thrill (BENEFIT)	.122	4.21***
Industry Losing Ground to Foreign Competitors (FOREIGN)	.499	2.04*
Change Status of Law (LAW)	.971	2.17*
Ordered (ORDERED)	.516	2.32*
Employee Hotline (HOTLINE)	−.543	−1.84[+]
Employee Recently Fired (EMFIRED)	−.796	−2.73**
Save Firm Large Amount of Money (SAVELG)	.716	1.89[+]
Increase Positive Reputation of Firm (POSREP)	.687	1.62[+]
CONSTANT	4.138	

Notes: [+]significant at .10;   *significant at .05;   **significant at .01;   ***significant at .001.
[a]Vignette items and informal controls added to equation 1.

analyses, it significantly increased offending proclivities.) Also included were the measures of informal sanction threats and personal benefit described earlier. Parsimonious models are reported in the table (only variables that reached a .10 level of significance).

Results from this second analysis reinforced the power of shame and morality to inhibit corporate crime. When acts were perceived as highly immoral or apt to produce personal shame if committed, offending intentions declined. Unexpectedly, in this analysis, costly informal sanctions (such as losing one's job and the respect of friends, family, and business associates) *did not* significantly influence offending levels.[18] Similarly, the measure of firm reputation (FIRMREP) that inhibited offending intentions in the first equation lost significance in the second. Suspecting that the two variables (i.e., informal sanctions and firm reputation) were highly collinear (negative publicity is, after all, a kind of informal sanction), the correlation coefficient between the two variables was examined. Not surprisingly, the two were highly correlated ($r = .621$; $p = .01$) In a supplemental analysis (not reported here), the same equation was run excluding firm reputation. Informal sanction threats demonstrated significant inhibitory effects over managerial offending proclivities in the new analysis ($p = .06$). The two variables are probably measuring similar processes, rendering their individual effects insignificant when both are analyzed within the same equation.

While most of the vignette items retained from Table 7.2 continued to show strong effects on offending decisions, several did not. For instance, COMFIRM, REVENUE, and MORALE failed to reach significance in the full model, although the directional effects were the same (positive). Similarly, the measure of employee acquittal lost its predictive power. Knowing that a manager was acquitted for a similar act had little influence on offending decisions once we controlled for respondents' perceptions of *their own chances* of discovery and the possible negative consequences that were associated with it.

For many people, the thought of going through a criminal investigation – even if it does result in acquittal – was enough of a painful undertaking to inhibit offending. One executive vice-president whom I interviewed for an earlier study mentioned the trauma he had experienced when required to testify before the grand jury. Even though he was not personally a suspect and the case did not move forward, testifying was such an emotionally painful process that "he never wanted to go through that again."[19]

The results in equation 2 also showed a lessened effect for formal legal sanctions. Once informal sanction threats, moral beliefs, shame, *and* the personal benefits that may be gained from the illicit act were controlled in the

---

[18] A similar finding was reported by Grasmick and Bursik, who discovered that a variable measuring a concept similar to our measure of informal sanction threats (e.g., losing the respect of significant others) failed to affect offending intentions when shame (feeling guilty) and legal sanctions were included in their analysis. See Harold G. Grasmick and Robert J. Bursik Jr., "Conscience, Significant Others, and Rational Choice: Extending the Deterrence Model," *Law and Society Review* 24 (1990): 837–861.

[19] Sally S. Simpson, "Corporate-Crime Deterrence and Corporate-Control Policies," in K. Schlegel and D. Weisburd (eds.), *White-Collar Crime Reconsidered* (Boston: Northeastern University Press, 1992), pp. 289–398.

analysis, criminal sanctions directed toward the individual (CRIMINAL) were rendered insignificant. None of the other formal sanction threats (whether directed toward the firm or emanating from other legal systems) shifted offending intentions downward (or upward, for that matter). Note, however, that when respondents perceived that they personally may benefit from the crime (either sensually – because the act is exciting – or career-enhancing), there was a significant increase in offending proclivity.

These findings suggest that the corporate offending decision emerges from a complex set of considerations, mostly personal (i.e., how will I feel, what do I believe, how might I benefit?); yet, the firm also figures into the process. Managers consider, for instance, the kinds of controls that are in place to guard against employee misconduct. Firms with serious programs (e.g., more than mere codes of conduct) that can uncover and punish miscreants appear to enhance self-regulation. There is also a clear deference to organizational command structures among these managers. When ordered to violate the law by their supervisor, they tend to do what they are told. Finally, managers' decisions demonstrate a sensitivity to their organization's circumstances. On the one hand, they do not want to subject the firm to negative publicity and thus are inhibited from misconduct; but, on the other, when they can challenge a law they perceive to be ridiculous or foreign competitors in the marketplace, illegal acts become more tempting, especially if they save the company a significant amount of money.

Thus far, we have tried to untangle the degree to which formal legal sanctions inhibit offending; whether the individual manager or firm offers a more salient sanction target; how morality, shame, and informal sanction threats affect offending decisions; and whether self-regulatory programs (and which programs) lessen offending intentions. The evidence more generally supports a cooperative strategy over one that is based in a deterrence framework. Yet the data do not allow us to completely reject deterrence models, especially those that target responsible managers. If both cooperation (through self-regulation, shaming, and informal controls) and punishment inhibit offending, we are brought back to Braithwaite's original question: "when to punish, when to persuade?"[20]

Braithwaite himself, in recent work with Toni Makkai, investigated whether certain kinds of managers were more sensitive to sanction threats than others.[21] Examining compliance among Australian nursing-home

---

[20] Ian Ayres and John Braithwaite, *Responsive Regulation: Transcending the Deregulation Debate* (New York: Oxford University Press, 1992), p. 21.

[21] Toni Makkai and John Braithwaite, "The Dialectics of Corporate Deterrence," *Journal of Research in Crime and Delinquency* 31 (1994): 347–373.

executives, Makkai and Braithwaite investigated whether a fully specified deterrence model (including multiple sanction sources and types) operated similarly across different emotionality levels. They speculated (and demonstrated) that compliance was improved by the threat of formal legal sanctions for executives who tested low on emotionality. The deterrence model worked just the opposite, however, for managers who scored high on emotionality. Compliance declined among these managers. Makkai and Braithwaite investigated whether a fully specified deterrence model (including multiple sanction sources and types) operated similarly across different emotionality levels. They speculated (and demonstrated) that compliance was improved by the threat of formal legal sanctions for executives who tested low on emotionality. The deterrence model worked just the opposite, however, for managers who scored high on emotionality. Compliance declined among these managers. Makkai and Braithwaite speculate that "the uncovering of the emotionality interaction suggests that lying behind a failure to find a deterrence effect are individual cases where sanctions work, other individual cases where they are irrelevant, and still others where they are counterproductive."[22]

Interaction Models

Although the factorial data did not measure emotionality, formal sanctions should be irrelevant for persons who believe that illegal acts are highly objectionable on moral grounds. With this in mind, the sample was divided into two groups – respondents who perceived the vignette acts to be highly immoral (equation 1 in Table 7.4) versus those who perceived the acts to be only modestly so (equation 2 in Table 7.4).[23] We then compared the regression coefficients between groups to assess whether there were significant differences in how the independent variables affected offending proclivities. Only variables that differed significantly across equations are reported in Table 7.5.

Generally persons who ranked high on perceptions of act immorality tended not to be as swayed by the costs and benefits of the illegal act as those for whom the acts were less morally offensive. Etzioni suggests that for this group, morality delimits the range of acceptable conduct. Right and wrong have been internalized and, "once internalization has taken

---

[22] Ibid., p. 362.

[23] The division point between the groups is the mean value on the measure of act immorality. Those falling at or below the mean (7) are classified as low morality, whereas those above the mean are classified as high morality.

Table 7.5. *Study One: Random-Effects Regression Model of Offending Intentions on High- and Low-Morality Respondents*

	High Morality (N = 188) (Rho = 0.19, R^2 = 0.36)		Low Morality (N = 127) (Rho = 0.29, R^2 = 0.37)	
	b	(t)	b	(t)
Criminal Sanction against Individual (CRIMINAL)	.002	0.60	−.010	−1.14*
Criminal Sanction against Firm (CRIMFRM)	−.009	−1.43	−.005	−0.37*
Civil Sanction against Individual (CIVIL)	−.005	−1.25	.013	1.45*
Civil Sanction against Firm (CIVILFRM)	.022	3.37	−.010	−0.77*
Regulatory Sanction against Firm (REGFIRM)	−.009	−1.60	.012	1.15*
How Morally Wrong Is Offense (MORAL)	−.820	−4.92	.069	0.58*
Informal Control (INFORMAL)	.000	0.27	−.000	−0.63*
CONSTANT	8.005		2.690	

* Difference in the slope coefficient between "high" and "low" morality is statistically significant.

place, individuals pursue what they consider to be a moral line of behavior even in the absence of external sanctions."[24] Braithwaite would refer to these managers as "good citizens" – persons who generally act in a prosocial manner; managers who want to do right and who are amenable to persuasion.

If we focus just on those who were classified low on morality, it appears that a rational calculus was at work. For these managers, offending decisions were predicted by whether they personally would benefit; whether an employee had been fired for or acquitted of a similar act; whether there was an opportunity to challenge an unfair law (defiance); and whether their conscience would bother them if they violated the law – even if they weren't officially "caught." Slope comparisons of these variables between low and high moral groupings did not differ significantly and thus it would be a stretch to call these managers "bad citizens." It does seem clear, however,

[24] Etzioni, *The Moral Dimension*, p. 46.

that when moral restraints failed to set behavioral boundaries, other factors drove decision processes. Variables that did discriminate between groups included the inhibitory effects of informal and formal sanctions threats. Managers who were more morally flexible considered the likelihood that they would be subject to criminal sanctions or that the firm would be sued. (The latter was perhaps an acknowledgment of the financial reach of punitive damages.)

It would be premature to conclude, however, that respondents who were highly moral were completely unaffected by personal benefits or cost considerations. Like their less moral counterparts, offending levels for this group significantly increased when respondents believed that they might personally benefit from the crime (BENEFIT). Results also provided some evidence that persons with high moral restraint were more apt than those with low moral restraint to preclude offending under certain formal sanction threats. Specifically, when regulatory and criminal sanctions threatened the firm or when civil sanctions were directed toward the respondent, offending propensities decreased. Finally, acting illegally might be more easy to justify among the morally committed when there was a symbolic threat (e.g., foreign competitors). It is worth noting that, after sorting respondents by their perceptions of act immorality, this variable (MORAL) *still* exerted a negative effect on criminality for those in the high morality grouping – a difference between groups that was statistically significant.

Additional analysis (not reported here) that included demographic controls and where high and low moral restraint groups were differentiated from one another using the median (8) instead of the mean (7)[25] were even more strongly supportive of the idea that criminalization of corporate illegal acts was superfluous for the morally committed. The fact that punitive models appear to work better for some people than for others supports the "benign big gun" enforcement strategy advocated by Ayres and Braithwaite,[26] a point that will be elaborated further in Chapter 8.

In the next section, data from a second vignette study that was administered to executives from a Fortune 500 corporation along with a new cohort of MBA and executive education students from one of the original research sites are used to confirm results from the earlier study. The revision process resulted in an instrument similar but not identical to the original vignette survey.

[25] For analyses that distinguish high- and low-morality groups along the median instead of the mean, see Paternoster and Simpson, "Testing a Rational Choice Model," pp. 575–577.
[26] Ayres and Braithwaite, *Responsive Regulation.*

Study Two

Instrument Revision

Because some of the scenarios from the original survey were characterized by respondents as "unrealistic" and confusing, a twofold strategy was pursued to revise the research instrument. First, focus groups were convened to discuss the old survey (drawing again from the MBA student population). Second, a careful review of the instrument eliminated questions that were redundant or theoretically irrelevant (and unrelated empirically to the dependent variable).

The focus groups identified problematic scenario combinations (i.e., those that were unlikely or potentially confusing) while providing feedback about the survey questions that followed the vignettes. Based on recommendations by these groups, one offense type (the sales fraud scenario) was dropped from the vignette design. A concern with survey length also led to the elimination of some vignette dimensions and survey questions. For instance, we dropped formal sanction threats from the vignettes because these items seemed redundant with follow-up questions that tapped respondent perceptions of formal sanction threats. We also eliminated some questions that differentiated among sanction outcomes (being arrested versus going to jail, being sued versus losing a lawsuit, etc.) Because the deterrence literature tends to estimate arrest probabilities and not jail prospects,[27] we retained the former (or its civil and regulatory equivalents) and discarded the latter. Finally, recognizing that ethical reasoning was poorly measured in the first study (e.g., a single item indicator of act immorality), we drew upon the business ethics literature to identify better measures, now using a multidimensional ethics scale.[28]

Vignette dimensions and levels that did not affect offending decisions in the first survey were carefully reviewed to determine whether the dimension itself was problematic or whether the levels within the category were poorly worded or not clearly differentiated. In some cases, both the dimension and levels were well conceptualized and carefully measured (e.g., managerial location, managerial tenure, and firm size), yet failed to affect offending

---

[27] Raymond Paternoster, "The Deterrent Effect of the Perceived Certainty and Severity of Punishment: A Review of the Evidence and Issues," *Justice Quarterly* 4 (1987): 173–217.

[28] The multidimensional ethics scale is drawn from R. E. Reidenback and D. P. Robin, "Toward the Development of a Multidimensional Scale for Improving Evaluations of Business Ethics," *Journal of Business Ethics* 9 (1990): 639–653. This scale has been used successfully to evaluate the perceived ethics of an action depicted in scenarios and to "explain" behavioral intentions. See N. C. Smith and E. Cooper-Martin, "Ethics and Target Marketing: The Role of Product Harm and Consumer Vulnerability," *Journal of Marketing* 61 (1997): 1–20.

intentions. These dimensions were dropped from the new vignettes. In place of firm size, a dimension was added that measured organizational diversification. In other cases, a vignette item was not a clear measure of the underlying concept. Law, for instance, did not capture a defiance effect (as conceptualized by Sherman, 1993) as much as it measured the opportunity to challenge the application of a law. Therefore, in the second survey this item is measured somewhat differently (e.g., the depicted manager believes that the law governing this illegal act is unreasonable). We also felt that some of the economic benefits of the illegal acts were act-specific – that is, it is unlikely that violating EPA standards will improve firm revenues. However, it is apt to save on firm costs. Similarly, acts of bribery or price-fixing are more apt to improve company revenues and not save money. Therefore, these items are rotated in the vignettes as they relate to specific illegal acts. EPA scenarios include indicators of cost savings while bribery and price-fixing scenarios rotate measures of revenue enhancement.

Some dimensions in the first survey blended levels that were conceptually distinct. For instance, pecuniary and nonpecuniary benefits of noncompliance were combined under firm benefits. In the new instrument, these are treated as separate benefits. The old measure of self-regulation was broken into three distinct dimensions: cultural support for crime at the firm and industry level, self-regulation program structure, and self-regulation program operation.

From these revisions, three vignettes were created. Samples are given here for comparison purposes.

Price-Fixing. Lee, a manager at Steelcorp, considers whether to order an employee to meet with competitors to discuss product pricing for the next year. Such an act is common within the firm. Steelcorp is currently experiencing growing sales and revenues in an industry that is economically healthy. If successful, the act may result in a positive impression of Lee by top management. Lee also believes that the act will modestly increase firm revenues. The firm has internally implemented audits and inspections at random intervals, but no action was taken against an employee who was discovered by the firm engaging in a similar act. Lee decides to order an employee to meet with competitors to discuss product pricing for the next year.

Violation of Environmental Standards. Lee, a manager at Steelcorp, is ordered by a supervisor to release into the air emissions that fail to meet EPA standards. Lee thinks that the law governing this act is unreasonably applied to companies like Steelcorp. Steelcorp is currently experiencing declining sales and revenues in an industry that is economically healthy. If successful, the act may result in a promotion and salary bonus for Lee. Lee also believes that the act will save the company a large amount of money. The firm has a code of ethics, and an employee was recently fired by the firm for engaging in a similar act. Lee decides to release into the air emissions that fail to meet EPA standards.

Bribery. Lee, a manager at Steelcorp, considers whether to order an employee to offer a payoff to a purchasing agent who has requested a cash payment in exchange for future purchasing agreements. Lee thinks that the law governing this act is unreasonably applied to companies like Steelcorp. Steelcorp is currently experiencing declining sales and revenues in an industry that is losing ground to foreign competitors. If successful, the act may result in a promotion and salary bonus for Lee. Lee also believes that the act will modestly increase firm revenues. The firm has internally implemented audits and inspections at random intervals, and an employee was recently fired by the firm for engaging in a similar act. Lee decides to order an employee to offer the payoff to the customer.

A final difference between the old and new survey was the demographic information sought. Because the new survey targeted managers in their work setting along with MBA students, it was now important to learn about respondent's employment history, knowledge and experience of unethical conduct within and outside of the company, comprehension of their firm's compliance program, along with the demographic information (sex, age, race, nationality, and so forth) asked in the first survey. The research instrument for the second study, along with the breakdown of response categories, is attached as Appendix C.

Results discussed here are drawn from responses to 78 surveys (78 × 3 = 234 observations). Of the 78 respondents (out of approximately 200 distributed), 30 are middle- or upper-level executives working within a Fortune 500 company.[29] A breakdown of the sample (see Appendix D) shows that respondents are mostly male (66 percent), in their mid-thirties (average age is thirty-five), white (92 percent), and of U.S. nationality (85 percent). They are, on average, well educated (the majority hold some

[29] Toolcorp is a Fortune 500 manufacturing company involved primarily in the manufacture of tools and accessories, small appliances, and securities hardware. Within its primary markets, the firm is a top competitor and global player.

type of graduate degree or have one year of graduate studies (68 percent), married (almost 60 percent), and have twelve years of business experience.

Generally, and not unexpectedly considering the inclusion of more working managers, the second set of respondents has been working longer than the first group (twelve years compared with five in the earlier study). The sample is older (by seven years, on average), with fewer females and minorities represented.

The survey was administered to MBA and executive education students in a manner similar to the first survey. At the company site, top management (and the legal office) agreed to let us administer the instrument, but cooperation from subunits was elicited primarily from managers within finance and finance-related areas (e.g., audits).

Results

As before, the analysis focused on offending propensities as the key *dependent* variable of interest. About half of these respondents indicated some likelihood of offending; however, the mean is relatively low (1.6). This suggests that most respondents were fairly cautious in their offending propensities (a 10–20 percent chance of offending). However, about 30 percent of respondents reported a 30–90 percent chance of offending. Thus, there was enough variation in the dependent variable to warrant GLS analysis. Because each respondent read and responded to three vignettes, it was again necessary to control for correlated error terms using random effects models.

In Table 7.6, the mean values for respondent perceptions of formal sanction probabilities and consequences, broken down by individual and corporate targets, are presented. Like the first set of respondents, these managers believed that companies are more apt to feel the sting of formal legal sanctions than are individual managers, and these differences are statistically significant for all types of interventions.

The data also show that respondents attached greater costs to sanctions directed against them than those against the company and there were significant differences in perceptions of consequences by sanction target. Recall in the earlier sample, respondents believed that sanctions were more likely to be directed at firms but would be more consequential for individuals. In the second study, this was also true. Overall, managers felt that criminal sanctions were the least probable for companies and only slightly more likely than civil sanctions for individual managers (3.88 versus 3.56 mean values, respectively). Regulatory interventions, while thought to be most likely for firms and individuals, were believed to carry the least consequence.

Table 7.6. *Study Two: Perceived Sanction Certainty and Severity by Source and Target (mean perceived risk and consequence)*

	Target	
Source	Individual	Company
Certainty		
Criminal	3.88	4.65**
Civil	3.56	5.05***
Regulatory	4.58	5.59***
Severity		
Criminal	9.48	8.42***
Civil	9.35	8.26***
Regulatory	NA	7.85

Notes: Mean differences (two-tailed test): **significant at .01; ***significant at .001.

Results from both studies support the contention that offending managers may feel protected from the long arm of the law (especially criminal law) by a largely impenetrable corporate facade. Equally obvious is that managers do fear the negative consequences that are associated with formal legal sanctions. It is not possible from this comparison to disentangle whether managers fear the damage done to reputations, the costly financial burdens associated with a lawsuit or criminal fines, or the possibility of going to jail. Moreover, we do not know if these perceived costs actually inhibited illegal conduct among this sample of respondents. However, we can and do explore these questions in the following analyses.

Vignette Analysis

In Table 7.7, a random-effects model is reported for the regression of offending intentions on the vignette items. As in the first survey, we dropped cases in which vignettes were perceived to be unrealistic or values were missing on the dependent variable.[30] Because of changes in the vignette dimensions and levels, results are not directly comparable with those in Table 7.2. With this caveat in mind, it is notable that some variables across the two samples

---

[30] Instrument revision appears to have been successful given that only 5 percent of vignettes are perceived as unrealistic compared with 14 percent in the first survey.

Table 7.7. *Study Two: Random-Effects Regression Model of Offending Intentions on Vignette Items (Rho = 0.53, $R^2 = 0.14$)*

	b	(t)
Diversification		
Diversified Company (DIVERSE)	.057	.24
Firm Pressures		
Declining Sales (DECSALES)	−.543	−2.19*
Self-Regulation (Structure)		
Mandatory Ethics Training (ETHICS)	.073	.21
Hotline (HOTLINE)	.023	.07
Ethics Audits (AUDITS)	.115	.33
Self-Regulation (Operation)		
Employee Severely Reprimanded (REPRIMND)	−.771	−2.57**
Employee Recently Fired (EMFIRED)	−.651	−2.19*
Manager Power		
Ordered by Supervisor (ORDERED)	.643	2.58**
Firm Benefits (Pecuniary)		
Save Firm Large Amount of Money (SAVELG)	−1.054	−3.19***
Greatly Increase Revenues (GREVENUE)	.661	2.41*
Firm Benefits (Nonpecuniary)		
Law Is Unreasonable (LAW)	.186	.79
Manager Benefits		
May Result in Promotion (PROMOTE)	−.302	−.97
Positive Impression by Management (MANAGE)	−.116	−.39
Environment Constraints		
Industry Economically Deteriorating (ECDET)	−.154	−.56
Losing Ground to Foreign Competitors (FOREIGN)	−.537	−1.77+
Corporate Culture		
Act Is Common within Firm (COMFIRM)	.486	1.59
Act Is Common within Industry (INDUSTRY)	.165	.53
CONSTANT	2.049	

Notes: +significant at .10;   *significant at .05;   **significant at .01;   ***significant at .001.

had similar effects on offending intentions. For instance, when respondents learned that a manager had been severely reprimanded or fired for his or her illegal conduct (in contrast to no action taken against a criminal employee – the excluded category), offending propensities decreased significantly. Also like the earlier study, offending was significantly more likely if a manager was ordered by a supervisor to commit the crime or if firm revenue was enhanced by the illegal act.

On the other hand, several findings were unexpected and/or contrary to prediction. In direct contrast to findings from the earlier study, the structure of self-regulation did not appear to affect offending decisions. Relative to ethics codes (excluded), additional layers of regulation (e.g., mandatory training, anonymous hotlines, and random audits) did not offer increased protection against corporate offending. Moreover, offending propensities *increased* when the firm was growing and if the act saved the company a small amount of money (relative to larger cost savings). Also unexpected was the lack of a defiance effect (law is unreasonable). Lastly, rather than being criminogenic when the depicted firm was "losing ground to foreign competitors," this condition appeared to slightly depress criminality, although not significantly so.

Similar to the first study, offending was unrelated to the manipulation of a variety of managerial benefits. Information about firm diversification also had no effect on offending propensities. When the act was a common practice in the company or industry, the effect on crime was positive (as predicted) but insignificant.

The common results across studies regarding the role of managerial power, firm benefits, and self-regulation (operation, not structure) in promoting or inhibiting corporate misconduct suggest that corporate illegality is attractive because the company gains from it. Crime flourishes because of the structure of decision making in organizations (e.g., from the top down). When given an order to break the law, these managers did so. However, results also indicate the crime control promise of self-regulation. A comprehensive compliance system that is serious about policing and punishing miscreants enhances crime prevention.

Effect Coding

In Table 7.8, offending judgments were regressed on effect-coded vignette dimensions in order to assess the relative importance of each dimension on criminal decision making. Some dimensions (e.g., manager benefits) might collectively have an important relationship with the dependent variable even though the specific items may not differ significantly from one another (e.g., promotion, peer admiration, positive attention from top management).

Six dimensions were significantly related to variation in the dependent variable. The most powerful dimension was crime types (beta $= .23$, $p < .001$). Clearly, managers differentiate between offending or not

Table 7.8. *Study Two: Random-Effects Models with Behavioral Intentions Regressed on Effect-Coded Vignette Dimensions* $(Rho = 0.53, R^2 = 0.19)$

	b	Beta	T-ratio
Crime type	1.00	.23	4.97***
Firm benefits (pecuniary)	1.00	.22	4.67***
Firm benefits (nonpecuniary)	0.83	.00	0.07
Firm pressures	1.00	.12	2.29*
Self-regulation (operation)	1.00	.16	3.17**
Self-regulation (structure)	1.02	.05	0.87
Manager power	1.01	.15	2.82**
Manager benefits	1.00	.08	1.40
Diversification	1.07	.01	0.15
Environment constraints	1.01	.12	2.28*
Corporate culture	1.00	.08	1.61
CONSTANT	−20.14		

Notes: *significant at .05;   **significant at .01;   ***significant at .001.

depending on the type of crime under consideration. Almost as important as crime type was the economic benefits that the firm would reap as a consequence of the illegal act (beta = .22, p < .001). This was in contrast to managerial benefits and noneconomic benefits that might accrue to the firm from the illegal act (nonpecuniary) which have no relationship with the dependent variable. The operation of the self-regulatory process and manager power (being ordered to commit the act) had similar collective effects (betas = .16 and .15, p < .01) followed by firm pressures and environmental restraints on the company (betas = .12, p < .05). It is important to remember, however, that the directional effects of some of the specific variables that make up these dimensions were not in the predicted direction. Hence, it is difficult to interpret why firm pressure and environmental restraints had the predictive power that they did.

Full Models

Next, we explored whether shame, informal sanction threats, and ethical reasoning inhibited offending in addition to the restraint derived from legal interventions and controlling for the personal benefits that may accompany the criminal act. The random-effects models depicted in Table 7.9 show results for two regressions. In the first model, offending intentions were regressed on formal sanction threats, shame, personal benefit, and a

Table 7.9. *Study Two: Random-Effects Regression Model of Offending Intentions on Formal Sanction Threats, Shame, and Morality*

	b	(t)
Equation 1 (Rho = 0.50, R^2 = 0.55)		
Criminal Sanction against Individual (CRIMINAL)	.001	.21
Civil Sanction against Individual (CIVIL)	−.004	−.65
Criminal Sanction against Firm (CRIMFRM)	.001	.20
Civil Sanction against Firm (CIVILFRM)	.015	1.75[+]
Regulatory Sanction against Firm (REGFIRM)	−.009	−1.47
Moral Equity Factor Score (MES1 FS)	−.641	−4.98[***]
Relativistic Factor Score (MES2 FS)	−.445	−4.00[***]
Contractualism Factor Score (MES3 FSR)	−.281	−2.39[*]
Sense of Shame (SHAME)	−.393	−1.02
Feeling Shame (SHAMESEV)	−.118	−1.89[+]
Tarnish Reputation of Firm (FIRMREP)	−.081	−1.49
Guilt If Tarnished Firm Reputation (FIRMREPS)	.245	.56
Informal Sanction Scale (ISS)	−.000	−1.66[+]
Career Advancement plus Thrill (BENEFIT)	.177	5.34[***]
CONSTANT	2.663	
Equation 2 (Rho = 0.53, R^2 = 0.57)		
Civil Sanction against Firm (CIVILFRM)	.015	1.76[+]
Moral Equity Factor Score (MES1 FS)	−.631	−4.95[***]
Relativistic Factor Score (MES2 FS)	−.404	−3.53[***]
Contractualism Factor Score (MES3 FSR)	−.322	−2.74[**]
Sense of Shame (SHAME)	−.668	−1.70[+]
Informal Sanction Scale (ISS)	−.000	−1.76[+]
Career Advancement plus Thrill (BENEFIT)	.156	4.68[***]
Employee Severely Reprimanded (REPRIMND)	−.591	−2.71[**]
Employee Recently Fired (EMFIRED)	−.366	−1.65[+]
Ordered by Supervisor (ORDERED)	.323	1.77[+]
Declining Sales (DECSALES)	−.317	−1.72[+]
CONSTANT	2.769	

Notes: [+]significant at .10;   [*]significant at .05;   [**]significant at .01;   [***]significant at .001.
[a]Significant variables from Table 2 added to equation 1, only variables significant at .10 are reported.

multi-dimensional ethics scale.[31] In the second model, significant vignette items and a measure of informal sanction threats were added to model 1.

---

[31] Respondents are asked to evaluate the illegal act by placing an X along a six-point scale that measures nine elements of ethical reasoning. The nine items are factor-loaded with the expectation that three unique dimensions will be identified. As expected, our items

Again, for brevity's sake only variables significant at a .10 level are reported in the second equation.

Equation I. Generally, these results show the pushes away from crime due to the power of ethical reasoning and informal controls along with the pulls toward offending based on the benefits it may bring. By far, the strongest predictor of offending intentions was our measure of personal benefit – a measure of excitement coupled with career advancement. Next, the various dimensions of ethical reasoning (MES1–MES3) exhibited strong inhibitory effects. When respondents perceived acts to be culturally or traditionally unacceptable, unfair or immoral, or in violation of an informal contract or promise, offending intentions declined. Shame also had a negative effect on offending primarily at the individual level. When respondents thought that feeling guilty (SHAMESEV) would be consequential for them, they were somewhat less likely to consider acting illegally (p < .10). Believing that the illegal act may tarnish the reputation of the firm (FIRMREP), along with an increased sense of personal shame (SHAME) for committing the crime, affected offending propensities in the predicted direction (i.e., negative), but both failed to reach significance.

None of the legal interventions brought a credible deterrent threat and the only one close to having a significant effect (civil sanction likelihood for the firm) had effects inconsistent with a deterrence argument (positive).

Equation 2. These results remained, even after demographic and other controls were added to the analysis (sex, age, years of business experience, and personal experience with illegal conduct),[32] but changed slightly when significant items from the earlier vignette analysis were included (see equation 2). As shown in Table 7.9, with the addition of vignette items, ethical reasoning still had a significant impact on offending decisions as did personal benefit. Now, however, those who admitted that they would feel guilty (SHAME) if they committed the illegal act were less apt to offend. The threat of informal sanctions (e.g., knowledge of crime and reaction to it by family, friends, and business associates) was also modestly associated with crime inhibition. Only two vignette items retained significance in the full model; the threat of an internal reprimand and declining sales both decreased

loaded on three separate factors: (1) act unacceptable traditionally or culturally; (2) degree of fairness and moral rightness of the act; and (3) act in violation of an unspoken promise or unwritten contract.

[32] Because none of the demographic items reach significance, these results are not reported. Runs are available on request.

offending intentions. Again, none of the formal legal sanctions deterred offending decisions, but offending chances increased significantly if the act was thought to be exciting or beneficial to one's career (BENEFIT).

Once again, the full regression model offers fairly strong support for some of the key elements of a cooperative corporate crime control strategy. The factors that are most strongly predictive of crime inhibition are not those found in a policy of criminalization (or, indeed, reliance on legal interventions generally), but rather those that build on the ethical foundations of managers and offer gentle punishments (reprimands) in contrast to more severe and stigmatizing ones (e.g., being fired or arrested). On the other hand, the strong impact of personal benefit in both equations raises the question of whether certain kinds of managers will be more susceptible to persuasion while others may be more amenable to punishment.

The final analyses explore this issue by dividing the sample into high- and low-morality groups. Divisions were made using one of the ethics measures that asked respondents to rank illegal acts along a continuum from not immoral at all to very immoral (0 through 6). (This measure was similar to the one used to divide the sample in the first study.) Mean scores were calculated for this measure, and persons falling above the mean were classified as highly moral while those falling at the mean or below were grouped as low.

Interaction Models

Results in Table 7.10 (only variables with significant slope differences across groups are reported) reaffirm many of those from the earlier study. While it is clear that both high- and low-morality respondents did not differ from one another regarding the inhibitory role of ethical reasoning in crime judgments or the attraction to crime for the personal benefits it brought (Career Advancement + Thrill), those who ranked lower in morality appeared to be much more concerned with costs to conscience, formal legal sanctions directed toward them (criminal and civil), and regulatory sanctions directed toward the firm. They were also more sensitive to the threat of job loss (EMFIRED).

According to the t-value for coefficients in each equation (and not the slope comparisons across groups), persons who tended to view the corporate acts in question as highly immoral were swayed by the threat of informal sanctions and seemed apt to experience a defiance effect (both of these results contradict findings from the earlier study). However, recall that defiance is measured somewhat differently across the two studies. In the second study,

Table 7.10. *Study Two: Random-Effects Regression Model of Offending Intentions on High- and Low-Morality Respondents, including Vignette Items Only*

	High Morality (N = 111) (Rho = 0.05, R^2 = 0.43)		Low Morality (N = 96) (Rho = 0.61, R^2 = 0.64)	
	b	(t)	b	(t)
Criminal Sanction against Individual (CRIMINAL)	.009	1.05	−.007	−.67*
Civil Sanction against Individual (CIVIL)	.004	.48	−.008	−.65*
Regulatory Sanction against Firm (REGFIRM)	−.012	−1.49	−.020	−1.58*
Feeling Shame (SHAMESEV)	.111	1.04	−.210	−2.35*
Tarnish Reputation of Firm (FIRMREP)	.024	.35	−.187	−1.82*
Informal Sanction Scale (ISS)	−.000	−2.46	.000	.42*
Employee Recently Fired (EMFIRED)	.205	.64	−.291	−.78*
Losing Ground to Foreign Competitors (FOREIGN)	−.479	−1.73	.201	.58*
Act Is Common within Firm (COMFIRM)	.040	.12	−.026	−.08*
Declining Sales (DECSALES)	.263	.95	−.966	−2.80*
CONSTANT	−.843		3.240	

Notes: *Difference in the slope coefficient between "high" and "low" morality is statistically significant.

LAW measures the perceived unfairness of the law as opposed to capturing an opportunity to challenge its application (study 1). Thus, subtle differences in measurement may account for the different findings, at least for this variable. Moreover, slope comparisons between high- and low-morality groups do not reveal significant differences in how LAW affects offending propensities, so this finding should be viewed as provisional at best. (A similar point can be made regarding the role of organizational authority in criminal decision making. The high-morality group seems somewhat more susceptible to supervisor's orders to commit crime than the low-morality group, but the difference is not significant.)

Apart from the specific variable differences, comparisons between the high- and low-morality groups in the second study are noteworthy for three features:

1. Both groups use ethical reasoning to inform offending decisions.
2. Both groups are attracted to crime for the personal benefits that it may bring (specifically, career advancement or "sneaky" thrills).
3. Generally, the chance that illegality may be officially discovered and sanctioned is more salient to persons low on morality than those ranked higher whereas the threat and consequence associated with informal discovery matters more to persons who perceive the acts as highly immoral.

Conclusions

Because corporate control strategies generally have not been subjected to much empirical evaluation, these vignette studies provide a useful tool to explore how corporate managers (current or anticipatory) are apt to respond to deterrence and compliance strategies. Generally, results challenge a strict deterrence model. Overall, managers tend not to adjust behaviors based on formal legal threats – even though they fear these threats and believe them to be consequential (to themselves and to their respective companies). Of greater significance and more important as far as prospective behavior is concerned are threats to significant relationships, feelings of guilt and responsibility for tarnishing the good name of their firm, and a system of internal compliance that is multifaceted and proactive.

It is also fairly clear that crime inhibition is related as well to manager's perceptions of corporate crimes on a moral or ethical dimension. To the extent that crimes are thought to violate an ethical contract, managers are unlikely to succumb to a corporate crime opportunity. Yet, even in the context of moral inhibition, some environmental, contextual, or personal factors enhance the attractiveness or perceived benefit of corporate offending. The most consistent finding along these lines is that corporate offending is attractive sensually to potential offenders. Although our study does not allow us to untangle what makes the acts exciting or thrilling (e.g., breaking the rules, the challenge of it, a sense of power over regulators or competitors), what is clear is that there are emotional rewards that act as powerful incentives for managers. This attraction exists regardless of whether managers perceive acts to be immoral or unethical. In addition, managers who believe that their chances for success on the job can be enhanced by crime are most likely to admit criminal propensities. Finally, being ordered to violate the law by one's supervisor generally increases offending likelihoods. Other factors that may increase corporate offending (but these findings are more equivocal) include doing business in an industry with foreign competitors; legal defiance; and economic enhancement, either through saving money or increasing revenues.

Andenaes argues that it is not possible to divorce mere deterrence (fear of formal legal sanctions) from inhibition derived from the educative effects of law and punishment (moral habituation).[33] Thus, our results do not necessarily imply that there is no role for criminal law in the compliance process. Indeed, our findings that managers who do not place moral opprobrium on corporate crime are more susceptible to formal sanction threats (and other kinds of threats to conscience or from significant others) suggest that punitive sanctions may be necessary to control the *behavior* of some and serve as *reminders* to the rest. However, it is not evident from our findings that criminal law should be the intervention of choice when selecting among legal systems. In the final chapter, we discuss the implications of the vignette survey findings for the deterrence-compliance debate.

[33] Johann Andenaes, *Punishment and Deterrence* (Ann Arbor: University of Michigan Press, 1974).

CHAPTER EIGHT

Shaping the Contours of Control

AT THE BEGINNING of a new century, the corporate crime front is fairly quiet.[1] In the United States, at least, political scandal and a booming economy seem to have muted criticisms of and lessened concerns about corporate malfeasance. However, the lull is bound to be short-lived. Because corporations, like people, are imperfect, there is always another Three Mile Island, Ford Pinto case, or savings-and-loan fiasco around the corner. Like these earlier cases, discovery will trigger public outrage, political opportunism, and the inevitable call for something to be done – usually ratcheting up the punishment in some way. Although this is clearly an appropriate time to launch investigations and probes into what went wrong, it is not the time to impose quick-fix solutions.

The Failure of "Strict" Deterrence

In his critical assessment of extant regulatory policy, Peter Grabosky suggests that the road to regulatory hell is paved with good intentions.[2] Policy failures often stem from implementation problems, bad science, and bad politics.[3] Policies are advocated for ideological reasons and put into place absent empirical considerations or, after implementation, lacking follow-up evaluation. There is much suggestive evidence that "strict" criminalization fits this characterization. Resistance, hostility, defiance, and obfuscation have

---

[1] The Ford Motor Company and Bridgestone Firestone tire cases not withstanding.
[2] P. N. Grabosky, "Counterproductive Regulation," *International Journal of the Sociology of Law* 23 (1995): 347–369.
[3] Ibid., pp. 356–362.

all been cited by others as evidence of counterproductive regulation. Our research shows that corporate crime control strategies based solely in a deterrence framework are unlikely to work – especially those that emphasize severe punishments instead of more certain and modest ones.[4]

As noted earlier, punishment is popular. It is a good sell to concerned and frightened citizens by politicians who care more about reelection than about what works. Punitiveness makes good copy, but not necessarily good policy. Daniel Nagin (who is a bit more optimistic about the evidence supporting deterrence than I) cautions against oversimplified policies based in deterrence. He notes that how or whether crime rates respond to changes in sanction policy depends on a number of factors:[5]

> The response . . . will depend on the specific form of the policy, the context of its implementation, the process by which people come to learn of it, differences among people in perceptions of the change in risks and rewards that are spawned by the policy, and feedback effects triggered by the policy itself (e.g., a reduction in private security in response to an increase in publically funded security). Further, the magnitude and possibly even the direction of the response to a policy may change over time.

Although Nagin is primarily interested in more conventional crime control policies and aggregate crime rates, his observations find support in our data as well. For instance, managers in both studies thought that formal legal sanctions directed toward them would be more consequential than those that targeted the firm. Yet, because it is much more difficult to successfully identify and prosecute individuals within companies than it is to bring the firm to court, a potentially credible deterrence threat is negated.

We also see how reliance on formal legal sanctions as a control mechanism may be more successful for some managers than others. Although our evidence is mixed (effects are stronger when the sample is divided at the mean instead of the median), managers who do not believe in the morality

---

[4] Recently, Mark Kleiman suggested that risk-aversion models that emphasize "an infinitesimally small risk of an enormous punishment" have a greater chance of working with corporate executives than with burglars. Kleiman's statement demonstrates the pervasiveness of the corporate deterrence argument among influential academic policy types. Yet, close examination of his remarks reveals an absence of any documented evidence supporting this supposition. See Mark A. R. Kleiman, "Getting Deterrence Right: Applying Tipping Models and Behavioral Economics to the Problems of Crime Control," in *Perspectives on Crime and Justice: 1998–1999 Lecture Series*, vol. 3 (November) (Washington, D.C.: U.S. Department of Justice, National Institute of Justice, 1999), p. 10.

[5] Daniel S. Nagin, "Criminal Deterrence Research at the Outset of the Twenty-First Century," in Michael Tonry (ed.), *Crime and Justice: A Review of Research*, vol. 23 (Chicago: University of Chicago Press, 1998), p. 4.

of the law and whose consciences are not offended by the illegal act may be more deterred through formal sanction threats than managers who need no additional incentives to obey the law. The implications of these findings are that different interventions work for different people. Thus, a mix of interventions will probably be more successful than policies based in strict deterrence.

Policy Challenges

At the very minimum, companies should formulate compliance programs that reinforce and teach (through training and example) good ethics. The system should be accessible to employees (via hot lines or open-door policies) *and* it should be credible. By this I mean that compliance teams should treat cases of misconduct seriously, impartially, and reasonably. Not all who transgress should be fired. But in some cases, termination may make the most sense. Lessons learned from discovered cases can be fed back to relevant managers and subunits. Although the threat of civil lawsuits is a challenge to full disclosure in the compliance process, it is also true that secrecy breeds mistrust. To the extent that individuals can be shielded and their mistakes instructional, openness should be the goal.

Managers need to understand that ethical lapses and gross misconduct are not tolerated, regardless of who and how powerful the players are. It is important to stress as well that while some internal crime control programs (especially those that increase employee surveillance by turning employees into conduct monitors and informants) can reduce white-collar crimes (such as pilfering), there is a fine line between efficient crime control and tactics that increase employee mistrust and alienation.[6] Each company should carefully assess whether its compliance process is moral and judicious.[7]

This advocacy for compliance programs recognizes that there are multiple organizational barriers to their success, some of which are identified in the vignette studies. Organizational norms may preclude open discussion of wrongdoing or ethics. Robert Jackall reports that morality in organizations is a social creature, sometimes encrypted in rational or technical speak of "cost-benefit," "trade-offs in efficiency," or sometimes determined, conveniently, by top management. "Managers know that in organizations right and wrong get decided by those with enough clout to make their views stick."[8]

[6] Stuart H. Traub, "Battling Employee Crime: A Review of Corporate Strategies and Programs," *Crime and Delinquency* 42 (1996): 244–256.
[7] See, e.g., Gary T. Marx, *Undercover* (Los Angeles: University of California Press, 1998).
[8] Robert Jackall, *Moral Mazes* (New York: Oxford University Press, 1998), pp. 104–105.

Evidence from our vignette study shows that offending propensities increase in the context of top management and normative support for corporate crime. Yet the results of the survey also suggest that a fair number of managers care deeply and feel strongly about ethical issues.[9] Corporate compliance can be best served by building on the strong moral base exhibited by most managers. If, as Jackall suggests, ethical concerns are treated as "inappropriate" within the business environment,[10] companies must, in addition to creating and maintaining a strong and effective compliance system, incorporate a moral dimension into meetings and group discussions where important and consequential decisions are made.

The question is not "Whose values will prevail?" but rather how to legitimate, maintain, or change ethical standards within organizations.[11] Both formal (leadership, orientation, and training) and informal systems (language, norms, rituals) within organizations figure into the puzzle. For instance, a recent national survey of 4,035 randomly selected employees found that corporate ethics programs (especially those that contained codes of conduct, ethics training, and ethics offices) increased employee awareness of misconduct and the likelihood that observed misconduct would be reported. However, employees preferred to turn to their direct supervisors for advice about ethical issues. In companies with well-developed programs, employees reported much higher levels of commitment to ethical conduct and believed commitment by others in the company was "about right."[12]

On the other hand, Peter Yeager warns that organizational morality is a complex affair – that managers tend to adopt different types of moral reasoning based on their duties and responsibilities within the corporate hierarchy. In the "moral division of labor," those responsible for strategic and tactical organizational planning (top managers) will emphasize a utilitarian mode of reasoning, whereas middle managers (who carry greater

---

[9] These findings are similar to those of other researchers who suggest that ethics issues and ethical dilemmas weigh heavily on managers. See also Kathy E. Kram, Peter C. Yeager, and Gary E. Reed, "Decisions and Dilemmas: The Ethical Dimension in the Corporate Context," in James E. Post (ed.), *Research in Corporate Social Performance and Policy*, vol. 11 (Greenwich, Conn.: JAI Press, 1989), pp. 21–54.

[10] Jackall, *Moral Mazes*; See also Kram et al., "Decisions and Dilemmas"; Jeanne Liedtka, "Managerial Values and Corporate Decision Making: An Empirical Analysis of Value Congruence in Two Organizations," in James E. Post (ed.), *Research in Corporate Social Performance and Policy*, vol. 11 (Greenwich, Conn.: JAI Press, 1989), pp. 55–91.

[11] See, e.g., Linda Klebe Trevino, "A Cultural Perspective on Changing and Developing Organizational Ethics," in *Research in Organizational Change and Development*, vol. 4 (Greenwich, Conn.: JAI Press, 1990), pp. 195–230.

[12] Ethics Resource Center, *Employee Survey on Ethics in American Business: Policies, Programs and Perceptions* (Washington, D.C.: Ethics Resource Center/NBES, 1994).

interpersonal responsibilities) are more apt to favor deontological or action-centered moral considerations.[13] Yeager concludes that moral reasoning is an essential part of organizational work and that conflicts over ethics are inevitable. The goal and challenge for advocates of compliance is to facilitate communication and discussion of ethical concerns in a setting that, too often, structurally discourages it.

A more insidious barrier to organizational compliance is what Diane Vaughan has called the normalization of deviance. Deviance normalization is not a "rational" process. Instead, culture, structure, and organizational characteristics combine to produce a world view that shapes manager's perceptions of doing right and doing wrong.[14] It is important to realize that this argument is distinct from the preceding one. Deviance normalization is a process through which incremental decisions, over time and in the aggregate, stretch the boundaries of what is acceptable and accepted within the work group, management team, or organization as a whole.

Ironically, it may be that the very organizations that prepare best for disaster, misconduct, and mistake are the ones most susceptible to this problem. "Training, often used to prevent errors, can create them; information richness introduces inefficiency, too little produces inaccuracy; teams have multiple points of view that enhance safety, but as they become a cohesive group they share assumptions, so the 'requisite variety' important to safety is lost."[15] Vaughan's case in point is NASA and the *Challenger* disaster but because her observations extend to other kinds of organizations and situations, she raises important questions about how organizational mechanisms (formal and informal) can both service and negate harmful outcomes. More research is necessary to determine the situations and context under which each condition is likely to occur.

These observations, however, should not lead us to reject the key elements of Braithwaite's pyramid (self-regulation, informal social control, persuasion, and punishment). The implications of Vaughan's research are that organizations and their managers cannot afford complacency – in putting compliance into practice or, once there, in assuming that the systems will continue to function as expected. Nagin, too, warned of feedback effects

---

[13] Peter Cleary Yeager, "Management, Morality, and Law: Organizational Forms and Ethical Deliberations," in Frank Pearce and Laureen Snider (eds.), *Corporate Crime: Contemporary Debates* (Toronto: University of Toronto Press, 1995), pp. 150–152.

[14] Diane Vaughan, *The Challenger Launch Decision: Risky Technology, Culture, and Deviance at NASA* (Chicago: University of Chicago Press, 1996), pp. 408–415.

[15] Diane Vaughan, "The Dark Side of Organizations: Mistake, Misconduct, and Disaster." *Annual Review of Sociology*, vol. 25 (Palo Alto, Calif.: Annual Reviews, 1999), p. 297.

from policy (although the ones noted by Vaughan are of a different nature than he imagined).

Another challenge to self-regulation, as our data document, is external to the firm. Regardless of how immoral corporate crimes are perceived to be and in spite of internal compliance programs, the organizational environment still manages to exert an independent effect on offending decisions. Because our results vary somewhat between studies, it is difficult to specify which conditions are criminogenic (e.g., in the first study highly moral managers would break the law if their company was losing ground to foreign competitors, whereas in the second study they were more likely to do so when the law was perceived as unfair). However, results do implicate the importance of the political and economic environments in which a firm operates. Developing compliance programs that are sensitive to crime hotspots and to the rationalizations that promote illegality will improve the likelihood that a company can dissuade most managers from crime and quickly uncover and respond to those who are not dissuaded.

In sum, our survey results give us some confidence that managers are not the immoral sociopaths often depicted in the corporate-crime literature and that a policy of persuasion – based on the assumption that most managers and executives want to do right – is apt to succeed most of the time. However, even among our small group of managers, there were a few who were not dissuaded from crime by moral concerns. Compliance benefits from recognizing that these persons exist and that persuasion may need some assistance from punitiveness.

Braithwaite's enforcement pyramid is founded in the notion that movement up the pyramid lessens official discretion and increases punitiveness. In the United States, there are multiple systems of formal control that could be used more effectively within the pyramid than they currently are. For instance, Braithwaite argues that the U.S. government has been locked into a predominantly punitive strategy (a "punitive, formal, and litigious regulatory regime").[16] He suggests that the regulatory justice system be the contact of first resort and that regulators (and not the Department of Justice) decide the manner in which to pursue a case.[17] Given that managers in this study perceive regulatory interventions to be most likely while they fear criminal sanctions the most, this suggestion has merit.[18]

---

[16] John Braithwaite, *To Punish or Persuade: Enforcement of Coal Mine Safety* (Albany, N.Y.: SUNY Press, 1985), p. 147.

[17] Ibid., p. 168.

[18] In fact, regulatory interventions have the predicted negative (albeit insignificant) impact on offending propensities once other variables are included in the analysis.

The greatest flexibility and oversight rests with the regulatory justice system. Giving regulators the power to flex the big stick of criminal prosecution when necessary should enhance the likelihood of maximum compliance. Limiting the use of criminal sanctions to cases that are egregious (either in terms of the offense or the blatant disregard of law and victims exhibited by responsible managers) retains the legitimacy and stigmatic significance of criminal law relative to other legal interventions. Our data offer little evidence that civil sanctions deter corporate crime. However, given that the main purpose of civil law is restitution and not retribution, there are other justifications for the use of civil law other than "mere" deterrence.

The vignette data highlight the importance of holding both managers and companies legally responsible for illegal acts. Most managers care whether they are apt to be the recipients of criminal sanctions, but they also care whether the firm is harmed by their illegal activities. A key consequence that figures prominently in their thinking is whether corporate crime is likely to damage the reputation of the firm. Shame is a potent inhibitor of unethical conduct. Thus, targeting responsible managers and the company for sanctions will be effective because the relationship between external (formal legal), organizational (self-regulatory), and personal (conscience) controls is mutually reinforcing.

> Formal sanctions directed against the firm are a critical part of an extensive informal system of social control. Formal firm-level sanctions maintain the credibility of informal sanctions (individual-level sanctions and shame) and a belief in the moral legitimacy of the law, all of which are effective deterrents to corporate crime.[19]

Nothing in these data, however, supports a policy of "pure" criminalization. Criminalization steps away from other legal alternatives (because they are not punitive enough). It fails to acknowledge the important role of self-regulation (because it does not trust that corporations or managers will do the right thing). It views informal sanctions (such as negative publicity, commitment and stigmatic costs) as not prohibitive in their own right. It does not consider that excessively punitive interventions can produce defiance, lack of cooperation, antagonism toward regulators, and potentially higher crime rates. In short, criminalization is uninformed by the empirical literature. It is "bad science" and therefore "bad policy."

---

[19] Raymond Paternoster and Sally S. Simpson, "Testing a Rational Choice Model of Corporate Crime," *Law and Society Review* 30 (1996): 579.

Future Directions for Compliance Research

The survey data offered here as a "test" of criminalization and cooperative strategies of corporate crime have their limitations. Thus, observations
are made and conclusions drawn with some circumspection. Clearly, results
from these studies need to be replicated among managers who are currently working within corporate environments. A random survey of working adults similar to the one recently conducted by the Ethics Resource
Center in Washington, D.C., is one way in which to establish the generalizability of results.[20] However, given the relevance of organizational culture,
managerial philosophy, and internal compliance programs to the offending decision, it is also important to conduct in-depth interviews and surveys
within companies to get a better sense of the relationship between workplace dynamics and corporate compliance. Finally, panel studies conducted
with the same set of respondents over time would be better able to capture the dynamic nature of corporate compliance. It would be especially
useful to measure how managers' perceptions over time are influenced by
different kinds of interventions and outcomes. These data would also allow
analyses beyond crime participation questions to include other elements
of corporate criminal careers (e.g., frequency, specialization, duration, and
desistance).[21]

It is also the case that offending intentions are not the same thing as
actual behavior. Scenarios are helpful at uncovering the kinds of things that
shift around managers' judgments in hypothetical situations. Decisions rendered from scenario conditions are "hyperrational" in that managers are
exposed to specific and clearly understood conditions and circumstances.
Thus, research scenarios approximate more closely the circumstances under which strategic decisions occur rather than those that underlie routine
or emergency decisions (raising another generalizability problem). Other
research techniques (e.g., randomized experiments, in-depth interviews,
case studies) would be better able to uncover how managers think and
act under a broader range of circumstances than those depicted in this
study.

[20] Ethics Resource Center, *Employee Survey*.

[21] Alfred J. Blumstein, Jacqueline A. Cohen, Jeffrey A. Roth, and Christy A. Visher (eds.),
Criminal Careers and "Career Criminals" (Washington, D.C.: National Academy Press, 1986).
For recent applications of the criminal career paradigm to white-collar criminals, see David
Weisburd, Ellen F. Chayet, and Elin J. Waring, "White-Collar Crime and Criminal Careers:
Some Preliminary Findings," *Crime and Delinquency* 36 (1990): 342–355; David Weisburd,
Stanton Wheeler, Elin Waring, and Nancy Bode, *Crimes of the Middle Classes* (New Haven:
Yale University Press, 1991); David Weisburd and Elin Waring (with Ellen F. Chayet), *White-
Collar Crime and Criminal Careers* (Cambridge: Cambridge University Press, 2001).

Additionally, our data do not tell us how much punishment is necessary to adjust offending likelihoods for those who are not legally habituated. Are these managers choice-indifferent (as described in Chapter 2) such that small adjustments to sanction certainty or severity will produce noncrime choices? Or are these managers so attracted to crime (because of individual traits or circumstances or structural inducements) that significant changes in sanction threats are necessary to inhibit corporate offending?[22] Although this is an empirical question, I doubt whether the latter is the case, given the life circumstances of most respondents. On average, the respondents in our sample are well integrated into social networks and highly educated, and either hold professional positions or (as MBAs) have a strong likelihood of doing so. If, in fact, this population is merely indifferent to crime (as opposed to committed to it), future deterrence studies may get better answers to questions about why and under what conditions people shift their crime or noncrime preferences by using corporate managers as research participants.

In the field of criminology and criminal justice, corporate crime and corporate criminals are understudied. Consequently, there is not a great deal of information from which to draw policy recommendations. Indeed, it is not the intention of this work to make policy recommendations per se, but rather to use empirical evidence to assess whether the apparent shift toward criminalization and deterrence is reasonable. The available evidence that does exist (including the vignette studies reported in this book) leads to the conclusion that it is not and such crime control strategies may, in fact, be socially harmful. On the other hand, the data do offer some evidence that a compliance process that builds on a foundation of self-regulation and cooperation (persuasion) has merit. While much more work on corporate compliance (and deterrence) needs to be done before any policy prescriptions can be justified, it is imperative that crime control policies be informed by science rather than political expediency.

[22] Philip J. Cook, "Research in Criminal Deterrence: Laying the Groundwork for the Second Decade," in Norval Morris and Michael Tonry (eds.), *An Annual Review of Research*, vol. 2 (Chicago: University of Chicago Press, 1980), pp. 211–268.

Appendix A. *Study One: Questionnaire Items and Responses*

	Responses (Mean/Percent)				
	Overall	Price-Fixing	Sales Fraud	Bribery	EPA
Question[a]					
1. What is the chance that you would act as the manager did under these circumstances?* (COMMIT)	2.06	2.42	1.94	2.26	1.62
2. Regardless of what you would do, is the situation described in this scenario believable or realistic? (SITREAL)	86% (yes)	77% (yes)	88% (yes)	87% (yes)	94% (yes)
3. How morally wrong do you think this incident is? (MORAL)	7.41	7.04	7.40	7.00	8.19
4. What is the chance you would be arrested for a criminal offense if you did what the manager did under these circumstances? (CRIMCH)	4.30	4.02	3.43	4.53	5.22
5. What is the chance that the firm would be criminally prosecuted if you did what the manager did under these circumstances? (CRIMFMCH)	4.81	4.78	3.89	4.43	6.12
6. What is the chance that you personally would					

Appendix A. *(cont.)*

	Responses (Mean/Percent)				
	Overall	Price-Fixing	Sales Fraud	Bribery	EPA
be sued if you did what the manager did under these circumstances? (CIVILCH)	3.73	3.26	3.27	3.97	4.44
7. What is the chance the firm would be sued if you did what the manager did under these circumstances? (CIVILFCH)	5.10	5.45	4.05	4.36	6.54
8. What is the chance that you personally would be investigated by a regulatory agency if you did what the manager did under these circumstances? (REGCH)	4.63	4.42	4.30	4.61	5.19
9. What is the chance that the firm would be investigated by a regulatory agency if you did what the manager did under these circumstances? (REGFMCH)	5.65	5.64	5.08	5.10	6.82
10. Suppose in fact you did what the manager did but neither you nor the firm came to the attention of the authorities. What is the chance that it would somehow become known to others such as					

Appendix A. *(cont.)*

	Responses (Mean/Percent)				
	Overall	Price-Fixing	Sales Fraud	Bribery	EPA
colleagues or friends that you had done this? (KNOWNINF)	6.26	6.81	6.10	6.29	5.82
11. What is the chance that you would be dismissed from the company? (DISMISS)	5.57	4.88	5.94	5.78	5.68
12. What is the chance that you would lose the respect and good opinion of your *close friends?* (FRIEND)	5.87	5.32	5.78	5.76	6.63
13. What is the chance that you would lose the respect and good opinion of your *business associates?* (BUSINESS)	6.36	6.28	6.45	6.06	6.66
14. What is the chance that you would lose the respect and good opinion of your *family?* (FAMILY)	4.97	4.39	4.81	4.94	5.74
15. What is the chance that you would jeopardize your future job prospects? (JOBCERT)	6.56	6.28	6.57	6.52	6.87
16. Would you feel a sense of guilt or shame if others knew that you had done this? (SHAME)	84% (yes)	82% (yes)	87% (yes)	76% (yes)	91% (yes)
17. What is the chance that your actions would tarnish the reputation of the firm? (FIRMREP)	6.20	6.38	5.98	5.46	6.98

Appendix A. *(cont.)*

	Responses (Mean/Percent)				
	Overall	Price-Fixing	Sales Fraud	Bribery	EPA
18. Would you feel a sense of guilt or shame if your action tarnished the reputation of the firm? (FIRMREPS)	79% (yes)	80% (yes)	79% (yes)	76% (yes)	79% (yes)

How much of a problem would the following circumstances create in your life?[b]

	Overall	Price-Fixing	Sales Fraud	Bribery	EPA
19. Being arrested for doing what the manager did. (CRIMSEV)	9.47	9.28	9.56	9.40	9.62
20. Having criminal charges brought against the firm. (CRIMFMSV)	8.17	8.18	8.22	8.00	8.27
21. Personally being sued for doing what the manager did. (CIVILSEV)	9.21	9.20	9.31	9.15	9.19
22. Having the firm sued for doing what the manager did. (CIVILFSV)	7.83	7.88	7.97	7.52	7.96
23. Having the firm cited by a regulatory agency for doing what the manager did. (REGFMSEV)	7.33	7.23	7.55	7.03	7.51
24. Being dismissed from your job for doing what the manager did. (DISCOST)	9.23	9.07	9.34	9.23	9.28
25. Losing the respect and good opinion of your *close friends* for doing what the manager did. (FRNDCOST)	8.60	8.63	8.68	8.33	8.74

Appendix A. *(cont.)*

	Responses (Mean/Percent)				
	Overall	Price-Fixing	Sales Fraud	Bribery	EPA
26. Losing the respect and good opinion of your *business associates* for doing what the manager did. (BUSCOST)	7.75	7.71	7.98	7.44	7.88
27. Losing the respect and good opinion of your *relatives* for doing what the manager did. (FAMCOST)	8.50	8.69	8.57	8.26	8.48
28. Jeopardizing your future job prospects for doing what the manager did. (JOBSEV)	8.86	8.87	8.96	8.78	8.85
29. Going to jail for doing what the manager did. (CONVICT)	9.78	9.84	9.78	9.69	9.79
30. Losing a lawsuit for doing what the manager did. (LAWSUIT)	8.89	8.97	8.95	8.76	8.88
31. The firm is criminally convicted and fined for doing what the manager did. (CONVICTF)	7.91	7.95	8.09	7.76	7.87
32. The firm loses a civil lawsuit for doing what the manager did. (LAWSUITF)	7.54	7.64	7.62	7.36	7.55
33. The firm receives a citation and fine from a regulatory agency for doing what the manager did. (AGENCYF)	7.02	6.96	7.27	6.74	7.13

Appendix A. *(Cont.)*

	Responses (Mean/Percent)				
	Overall	Price-Fixing	Sales Fraud	Bribery	EPA
34. Tarnishing the reputation of the firm for doing what the manager did. (FIRMRPSV)	7.25	7.20	7.35	7.12	7.33
35. Feeling a sense of personal shame and guilt for doing what the manager did. (SHAMESEV)	8.25	8.19	8.31	8.20	8.30
36. How much would it advance your career if you did what the manager did under these circumstances? (CAREER)	3.12	3.23	3.43	3.00	2.82
37. How exciting or thrilling would it be for you if you did what the manager did under these circumstances? (THRILL)	1.32	1.76	1.35	1.21	.94

[a] Questions 1–18 are based on a 0–10-point scale ranging from "no chance at all" to "100% chance," except as otherwise indicated.

[b] Questions 19–35 are based on a 0–10-point scale ranging from "no problem at all" to "a very big problem."

Appendix B. *Study One: Sample Characteristics*

Gender	60% male	40% female
Age	22–55 range	28 average age
Race	85% white	15% other
Nationality	82% United States	18% other
Years of business experience	0–30 range	5 average
Offending intentions	0–9 range	2.15 average probability, 66% would offend

Note: Missing cases excluded.

Appendix C. *Study Two: Questionnaire Items and Responses*

	Responses (Mean/Percent)
Question[a]	
1. What is the chance that you would act as the manager did under these circumstances?* (COMMIT)	1.66
2. Regardless of what you would do, is the situation described in this scenario believable or realistic? (SITREAL)	93% (yes)
3. Please think about the paragraph you have just read. Then give your beliefs as an individual about the manager's action by placing a check between each of the opposites to the right. What the manager is doing is:	
Culturally acceptable/unacceptable	4.1
Morally fair/unfair	4.7
Just/unjust	4.9
Violate/not violate unwritten contract*	1.6
Traditionally acceptable/unacceptable	4.1
Morally right/not morally right	5.3
Violate/not violate unspoken promise*	1.7
Acceptable/not to family	5.23
Very unethical/ethical*	.96
4. What is the chance you would be arrested for a criminal offense if you did what the manager did under these circumstances? (CRIMCH)	3.94
5. What is the chance that the firm would be criminally prosecuted if you did what the manager did under these circumstances? (CRIMFMCH)	4.70
6. What is the chance that you personally would be sued if you did what the manager did under these circumstances? (CIVILCH)	3.58
7. What is the chance the firm would be sued if you did what the manager did under these circumstances? (CIVILFCH)	5.13
8. What is the chance that you personally would be investigated by a regulatory agency if you did what the manager did under these circumstances? (REGCH)	4.65
9. What is the chance that the firm would be investigated by a regulatory agency if you did what the manager did under these circumstances? (REGFMCH)	5.63
10. Suppose in fact you did what the manager did but neither you nor the firm came to the attention of the authorities. What is the chance that it would somehow become known to others such as colleagues or friends that you had done this? (KNOWNINF)	6.68

Appendix C. *(cont.)*

	Responses (Mean/Percent)
11. What is the chance that you would be dismissed from the company? (DISMISS)	5.40
12. What is the chance that you would lose the respect and good opinion of your *close friends?* (FRIEND)	6.54
13. What is the chance that you would lose the respect and good opinion of your *business associates?* (BUSINESS)	6.41
14. What is the chance that you would lose the respect and good opinion of your *family?* (FAMILY)	6.46
15. What is the chance that you would jeopardize your future job prospects? (JOBCERT)	6.65
16. Would you feel a sense of guilt or shame if others knew that you had done this? (SHAME)	90% (yes)
17. What is the chance that your actions would tarnish the reputation of the firm? (FIRMREP)	6.44
18. Would you feel a sense of guilt or shame if your action tarnished the reputation of the firm? (FIRMREP)	90% (yes)

How much of a problem would the following circumstances create in your life? [b]

19. Being arrested for doing what the manager did. (CRIMSEV)	9.50
20. Having criminal charges brought against the firm. (CRIMFMSV)	8.49
21. Personally being sued for doing what the manager did. (CIVILSEV)	9.37
22. Having the firm sued for doing what the manager did. (CIVILFSEV)	8.33
23. Having the firm cited by a regulatory agency for doing what the manager did. (REGFMSEV)	7.92
24. Being dismissed from your job for doing what the manager did. (DISCOST)	9.34
25. Losing the respect and good opinion of your *close friends* for doing what the manager did. (FRNDCOST)	8.72
26. Losing the respect and good opinion of your *business associates* for doing what the manager did. (BUSCOST)	8.13
27. Losing the respect and good opinion of your *relatives* for doing what the manager did. (FAMCOST)	8.81
28. Jeopardizing your future job prospects for doing what the manager did. (JOBSEV)	9.10
29. Tarnishing the reputation of the firm for doing what the manager did. (FIRMRPSV)	7.72

Appendix C. *(cont.)*

	Responses (Mean/Percent)
30. Feeling a sense of personal shame and guilt for doing what the manager did. (SHAMESEV)	8.57
Question (a great deal/not at all)	
31. How much would it advance your career if you did what the manager did under these circumstances? (CAREER)	3.03
Question (not exciting/very exciting)	
32. How exciting or thrilling would it be for you if you did what the manager did under these circumstances? (THRILL)	.82

[a] Questions 1–2 and 4–18 are based on a 0–10-point scale ranging from "no chance at all" to "100% chance," except as otherwise indicated. Question 3 is based on a 0–6-point scale; asterisk designates items that are reverse coded.

[b] Questions 19–30 are based on a 0–10-point scale ranging from "no problem at all" to "a very big problem."

Appendix D. *Study Two: Sample Characteristics*

Gender	66% male	34% female
Age	22–55 range	35 average age
Race	92% white	8% other
Nationality	85% United States	15% other
Years of business experience	0–30 range	12 average
Offending intentions	0–9 range	1.6 average probability, 50% would offend

Note: Missing cases excluded.

Name Index

Subject Index

CPSIA information can be obtained
at www.ICGtesting.com
Printed in the USA
LVOW03s1923231217
560663LV00002B/224/P